DIPLOMACY AT THE UN

DIPLOMACY AT THE UN

Edited and Introduced by
G. R. Berridge and A. Jennings
Leicester University

MACMILLAN
PRESS

First edition 1985
Reprinted 1986

Published by
THE MACMILLAN PRESS LTD
Houndmills, Basingstoke, Hampshire RG21 2XS
and London
Companies and representatives
throughout the world

Printed in Great Britain by
Antony Rowe Ltd
Chippenham

British Library Cataloguing in Publication Data
Diplomacy at the UN
1. United Nations   2. Diplomacy
I. Berridge, G. R.   II. Jennings, A.
327.2   JX1977
ISBN 0–333–36019–2

Contents

Preface

In 1981 the Noel Buxton Trust, which, since its inception in 1919, has had as one of its principal concerns the study of the causes of war and the promotion of international peace, invited the University of Leicester to hold a series of lectures on a theme of the University's choosing in the field of international relations. The University acknowledges the generosity of the Trust in supporting these lectures, which were given by Peter Calvocoressi, Geoffrey Goodwin, Alan James, Maurice Keens-Soper and Susan Strange in the spring term 1982 under the title of 'The United Nations and Diplomacy'. It was from this series that the idea for the present book emerged. A special debt is owed for the assistance of Margaret Beard, Secretary of the Noel Buxton Trust.

The editors are grateful to the contributors for advice on editorial policy and to Geoffrey Goodwin, Maurice Keens-Soper and Jack Spence for their helpful comments on the introduction as well.

G. R. B. and A. J.

The University
Leicester

List of Acronyms

ACT   Agreement on Commodity Trade
ASEAN   Association of South-east Asian Nations
CIEC   Conference on International Economic Cooperation
COMECON   Council for Mutual Economic Assistance
ECWA   Economic Commission of Western Asia
EEZ   Exclusive Economic Zone (Law of the Sea Conference)
FAO   Food and Agriculture Organisation
GATT   General Agreement on Tariffs and Trade
IBRD   International Bank for Reconstruction and Development
ICJ   International Court of Justice
ICNT   Informal Composite Negotiating Text (Law of the Sea
           Conference)
ILO   International Labour Organisation
IMCO   Inter-governmental Maritime Consultative Organisation
IMF   International Monetary Fund
ISA   International Seabed Authority
LDCs   Least Developed Countries
MFA   Multi-fibre Agreement
MTN   Multilateral Trade Negotiations
NICs   Newly Industrialised Countries
OAU   Organisation of African Unity
OECD   Organisation for Economic Cooperation and
           Development
PLO   Palestine Liberation Organisation
PTO   Production and Trade Organisation
SNPA   Substantial New Programme of Action (United Nations
           Conference on Least Developed Countries)
SWAPO   South West African People's Organisation
UN   United Nations
UNCLDC   United Nations Conference on Least Developed
           Countries
UNCLOS   United Nations Conference on the Law of the Sea
UNCTAD   United Nations Conference on Trade and Development

UNDOF	United Nations Disengagement Observer Force
UNDP	United Nations Development Programme
UNEF	United Nations Emergency Force
UNEP	United Nations Environment Programme
UNIFIL	United Nations Interim Force in Lebanon
UNRWA	United Nations Relief and Works Agency

Notes on the Contributors

E. R. Appathurai teaches international politics at York University, Toronto. Between 1950 and 1963 he served tours of duty in India, Pakistan, Egypt, West Germany and the Soviet Union as a member of Ceylon's diplomatic service. He is the author of, amongst other things, *Les missions permanentes auprès des organisations internationales*, tome 3 (Bruxelles: Bruylant, 1975), which is about UN permanent missions in New York.

John Barratt is Director General of the South African Institute of International Affairs and an Honorary Professor in International Relations at the University of the Witwatersrand. Formerly a member of the South African Foreign Service, he was stationed in New York with the mission to the UN from 1958 to 1965. He has written widely on South African foreign policy.

R. P. Barston teaches international relations in the Department of Politics at the University of Lancaster, and is also a World Bank consultant in the Far East. He specialises in foreign-policy analysis and maritime law. He is a former member of the Foreign and Commonwealth Office, where he worked on a number of law-of-the-sea issues. He has edited *The Other Powers* and written, amongst other things, *The Maritime Dimension* (with Patricia Birnie).

G. R. Berridge teaches politics at the University of Leicester. His main publications have been on South Africa, and he is currently completing a study of the politics of the Europe–South Africa shipping conference.

Peter Calvocoressi is a writer, teacher and publisher. He has been a Reader in International Relations at Sussex University, and served for ten years on the UN Subcommission on Prevention of Discrimination and Protection of Minorities. His books include *Total War, World Politics since 1945* and *Top Secret Ultra*. He is presently working for the *Sunday Times* and writing a new book about pacifism and peace movements.

G. L. Goodwin is Emeritus Professor of International Relations of the University of London, having held the Chair at the LSE from 1962 until 1978. Previously he was a Lecturer at the LSE, before that having served in the British Regular Army and the Foreign Office. He was Commissioner on International Affairs, World Council of Churches, 1968–75, and Honorary President of the British International Studies Association, 1977–80. Amongst his publications are *Britain and the United Nations* and, most recently, an edited collection, *Ethics and Nuclear Deterrence*.

Rosemary Holland graduated from King's College, London, in 1975 with an MA in war studies. She subsequently did research on Middle Eastern history in London. She is currently completing a PhD in Political Science with a Middle East speciality at George Washington University in Washington, D.C., and teaching a course entitled 'Politics and Values'.

Alan James is Professor of International Relations at the University of Keele. The political activities of the United Nations have for long been one of his major research interests and he has written widely on the role of the Secretary-General and on United Nations peace-keeping. Currently he is completing a study of sovereignty in international relations.

A. Jennings teaches economics at the University of Leicester. He was formerly employed as a senior economist by the governments of Malawi and Botswana and has worked for the Ministry of Overseas Development (UK), the UN and UNCTAD (Special Programme for Least Developed Countries). His publications include contributions to *The Challenge of Development in the Eighties* (edited with Thomas G. Weiss), *Monetary Economics in Developing Countries* (with S. Ghatak) and *Our Response to the Poorest of the Third World*.

Maurice Keens-Soper teaches politics at the University of Leicester. From 1966 until 1968 he was a Research Fellow at the Graduate Institute of International Studies in Geneva. He conducted research at the United Nations in 1981 and 1982. His most recent publication (with Karl W. Schweizer) is a critical edition of François de Callières: *The Art of Diplomacy*.

Sir Anthony Parsons was born in 1922 and educated at Oxford

University. He worked for the Diplomatic Service, mainly in Middle East posts, London and the United Nations. He was British Ambassador in Tehran from 1974 until 1979 and Permanent Representative to the UN in New York in 1979–82. During 1983 he was Foreign Affairs Adviser to the Prime Minister.

Bernard Reich teaches political science and international affairs at George Washington University in Washington, D.C. His research has focused on various aspects of the politics and international relations of the Middle East. His latest book is *The United States and Israel: Influence in the Special Relationship*.

J. E. Spence has been Professor of Politics at the University of Leicester since 1973 and a Pro-Vice-Chancellor since 1981. Previously he taught at the Universities of Natal, California and Wales. His principal publications have been on South Africa, while from 1975 until 1981 he was the editor of the *British Journal of International Studies*.

Susan Strange has been Professor of International Relations at the London School of Economics and Political Science since 1978, and was previously Senior Research Fellow at the Royal Institute of International Affairs, Chatham House. Before that she taught at University College and wrote for the *Observer* and the *Economist*.

Thomas G. Weiss is an economic-affairs officer in UNCTAD's Special Programme for Least Developed Countries. Formerly a staff member at the Institute for World Order, UNITAR and the ILO, as well as a lecturer at Colgate, Princeton and New York Universities, his books include *International Bureaucracy, The World Food Conference and Global Problem Solving* (with R. S. Jordan) and *More for the Least? Prospects for Poorest Countries in the Eighties* (with A. Jennings).

Introduction

G. R. BERRIDGE and A. JENNINGS

This book has two main purposes. The first purpose is to clarify the diplomatic work of the United Nations, that is to say, to locate it in the broader world of international politics. The second is to say something about the value of the UN's contribution to the diplomatic solution of the problems which face states individually and collectively.

The experience of the League of Nations demonstrated that in modern conditions and given modern prejudices, a collective security system could not be expected wholly to replace an alliance security system. Accordingly, when the United Nations was created at the end of the Second World War it was given a less ambitious brief: to graft a cutting of collective security onto the wild briar of the balance of power. When – but only when – the great powers and the alliances which they might be expected to lead were not involved in a dispute, the United Nations would be able to take action. This was the principal rationale of the United Nations and the chief task of its most powerful organ, the Security Council.

However, the United Nations was also charged with preserving 'international peace and security' by less dramatic means: by encouraging negotiation, enquiry and mediation (as well as providing for arbitration and judicial settlement)[1] and, *inter alia*, serving as a general forum for the discussion of political, colonial, economic and social questions. In short, the United Nations was conceived as an entity which would not only operate collective security, arbitration and judicial settlement but also nurture two traditions of diplomacy which were by this time well established: diplomacy assisted by a neutral third party, and 'multilateral' or 'conference' diplomacy. Despite the absence of unequivocal Charter reference to it, it also seems clear that the founders assumed that the UN would in addition be a place where old-fashioned bilateral diplomacy would occur.[2]

In third party diplomacy the parties to a dispute have failed to reach agreement and vest in a third party more or less limited powers to help them proceed. The parties to the dispute themselves (of whom there may be more than two) may or may not be prepared to negotiate face-to-face following the intervention of the 'third party'. For its part, the third party must be seen to be impartial with regard to the *shape* of any settlement but not necessarily impartial with regard to the question of a settlement *as such*. On the contrary, the anxiety of the third party for a settlement will often be regarded as a qualification since it can be assumed that such an attitude will lead him to pursue his task with energy. This was the case with Henry Kissinger's mediation in the Middle East following the Yom Kippur War in 1973.[3]

By contrast, in both bilateral and multilateral diplomacy the negotiation is always face-to-face and *each* of the parties has an interest in the shape of the settlement. They do not, however, share an anxiety for *any* settlement. The casual distinction between bilateral and multilateral diplomacy is simply that in the former case contact is confined to two states while in the latter it occurs between three or more, but this is not sufficient. Thus, while 'multilateral diplomacy' suggests little more than the activity of negotiation itself, 'bilateral diplomacy', or 'old diplomacy', conjures up the idea of the conduct of *general* business between states as well. In short, there is a functional as well as a numerical connotation to the distinction. This, at any rate, is the sense of the distinction as it shapes the structure of this book.

If these ideas are reasonably clear in the language of diplomacy in general, they are not always clear in either the language or the practice of the United Nations. To begin with, the distinction between third party and multilateral diplomacy tends to be blurred since when the UN acts as a third party it does so – except in the shape of the Secretary-General himself – via a standing diplomatic conference; this in the main, and at any rate formally, is the Security Council. Obviously, however, the conclusion to be drawn from this is not that the distinction between third party and multilateral diplomacy is without force in the UN context (UN conferences do not normally act as third parties) but simply that the UN is in one of its aspects a 'collective third party'.[4]

Secondly, the distinction between bilateral and multilateral diplomacy at the UN tends to be confused by the common use of phrases such as 'corridor diplomacy', 'quiet diplomacy', and so on. While setting and decibel count are some guide to the nature of diplomatic activity, such clues do not take us very far. In fact, some of the offstage activity at the United Nations is essentially bilateral in character; here, the informal exchanges which occur between foreign ministers at the annual opening of the General Assembly represent a case in point. Equally, much of this activity is multilateral. The best-known examples of the latter are to be found in the regional caucuses which regularly meet to thrash out joint positions in advance of General Assembly and Security Council debates.

The final confusion is the application of the terms 'conference diplomacy' or 'multilateral diplomacy' to UN meetings which bear little resemblance to diplomacy. This is particularly the case with the General Assembly and the public sessions of the Security Council. The alternative phrase which is often applied here, 'parliamentary diplomacy', is more accurate, at the price of introducing a contradiction in terms. This sort of 'diplomacy' is really propaganda. The real multilateral diplomacy, other than that conducted in the General Assembly caucuses, is found in the *ad hoc* conferences which the UN has spawned. Such conferences have for some time now supplemented bilateral diplomacy,[5] and whereas formerly political issues predominated, increasingly economic, financial, social and cultural questions have become agenda items. The last decade, in particular, has witnessed an impressive growth in the number of international conferences.[6] They normally focus on a manageable problem and have a secretariat which provides organisational support. The open, plenary sessions are mainly designed for 'home' public consumption, in the manner of the General Assembly and the Security Council, and to the extent that real negotiation occurs, it usually takes place in private committees and 'contact' group sessions.

The scene is set for the book as a whole by a first chapter on the impact of power politics on the United Nations. Since the Organisation was conceived principally as a 'collective third party' which would help by diplomacy, *inter alia*, to preserve international peace and security, the following chapters – which form the first main part of the book – deal with the chief instruments of third party diplomacy at the UN. These are the Security Council and the Secretary-General.

The second part of the book deals with multilateral diplomacy. Here the General Assembly is examined since it is customarily – if inaccurately – regarded as the paradigm case of multilateral diplomacy. Permanent missions in New York are also dealt with in this part because they were invented to cope with conference diplomacy and derive their characteristic style from it. Multilateral economic diplomacy in general within the UN context is then considered, while the subsequent chapters in Part II deal with two *ad hoc* conferences: the Conference on Least Developed Countries which was held in Paris in 1981, and the third UN Law of the Sea Conference. These case studies have been chosen not only because of their intrinsic interest but because they test the proposition that focusing on a discrete problem rather than waiting in anticipation of a 'grand' solution to all the problems facing developed and developing countries is more likely to produce success.

The discussion of bilateral diplomacy at the UN in New York is reserved – as befits a subterranean activity – to the final part of the book. Here a notion put forward by Hedley Bull is put to crude test: 'Much of the importance of conferences and international organis- ations', he says, 'lies not in the multilateral diplomacy to which they give rise but in the opportunities they provide for bilateral diplomacy.'[7] A general examination of bilateral diplomacy in New York thus precedes two case studies. These cases – South African diplomacy and Israeli diplomacy – were chosen for their intrinsic interest and obvious political importance. There was, however, a further consideration. Having few formal relations in entire regions of the world, both South Africa and Israel might be expected to find the vast diplomatic corps attached to the UN in New York useful for their bilateral diplomacy, despite the fact that many of the members of this corps fiercely attack their policies. If, in such circumstances, these two countries do indeed find that the UN has certain diplomatic advantages, then the general supposition supported by Bull – at least in so far as it covers bilateral relations between hostile states – is thereby strengthened.

Some of the contributors to this volume are, either explicitly or implicitly, more impressed than others by the opportunities for genuine diplomacy afforded by the contemporary United Nations. Everything seems to turn on the nature of the conflict or other problem under discussion, as well as on the bureaucratic context within which the diplomacy is conducted. But even this indicates that the United Nations has diplomatic compensations as well as diplomatic drawbacks; that it is not, in other words, *merely* 'a dangerous place';[8] and that, in con- sequence, it is still an instrument of some significance in the search for international peace, security and welfare.

NOTES

1. For further elucidation of these and related distinctions, see Lord Gore-Booth (ed), *Satow's Guide to Diplomatic Practice*, 5th edn (London and New York: Longman, 1979) ch. 38.
2. Sir Geoffrey Jackson, *Concorde Diplomacy: The Ambassador's Role in the World Today* (London: Hamish Hamilton, 1981) p. 31.

3. For a more elaborate discussion of the concept of 'third party' diplomacy, see O. R. Young, *The Intermediaries: Third Parties in International Crises* (Princeton University Press, 1967) pp. 34 ff.

4. The 5th edition of *Satow's Guide* employs this phrase to describe the entirety of the UN's work, though this is obviously misleading. On the application of the 'third party' concept to the UN, see also Young, *The Intermediaries*, pp. 110–14.

5. See J. Kauffmann, *Conference Diplomacy* (Leiden: Sijthoff, 1970), for a theoretical and historical discussion.

6. Recent examples of conference diplomacy include meetings on the human environment (Stockholm, 1972), human habitat (Vancouver, 1979), women (Mexico City, 1975 and Copenhagen, 1980), food (Rome, 1974), population (Bucharest, 1974), agrarian reform (Rome, 1979), new and renewable sources of energy (Nairobi, 1981), the law of the sea (several sessions since Caracas, 1970), least developed countries (Paris, 1981), and more continuous sessions on trade (UNCTAD) and overall economic development during special sessions of the General Assembly (1974, 1975, 1976 and 1980).

7. Hedley Bull, *The Anarchical Society: A Study of Order in World Politics* (London: Macmillan, 1977). p. 165.

8. D. P. Moynihan, who was US Ambassador to the UN for a period in the early 1970s, called his UN memoirs *A Dangerous Place* (London: Secker & Warburg, 1979), while an earlier attack on the UN had been given the same title – A. Yeselson and A. Gaglione's *A Dangerous Place: The United Nations as a Weapon in World Politics* (New York: Grossman, 1974).

1 Power Politics and the United Nations

G. L. GOODWIN

The growth of international political institutions has been one of the more notable features of the twentieth-century diplomatic scene. Yet the United Nations, like the League of Nations before it, far from transforming a world of power politics into a more orderly and law abiding world society, threatens to become engulfed in a particularly tumultuous brand of power politics, what the present Secretary-General (J. Pérez de Cuéllar) has called 'the current tendency to resort to confrontation, violence and even war in pursuit of what are perceived as vital interests, claims or aspirations'.[1] Both organisations were, of course, products not only of a concert of victorious powers only momentarily brought together by the needs of their wartime alliances, but also of the fleeting and often illusory hopes engendered by the ravages of war. Is it perhaps inevitable that, as power relationships shift and memories of the 'pity of war, the pity war distilled' (Wilfred Owen) grow dim, so confidence in the efficacy of these would-be world organisations as a basis for world order steadily wanes?

Certainly, at the time of the inception of the League of Nations the widespread revulsion at the long-drawn-out bloodletting of the trench warfare just across the Channel – the carnage of Passchendaele and the Somme – was instrumental in mobilising public support for this new venture in international diplomacy. Even the official historian to the Foreign Office, Sir James Headlam-Morley, was moved to write of the European diplomatic system preceding 1914 which had allowed it to happen: 'on one thing everyone will be agreed, that this is not the way in which public affairs should be managed. The unvarnished record is the most complete condemnation of the system.'[2] Similarly, to the architects of the United Nations the 1930s seemed in retrospect a tragic commentary on the failure of the democracies to face up to the Axis dictators and to shoulder their obligations under the Covenant, while the bestiality of Nazi excesses in occupied Europe and the brutality of the war in the Pacific gave fresh impetus to the search to 'save succeeding generations from the scourge of war' (Preamble to the Charter).

In 1919 there were, of course, those who were mainly intent on renovating or repairing the concert system, particularly so as to enable it to meet automatically in times of crisis, just as in 1943 much attention was paid to remedying what were deemed to be the main weaknesses in the League system. Nevertheless in the early 1920s, apart from the Bolsheviks newly installed in power in Russia – Lenin called the League of Nations 'this plague of nations', while the accompanying International Labour Organisation was to him 'an abominable masquerade to trick the proletariat' – most liberal and radical opinion was more ambitious; it saw the League as the beginning of a process of transforming an anarchical world of power politics into a more orderly and civilised society of states. This was to be achieved by the institution of a security system through which, in Lockean terms, the great powers would learn to act with greater self-restraint – the great powers were, in Sir Alfred Zimmern's words, to become the 'Great Responsibles' and not merely the 'Great Indispensables' – and the normally peace-loving majority of states would cooperate together 'to conclude the fraud and violence of the minority'. In the United Nations the emphasis was somewhat different, for the Charter's security system was to be built around President Roosevelt's more Hobbesian conception of an armed concert of the three main victorious powers. The United States, the Soviet Union and Britain, charged with keeping the peace in a relatively disarmed world, were to constitute a new Leviathan capable of 'keeping them all in awe'. However, this new Leviathan was to be, in Sir Charles Webster's words, 'embedded in a larger organisation and subjected to the restraints of an ordered constitution expressing a moral purpose'.

Yet hardly had these new organisations been inaugurated than the realities of power politics reasserted themselves. Governments might make ritual genuflections to the ideals they embodied, but memories of the tragedy of war soon faded and prophetic visions of 'swords beaten into plowshares' gave way to the determination of member states to harness the new institutions to their own particular needs. In 1920 France, faced by a still potentially more powerful Germany, suffered the collapse of the Anglo-American guarantee of the new French frontiers consequent upon American defection from the League. With little prospect of renewing her traditional alliance with Russia, with the Bolsheviks now in power, France turned not only to building a system of continental alliances to contain Germany, but her main objective in the

League was to *strengthen* its security system by supplementary arrangements (such as the Draft Treaty of Mutual Assistance in 1924). Thus for France the League was primarily an instrument to help contain and if necessary coerce a possibly resurgent Germany. By contrast, in Britain the League had been viewed by a somewhat sceptical government as mainly a means of institutionalising the conciliatory potential of the concert system, which had granted Britain the right to be consulted without imposing a duty to be involved – consultation without commitment. But a League without the United States was not the League Britain had expected to join. 'Half-a-League Onward' its supporters might cry, as Charles Manning put it; but from that moment on British – and Dominion – efforts were concentrated on *diluting* their obligations under the Covenant security system which was decried by most politicians and officials alike as either 'impracticable', 'too demanding' or 'potentially dangerous'.

Anglo-French differences (as well, of course, as the absence of the USA) were fundamental to the strains within the League security system, between its coercive and conciliatory roles. But the Abyssinian crisis in 1935 also highlighted the extent to which a League collective security policy, in this case of collective sanctions against Italy, could run directly counter to a balance of power policy, in which Italy was seen as an essential partner with France and Britain in providing an effective counterweight to the growing strength of Hitler in the West and of Japan in the Far East. The dilemma was real, especially for France, but the consequent vacillations and half-hearted sanctions reflect the crippling schizophrenia in the Franco-British handling of the crisis, which effectively alienated Italy and destroyed the League. In Duff Cooper's bitter comment: 'Doing the minimum of harm we incurred the maximum of ill will and at a time when the wind of fear was rising and the nations of the world were anxiously watching for indications of weakness or strength, Great Britain appeared as a friend not to be relied upon and a foe not to be feared.'[3] The League that could have helped give legitimacy and wider support to the efforts of the democracies – or perhaps more aptly *status quo* powers – to check the rising revisionist challenge of the dictators – the Armed Covenant advocated by Churchill – was in practice fatally flawed by the vacillation, as Professor Northedge once remarked, 'between the desire to enjoy the benefits of collective security and the urge to avoid paying the price for it'. From 1936 the League became an irrelevance incapable of checking the steady drift towards the Second World War. In June 1950 President Truman showed himself very conscious of this 'lesson of history' in taking the decision, which he felt incumbent on a 'good' UN member, to commit American troops to the defence of South Korea, a decision in which he was vigorously supported by the then British Prime Minister, Mr Clement Attlee.

In 1945 expectations of the United Nations were more sober at the public as well as at the official levels. Unlike its predecessor which could look back to a long period of order, tranquillity and progress, the United Nations was born into a world in which power politics of a peculiarly ruthless character had prevailed, little disguised, for over a decade. In the early postwar years there were few signs of that split between the rational idealism of 'popular' thinking, and the more coventional realism of official thinking, which had injected such a dangerous schizophrenia into British attitudes towards the League. Men's minds had become accustomed to unrest and upheaval and were more inclined to regard the harsh realities of 'power politics' as an inescapable fact of international life. Nevertheless, the new organisation might help curb the more blatant misuse of power so as to work towards a more civilised international society. And the idealism for a 'better world' was there. For the most part, however, the mood was apprehensive rather than optimistic – an apprehension reinforced by the horrors of Hiroshima and Nagasaki. This apprehension was also sharpened by the early realisation that the two basic premises upon which in 1944 the Charter's elaborate security structure was built were invalid. The first premise was that the major threat to peace in the postwar world was likely to come from a resurgent Germany and Japan; and that this would help hold the armed concert of the victorious powers together. By the late summer of 1945 it became clear that they would constitute no such threat. The second premise was the expectation, at least in British eyes, that the elaborate machinery for enforcement action under the Charter might be invoked against one of the great powers themselves. The veto put an end to that possibility and even at the time of the inaugural San Francisco Conference in April 1945 it was evident that, as Professor Brierly put it, 'we have discarded the system of the Covenant which, though not certainly, might possibly have worked, and we have substituted for it one which hardly even professes to be workable'. The system had been given, as Alan de Russett put it, 'teeth and lock jaw at the same time'. Hence, of course, the importance, recognised at San Francisco, of Article 51 which legitimised the alliance systems which were shortly to proliferate and provide the major poles in the emerging balance of power system.

Nevertheless, the American commitment to the objective of world security seemed genuine enough, given the existence of the veto rights under Article 27 and of the 'special arrangements' under Article 43 which would spread the responsibility for enforcement action. For Britain, now a 'consumer of security' and fearful of Soviet designs in Europe, the organisation could help both to perpetuate the very close wartime Anglo-American military collaboration and act as a brake on any tendencies to renewed American isolationism. For the Soviet Union the thought no doubt occurred that, if an organisation were to be set up, it would be better to be in it if only to prevent decisions being taken there which might be detrimental to Soviet interests; and it might always serve both as a useful 'listening' post on Western intentions and capabilities and as a means of exploiting dissension within the Western world and between it and the 'exploited masses' in the colonial world. At least it seemed that, whereas the League had essentially been 'Europe and its periphery' the United Nations had the makings of a truly world body. This was one of the few early expectations that was to be fulfilled.

The early disintegration of the armed concert of the victorious great powers and the emergence of alliance systems structured around the 'core' adversary powers, the United States and the Soviet Union, 'in posture of gladiators', brought the virtual demise of the Charter security system. Moreover, most efforts at the United Nations in the security field were henceforth directed not to replacing but to injecting a greater element of stability into what was held to be a 'delicate balance of terror' between the two armed camps. In a modest way the Organisation has fulfilled this hope for much of its history. It has served as a valuable point of diplomatic contact at times of high tension, for instance during the Berlin blockade in early 1949 and the Cuban crisis in 1962 and in successive Arab–Israel encounters; it has occasionally thrown up mediatory resources, as in India's role in securing an acceptable formula which brought about the ending of the Korean War in 1953, or in the successful efforts of Dag Hammarskjöld in 1955 to ease the repatriation of American prisoners of war held by the Chinese, to cite only a few examples. The record in the peace-keeping field has been mixed but not unimpressive and it can be claimed that in several instances, Suez (1956), Lebanon (1958), the Congo (1960), in the Sinai (1973) and intermittently in Cyprus, UN peace-keeping forces have helped to contain conflicts which could have further exacerbated great power tensions.

Against these constructive roles is to be set the extent to which the United Nations came to be seen by many Americans, particularly during the Korean War and for the greater part of the 1950s, as primarily an instrument of American policy in 'standing up' to the Russians. In my view this had a good side to it, in, for instance, President Truman's already mentioned decision to commit American forces to the defence of South Korea and to put them, and not just as a matter of form, under a so-called United Nations command. More significantly it meant that in this period American policy-makers were willing to pay considerable heed not only to the views of the majority of United Nations members – Truman's dismissal of General MacArthur in April 1951 owed not a little to his concern at the mounting criticism at the UN of the latter's belligerency – but also to what they deemed the prohibitions of the Charter on the use of force 'except in the common interest'. President Eisenhower, in adding his 'footnote to history' on the 1956 Suez crisis, claimed that he had made it very clear that the United States was going to stand by its interpretation of UN policy and the Charter; that meant 'we should apply this to anybody – those we thought our closest friends as well as those we thought were in another category'. Nevertheless, by many American policy-makers in the 1950s and well into the 1960s, the United Nations came to be treated as mainly an arena of 'competitive coexistence' with the Russians – a term incidentally the latter had themselves coined and exploited – in which 'neutrality' was seen as inconsistent with the moral obligations of UN membership; protestations that the organisation's main utility was to act as a bridge and a means of reconciliation between the two arming camps were apt to be denounced privately as rank treachery.

The disintegration of the armed concert was, of course, more than matched by the dissolution of the Western European colonial empires which has brought independence for not far short of one billion of the world's peoples and has led to the expansion of UN membership from the 51 original members in 1945 to the 157 of today. Some of the implications of this tremendous expansion have been well spelt out by Maurice Keens-Soper (see Chapter 6) in terms, for instance, of the extent to which the General Assembly has become a stage for the deployment of rhetorical skills – 'weak point, shout'; for dramatising issues which it cannot resolve; and for a process of voting-power politics through which the 'powerless' wield their numerical majorities to bring more effective pressure to bear on the powerful. It is true that in the occasionally painful process of decolonisation the UN has acted as something of a 'midwife' and 'wet nurse', both easing the process (Indonesia, Libya, several African states, for example) and assisting newly independent states towards an often highly precarious viability. But in the two most difficult cases – Indo-China and Algeria – the UN played virtually no role. Furthermore, the readiness to admit to UN membership every territory, however small or lacking in resources, which became sovereign on achieving independence, has led to a crippling divorce between the arithmetical majorities which the very large number of miniscule states can help the so-called 'Third World' to muster at the UN and their powerlessness to give effect to the resolutions they pass with such acclaim. This practice recently induced even the sober-minded *Economist* to write of 'that drones' hive of indecision', recalling Churchill's acid comment on the Assembly as 'babble tempered by skilful lobbying'.

What is then the situation in the UN today? It is certainly a far cry from 1961 when in Dag Hammarskjöld's final report he could write of the Organisation as having a sense of direction with principles generally accepted by members which 'gave emphasis to the concept, clearly implied in the Charter, of an international community for which the Organization is an instrument and an expression'.[4] My contention is that today not only have such hopes been shown to be largely illusory but that indeed the whole notion of an international society, let alone of a more tightly-knit international community, is under attack. That society, made up as it is of sovereign states lacking any overall system of government, is necessarily in large measure an anarchical society – to use Hedley Bull's term – and the very idea of it constituting a society depends upon the acknowledgement by the majority of sovereign states, especially by the most powerful, that their conduct is to be governed not solely by the facts of power or by the imperatives of their own ideology, but also by a generally accepted set of rules, conventions and norms of behaviour for the more orderly management of their relations.

The disciplines of the central nuclear balance, the spreading ethos of 'modernisation' on Western lines, the communications revolution – the world as a 'global village' – and the growing network of transnational and transgovernmental relations (reflected particularly in the operations of multinational corporations and functional agencies), have conditioned perceptions, it is claimed, to the point where the idea of an international society is increasingly taken for granted both within the United Nations and in the world at large. This is not a view I share. The other side of the coin is that the last 40 years of remarkably rapid change have seen not only the steady process of political fragmentation already referred to, but also a widespread reversion to the seamier aspects of Renaissance diplomacy and the accompanying disregard for diplomatic proprieties a marked disdain for many well-established tenets of international law as a relic of a colonial past; and an appalling disregard for the rights of the weak. The resurgence of Islamic and other forms of religious fundamentalism, induced in part by a revolt against what is seen as the materialist secularism of Western type modernisation, has accentuated the drive in many parts of the world for an indigenous, cultural identity; while in economic terms interdependence is seen by many developing countries as little more than a euphemism for the dependence of the 'peripheral' poor on the rich 'core' of industrial states, a dependence which both threatens to perpetuate their poverty and to increase their vulnerability to the ups and downs of the world capitalist economy. Moreover, the speed at which change has taken place is in itself deeply unsettling both for the governability of many states, and not only the newly independent states, but also for adapting the structures, norms and institutions of international society to the needs of its expanded membership. And there is the further complication that in an interconnected world the shock waves of what previously might have been regarded as mainly local conflicts are more likely both to have worldwide reverberations and to spark off crises requiring urgent and exceptionally skilful handling.

This is a depressing picture. And to it must be added the achievement by a Soviet Union, which however cautiously still sees itself as the agent of a worldwide revolutionary process, of a capacity to project its power, either directly or by proxy, into virtually every part of the globe. And then there is the apparent American determination to reverse what is seen as a decline in American influence and resolve; the emergence of China with at least the potential of a super power; and the continuing turbulence in so much of the so-called Third World. All of this has not only done little to assuage persistent East–West tensions but has also opened up opportunities for external interventions where super power rivalries come only too readily to be superimposed upon local conflicts.

The strains on what is an already fragile international society are thus deep-seated and persistent and it is to be expected that they will be mirrored – in however distorted a fashion – in the United Nations itself. Despite the genuine and not altogether ineffective attempts to agree upon new 'norms' of diplomatic and legal conduct which will reflect more closely both the needs and attitudes of the more recently independent countries and the requirements of a more orderly inter-national system, these strains may prove so great as to lead not to the disintegration of the Organisation but rather to a kind of pensioning off into benign – or even derisory – neglect. It is just possible that the challenges to world order that are likely to arise in the coming decade may disclose a resilience and untapped resources which may lead the United Nations back from the 'fringe' nearer to the centre of the world stage. Much will depend on whether the super powers are prepared to exercise their power with restraint, to acknowledge each other's essential security interests and to act together, wherever possible through the Security Council, to check conflicts which threaten to escalate to global proportions. None of this will be easy. The element of rivalry will continue to inhibit, while there is always the possibility that rash acts by lesser powers can put the super powers in difficult situations not of their own making. Nevertheless, although there is a 'tendency to avoid bringing critical problems to the Security Council, or to do so too late for the Council to have any serious influence on their development',[5] the Security Council has in the past served as a useful device for defusing crises. Even though the leverage the main powers can exercise over recalcitrant lesser powers (especially when the latter have powerful backers) has considerably diminished, its potentialities for the rather more peaceful management of change are not to be neglected and could indeed be strengthened (see Chapter 4). And much the same could be said of the UN's peace-keeping capacity.

It must be confessed, however, that on present evidence the United Nations may itself, if present trends develop further, render the task of achieving a more orderly world more difficult. I have three sets of issues in mind. The first is the use of the UN system, especially the UN's own General Assembly, to achieve a drastic restructuring of the international economic system so as to secure a more equitable distribution of the world's wealth, this being one of the main demands of supporters of a 'New International Economic Order'. The sense of frustration and bitterness which lies behind this pressure is easy to appreciate and it is not surprising that the in many ways outmoded Bretton Woods system – the 'rich men's club' – has lost much of its legitimacy in the eyes of the many states still sunk in abject poverty. There is also an understandable inclination to look back to the 1950s, when pressure by the 'powerless' brought not the United Nations Economic Development Fund they had sought, but at least two new affiliates of the World Bank (the International Finance Corporation in 1954 and, more indirectly, the International Development Association in 1958) as well as the UN's own Special Fund in 1960. What is overlooked, however, is that their success at that time was in large part a function of the then heightened East–West competition for influence in the developing world, which greatly enhanced the latter's bargaining power, together with the continuing belief amongst Western legislators, particularly in the US Congress, in the enlightened self-interest of a positive response to the developing world's pressure. Demands for a New International

Economic Order from 1976 onwards similarly have been based upon the assumption that the energy crisis – as we in the West call it – following the Yom Kippur War in 1973 had both exposed the vulnerability of Western economies and greatly strengthened the bargaining power of the so-called Group of 77. The demand for 'global negotiations' at the UN which might produce bodies more amenable to the Group's needs than the Western-dominated Bretton Woods institutions, and which was reiterated at the Cancun conference in 1981, has, however, lacked the expected bargaining muscle; the most vulnerable economies have turned out to be non-energy producers in the developing world while few of the major oil producers, and especially Saudi Arabia, have been prepared to give the Group the kind of backing which could make the Group of 77's pressures really effective. One damaging consequence – and the matter is far more complicated than I have space to indicate here – is that the developing world's attention has been unduly concentrated on the issue of 'global negotiations' – which will almost certainly prove a cul-de-sac – to the neglect of mobilising their potential bargaining power on specific issues within existing institutions. In the commodity, commercial, monetary and energy areas, this potential power might secure significant concessions if used skilfully.[6] As a collectivity the Group of 77 are relatively powerless; but within the Group there are, for example, producer interests which have real muscle and sources of leverage – if they could only learn to use them. If they fail, the sense of frustration and bitterness is likely to grow and to be damaging not only to North–South relations and to precariously viable developing states but, more importantly, to the tragically growing number of those in the South suffering from poverty and destitution. Even in a world of power politics the 'powerless' are capable of gaining a more sympathetic hearing if they can learn to argue their case more cogently and realistically. So far the United Nations has on balance, I fear, inhibited them from doing so.

The second threat to world order which may well be increased by the UN itself is the readiness, as Conor Cruise O'Brien once put it, 'of the majority of the United Nations . . . to pursue justice, at some risk of war'. For much of its history, anti-colonialist thinking at the UN has been impregnated with the concept of the 'just war', a concept covering virtually all so-called 'liberation' wars. Colonialism was, in Krishna Menon's term, 'permanent aggression' and force could properly be used to secure its rapid demise. Apartheid in South Africa is widely denounced, not without reason, as a form of war against the black African inhabitants which would justify armed intervention on their behalf, as it would be to 'free' Namibia, *if* the requisite force were available – which it is not. And there are still those in the Arab world who would deny the existence of Israel as a state and welcome a 'holy war' to expunge it from the map. Nor is it altogether irrelevant to recall that during the Korean War the view was expressed that a war conducted on the UN's behalf against a criminal aggressor was one in which the latter retained few rights; victory was more important than respecting the rules of war. This frame of mind is somewhat akin to the Chinese and North Vietnamese delegates' insistence, of which Geoffrey Best reminds us, during the negotiations in the 1970s to update the Geneva conventions on the laws of war, that 'every military enterprise of states other than (self-defined) socialist people's republics were morally and legally damned from the outset, while anything done against them by (self-styled) national liberators must by definition be all right'.[7]

Attitudes such as these are deeply destructive of the whole concept of an international society and it must be said that the United Nations has tended to sustain rather than to inhibit them. Moreover, even the legal position is unclear. Probably a majority of delegates at the UN would argue that Article 2.4 of the Charter (prohibiting the threat or use of force against the territorial integrity or political independence of any state, or in any other manner inconsistent with the purposes of the United Nations) gives *carte blanche* to those claiming to be acting against a colonialist or racist regime in furtherance of the concepts of justice enshrined in the Purposes of the Charter. Yet to the founding fathers this is to put a thoroughly misleading construction on an article intended to outlaw the use of force except in self-defence or in enforcement action taken through the Security Council. The tragedy of the nearly 20 million deaths in the so-called conventional wars of the last 30 years and the many millions of refugees still driven from their homes in the aftermath of fighting might have been expected to call forth from the United Nations, and particularly from the Security Council, a much more explicit and forthright condemnation of the use of force 'save in the common interest'. Moreover, even when such condemnation is forthcoming, Security Council resolutions 'are increasingly defied or ignored by those that feel themselves strong enough to do so' (Javier Pérez de Cuéllar). As Martin Woollacott wrote in the *Guardian*: 'only too often, the UN is a place where wars are pursued, proclaimed, planned, justified; and that they have occasionally been ended in the UN, or under UN auspices, should not give rise to too much optimism'.[8]

Finally, there is the UN's role in the arms control and disarmament field. The rigidity in much of nuclear deterrence thinking is a serious obstacle to meaningful arms control negotiations. Strategic parity may have been conceded by the United States in SALT ɪ and ɪɪ, but the hankering after superiority still remains. In the Soviet Union superiority over the United States seems to be regarded as the only acceptable correlation of forces if only because the Soviet Union is confronted by more than one major military adversary, that is to say, China as well as the United States; the Soviet Union's political environment is thus fundamentally different from that of the United States, a fact which the latter is loth to recognise. It is platitudinous to remark that a world security system which is predicated upon a competitive balance of deterrence – both sides seeking a margin of power rather than a balance of power – is in the long term potentially disastrous. As each side tends to take a pessimistic view of the other side's capabilities and intentions – as they habitually do – each sees the need to 'catch up' with the other and attain a new balance at a higher rather than a lower level. This kind of leap-frogging deterrence is a recipe for spiralling madness and constitutes an appalling and wasteful diversion of human and material resources. My own belief is that the central nuclear balance is a good deal more robust than is generally held and that consequently considerable risks can be taken by way of unilateral steps to initiate a process which could lead, *if* reciprocated, to a step by step reduction of present levels of nuclear and eventually conventional armaments to a minimal level consonant with a credible deterrence.[9] Initiatives at the UN have been a factor in securing a Partial Test Ban Treaty and a Non-proliferation Treaty, while the Committee of Disarmament (which takes decisions on the basis of consensus) has played a part in achieving the Conventions on Biological Weapons (1970) and on Inhumane Weapons (1980). But most of the debates at the UN have been occasions for the super powers and their allies to take a 'holier than thou' stance and to succumb to 'disarmament by declaration'. Given the entrenched position of the super powers and the eagerness of many of the lesser powers to obtain arms they cannot produce themselves from wherever available at the least cost,[10] this should come as no surprise. But it does rather make a mockery of the hopes placed by much of Western Europe's peace movement in the 1978 UN Special Session on Disarmament, as in the Second Special Session of June 1982, whilst at the same time threatening to distract attention from the urgent need for both the super powers to negotiate more seriously on issues which have some prospect of being amenable to negotiation.

The question then is whether the United Nations can still be looked to as a serious forum of negotiation on the kind of issues I have mentioned, a forum which is committed to the reconciliation of what are inevitably very diverse and often conflicting interests, a forum in which there will be some 'give and take' in negotiating, one in which the deeply rooted egoism of states will be curbed by a realisation of their common predicament, a predicament which calls especially in a nuclear age for the underpinning and renewal of sadly battered habits of civilised conduct. Or will they see – continue to see? – the United Nations as little more than a strutting ground for expressing their national and personal vanities and for mobilising support for exclusively and narrowly defined self-interest? Herbert Butterfield once wrote that the tragic element in international conflict is that such conflict is far too often seen as a simple picture of good men fighting bad. He urged the need to appreciate that the very structure of international society produces situations of Hobbesian fear. The tragedy, he wrote, is that conflict is so easily 'embittered by the heat of moral indignation on both sides, just because each is so conscious of its own rectitude, so enraged with the other for leaving it without any alternative to war'.[11] Butterfield was writing about the early stages of the 'Cold War', but it is still this conflict between 'embattled systems of self-righteousness', in which statesmen delude themselves into thinking they are gods and that 'inhuman means are justified by the superhuman ends',[12] which is so disruptive of our shared humanity and of the whole concept of a civilised world society. There are some signs that the perils inherent in such pharisaical attitudes are becoming more generally recognised at the UN: in the stress on its value as a point of diplomatic contact, and on registering consensus rather than scoring 'illusory voting victories'; in the use of the mediatory resources of the Organisation, particularly of the Secretary-General (often alongside bilateral or regional initiatives); in the growth of 'informal consultations' through the Security Council; and in the readiness to accept UN peace-keeping presences even in such difficult and highly charged situations as Southern Lebanon or Namibia. So the prospects are certainly not without hope. If, however, the UN were merely to encourage 'vast rhetoric and meagre expertise', to foster confrontation rather than compromise and to magnify rather than assuage the fear and distrust inevitably rampant in an anarchical interstate system, then indeed there would be reason to wonder whether the UN, in Woollacott's words, 'far from simply reflecting an ugly world could in some ways be making it uglier'.[13]

NOTES AND REFERENCES

1. *Report of the Secretary-General on the Work of the Organization, 1982*, p. 3.
2. Sir J. W. Headlam-Morley, *Studies in Diplomatic History* (London: Methuen, 1930) p. 6.
3. Duff Cooper, *Old Men Forget* (London: Rupert Hart-Davis, 1953) p. 193.
4. *Introduction to the Annual Report of the Secretary-General on the Work of the Organization, 1961*.
5. *Report of the Secretary-General on the Work of the Organization, 1982*, p. 7.
6. See A. Jennings and Thomas Weiss in Chapter 9 for an alternative approach to North–South negotiations. Also *The North–South Dialogue: Making it Work*, Report by a Commonwealth Group of Experts (Commonwealth Secretariat, 1982).
7. 'International Humanitarian Law: Principles and Practices', in G. L. Goodwin (ed), *Ethics and Nuclear Deterrence* (London: Croom Helm, 1982) p. 146.
8. *Guardian*, 22 February 1982.
9. See Charles E. Osgood, 'The GRIT Strategy', in *The Bulletin of the Atomic Scientists*, May 1980. (GRIT stands for *G*raduated *R*eciprocated *I*nitiatives in *T*ension-reduction.)
10. As Nicholas Sims has observed: 'Attempts through the United Nations even to raise the possibility of re-introducing the kind of register of arms transfers published by the League of Nations, let alone to restrict the trade, have met with anger and contempt from the majority of Third World countries', *Approaches to Disarmament*, rev. edn (London: Friends Peace and International Relations Committee, 1979) p. 100.
11. H. Butterfield, *History and Human Relations* (London: Collins, 1952) p. 21.
12. E. Voeglin, *The New Science of Politics* (University of Chicago Press, 1962) p. 169.
13. *Guardian*, 23 February 1982.

Part I
Third-party Diplomacy

2 Peace, the Security Council and the Individual

PETER CALVOCORESSI

The Security Council is the sharp end of the United Nations. It is popularly, and not inaccurately, regarded as the executive body of an organisation in which the General Assembly fills the role of a popular assembly and the Secretariat provides the bureaucracy which makes the wheels go round. What the UN does it does through its councils, above all the Security Council. What it fails to do is imputed as failure to the Security Council. To a large degree the repute of the UN is measured in terms of the activity and effectiveness of the Security Council.

The composition, functions and procedures of the Security Council are dealt with in the ten articles which comprise Chapter v of the Charter – Articles 23 to 32. The last five are headed 'procedures' but one of these is among the most important in the whole chapter. It requires the Council to be so organised that it can function continuously. In other words the Council is in permanent session. So far as I know the UN is the only international body in the world whose executive is in permanent session, and there have been occasions on which it has been summoned for deliberation in a matter of hours. It is always on stage.

The members of the Council are divided into two classes: the permanent and the non-permanent. This is indeed the best-known fact about the Council, perhaps the best-known fact about the whole UN. The permanent members are not merely ever-present. They also have the veto. They are recognised as belonging, by virtue of their superior power, to a separate category within the community of sovereign nations. The non-permanent also have, as a class, certain distinguishing features besides their non-permanence – or are supposed to have. In electing them the General Assembly is required by the Charter to bear in mind two things: in the first instance (those are the words of the Charter)

17

the contribution made by members to the maintenance of international peace and security and, secondly, equitable geographical distribution. Both these considerations are new in the sense that there was nothing like them in the Covenant of the League of Nations. The second, which imports the representational principle into the Council, has become increasingly important as the UN has become a truly worldwide body, something that the League never was; and due regard is paid to it in the election of members. Geography is not the only possible basis for a representational system but it is the basis specified by the Charter and it has been observed. For the primary consideration on the other hand – members' records in the maintenance of peace and security – little, if any, regard has ever been paid. Bad guys have as good a chance as good guys when it comes to getting a stint on the Council.

The duties of the Council are laid down in broad terms in Chapter v and elaborated in subsequent chapters. The crucial articles are 24 and 25 and at first sight they give the Council very wide powers indeed. By Article 24 members of the UN confer on the Council primary responsibility for the maintenance of international peace and security and they agree that in carrying out these duties the Council acts on their behalf. Furthermore, by Article 25, they agree in advance to accept and carry out the Council's decisions. The amplitude of this brief is offset by the fact that the Council can act only on the authority of a majority of its members and with the concurrence of every permanent member. The Council is given wide powers subject to strict restraints on the exercise of these powers in any particular instance.

There follows an article (26) which I confess to finding exceptionally obscure. It places on the Council a responsibility for formulating (in the context of peace and security) plans for establishing a system for regulating armaments. I do not understand what these words mean but they are clearly ancillary to the Council's central substantive duty to maintain international peace and security. They were drafted at a moment beset by conflicting views about armaments. On the one hand there was the widely held assumption that armaments are in themselves a threat to peace and a cause of war; on the other, the view that peace was endangered less by the existence of armaments than by their existence in the wrong hands, specifically in Fascist and Nazi hands. And behind both these attitudes was the glimmer, reflected in the provision of a Military Staff Committee, that armed force ought to be deployed and used internationally rather than nationally. This confusing moment, moreover, was also a passing one since the Charter was drafted at a time when weapons of war were regarded as more destructive than deterrent. Their deterrent power had been discounted because of the failures of collective security in the 1930s and had not yet reemerged as a major factor in international politics with the development of nuclear weapons.

The Charter was signed 37 years ago, in June 1945; it came into force in October of that year. I do not propose to present a history of the Council's activities over those years. I prefer to examine two broad questions: first, the internal weaknesses and constraints which have affected the Security Council's work and, secondly, the changes which have come over the international scene upon which it is required to keep the peace.

INTERNAL CONSTRAINTS

I have described the Council as an executive or quasi-executive flanked by a popular assembly and a bureaucracy. I was careful not to describe the General Assembly as a legislative or quasi-legislative body. It is not, and the UN has nothing remotely resembling a legislature. Consequently the legal basis of the Council is weak and it cannot easily be strengthened. There is of course the Charter itself, but the Charter goes no further than, say, Magna Carta. Constitutionally the UN and its principal organs have a less solid legal foundation than early Plantagenet England.

Besides the Charter there is the International Court of Justice. The ICJ is virtually a carbon copy of the Permanent Court of International Justice which was set up in 1920 as an autonomous body loosely associated with the League of Nations. The ICJ is, by virtue of Article 7 of the Charter and of its own statute, an organ of the UN but its competence is strictly limited and the growth of international public law is notoriously slow. This branch of law has been slow too in developing precedents by action outside the courts. It can be done but not expeditiously. Precedents are created by action but action is inhibited by lack of precedents and by the dangers of skating on thin law. Dag Hammarskjöld was concerned with this problem. He wanted to create precedents in order to fortify the bare bones of the constitution provided by the Charter: in effect, to expand the Charter by doing this. But the members of the UN, particularly the major powers, were hostile to this endeavour and Hammarskjöld himself came to see that he was going too fast for the times. He was affronting a cardinal principle of the UN – the sovereignty of the several states which are its members. Any hint, in the

Congo crisis for example, that the Secretary-General might be trying to enlarge the automotive capacity of the Security Council was greeted with thumbs down.

The Secretary-General is no match for sovereign states. He is part of an international organisation which was born with a split personality. It rests upon a fiction, but a fiction which is stronger than many facts. It is a fiction in the sense that what lawyers mean by sovereignty is a status. But status does not confer power; and few of the states in possession of sovereignty can exercise it fully or even considerably. It is more an adornment than an asset. Nevertheless, sovereignty remains fundamental to the international system, and the Charter hastens to affirm in its opening articles that the members of the UN are states and that (with one reservation of no practical consequence) the UN may not interfere in matters essentially within the domestic jurisdiction of a state (Article 2.7). This is an article of faith as well as an article in the formal sense. Many questions arise in its interpretation. For example, is apartheid a purely domestic concern of the Republic of South Africa? Was the attempt by the USSR to station nuclear weapons in Cuba – with the full agreement of the Cuban government – no concern of the USA? But whatever the arguments on points like these, the paramountcy of the state over international organisations and over the international idea is clear and is embodied in the Charter itself.

Consequently the Security Council can be expected to transcend the interests of particular members only occasionally, and to that extent it is bound to disappoint some of its members some of the time and a very great number of ordinary people a lot of the time. At this point appearances become important. No sensible person expects the Council to fly in the face of strongly vested national interests and in the case of the permanent members it is expressly rendered incompetent to do so. But it should at least sometimes be seen to be acting or debating at what one may call a higher level. Part of the reason for creating an international organisation is the conviction that there is a common good above particular interests and, if that is so, the Council ought to display an awareness of this common good and be seen to be seeking to promote it. It would be unfair to say that it has never done so, but its image is other. For this there have been two main reasons: the Cold War and the fact that in its early days the Council adopted a general rule of procedure that it would do its business in public.

Publicity has been regarded as a major element in making the peace of the world safer. A line of eminent statesmen from Woodrow Wilson onwards has testified to the virtues of public over secret proceedings and their arguments are powerful. But no other executive in the world is constantly on public parade and the incidence of the Cold War ensured that, for most of the postwar period (which is the same as the lifetime of the UN), the publicity has been bad. The pervasive super power conflict has ensured that the contacts between statesmen which the UN exists to promote and fructify have been publicly hostile. For much of its life the Security Council has been seen – in the USA seen on television – as a scene of wrangling and even abusive obstructiveness, a vast chamber occupied by a handful of contestants addressing unhelpful remarks to microphones. Such virtues as subtlety have been conspicuously absent. There are, however, signs of change. Members of the Council have increasingly taken to prior private confabulation and it has been alleged that behind the scenes they exhibit glimmerings of an *esprit de corps* which, in public, they seem bent on eschewing in deference to their purely national loyalties and obligations. It is in such pragmatic deviations and compromises that hopes can be glimpsed for a more beneficial international contribution to the defusing of national disputes which is the Council's principal function.

The one undoubtedly international face to be seen at the Council table is the Secretary-General, who heads what the Charter calls the 'organisation' of the UN and also attends the meetings of its principal organs (other than the ICJ). The Secretary-General has a special relationship with the Security Council because, by Article 99 of the Charter, he is entitled at his own discretion to bring to the Council's attention any matter which in his opinion may threaten the maintenance of international peace and security. He may, in other words, activate the Council. Apart from this he is a curiously indeterminate figure. He is described in the Charter as the chief administrative officer of the organisation – not, in normal English parlance, a title of great distinction.

The Security Council has the determining voice in the Secretary-General's selection since the Council recommends him for appointment by the General Assembly, so that he must in effect be acceptable to all the permanent members of the Council as well as to each of the main geographical blocks in the Assembly. The process of election, often contentious and prolonged, gives him a bad start, although once installed in office he is protected by the Charter from any attempt by members to nobble him. He has a large, if ill-assorted, bureaucracy at his back but he is less well informed than many foreign ministers and members of the Council. He has no diplomatic service covering the world on his behalf and only a rudimentary information-gathering service from such special missions as happen to be around. One consequence is that the Council as a body has a chief officer who is no more than averagely aware of what the future may have in store and, unlike the head of a typical British government department, is not necessarily more expert than his political masters. Long-range political weather forecasting is not his strong suit and so the Council is ill equipped to meet crises half way. It waits for them to come along.

To resume: the Security Council is the sharp end, as I have called it, of an anomalous worldwide organisation, based on a states-system and designed above all to prevent or contain armed clashes between these states. Its political rationale is therefore insecure. It has also a weak legal base and inadequate bureaucratic and intelligence supports. It has no force of its own. It has not developed an *esprit de corps*. It does not look impressive but it is always there to be looked at. Against these strictures must be put these facts: that there is no serious move anywhere in the world to get rid of it; that it regularly debates important questions; that its proceedings are studied with attention by governments, the media and to some extent the public; that its members nominate as their representatives persons of weight and experience. It is, in sum, an established and substantial piece on the international scene. The question to be asked is this: is its capacity to keep the peace, either in ways envisaged by the Charter or by subsequently improvised means, growing or waning? Does it count for more or less in the Game of Nations and in the hopes of people all over the world?

EXTERNAL CONSTRAINTS

Both the Charter and, before it, the Covenant of the League presuppose two broad ways of resolving conflicts likely to lead to war. The first consists of a variety of mechanisms for the peaceful settlement of disputes: negotiation, arbitration, adjudication – the extension to international affairs of methods tried with good effect in the internal affairs of states. None of them is new. The Covenant and the Charter put them in the shop window, urge recourse to them, offer help in getting things going. In any given case the Security Council may recommend appropriate measures, even recommend precise terms for an agreement. It is given an active role but no way, under this heading, of enforcing a solution which it thinks right. There is no way of measuring the effectiveness of these services but it is obviously a service to emphasise their availability and provide them.

It is equally obvious that there will be disputes that resist peaceful settlement. This is the crux of the matter. The League put its faith in collective security. It failed and the story of the failure can be read in numerous history books. The essence of collective security was the use of force to deter or, in the last resort, defeat a party to a dispute who insisted on using force to get his way. Collective security was meant to conjure up more force than that party would care to confront, to make him think twice or take the consequences. It was supposed to meet force with more force in order to deter.

In 1945 the founders of the UN were acutely conscious of the fact that collective security had failed to marshal the international force required to deter aggressive national ambitions. But they could think of no alternative. They decided, not to write it off, but to make it better and try again. So Chapter VII of the Charter – headed threats to the peace, breaches of the peace and acts of aggression – vests in the Security Council the right to determine whether any one of these situations exists. The Council is made judge of the facts and there is no appeal from its decision. The consequences are emphatic. The Council may call on members to levy a range of sanctions against the culprit, and, provided these do not include the use of force, members are under an obligation to do what is asked of them by the Council. The Council is empowered to go even further and use force to maintain or restore peace, provided that no particular member may be required to contribute to forcible action against his will. These provisions of the Charter show that its draftsmen wanted the UN to be in a position to take action sharper than anything deemed feasible by the League.

The founders of the UN have been disavowed by their own successors. The articles of the Charter which were intended to give teeth to the Security Council have been a dead letter. The members of the Council have converted wide powers into a minimal programme. Initially the Cold War operated to restrict the Council's ambit, and this trend has been confirmed by the advent of nuclear weapons. Chapter VII has been unused because it inspires more fear than confidence, because the logic of invoking it in the cause of peace is to threaten or make war, and because members of the Council recoil from using these paradoxical threats. I shall came back to Chapter VII.

The Cold War undermined a crucial presupposition of the Security Council. The Charter created a small executive directorate which, subject to certain restraints such as the veto, could operate as a corporate entity and frequently would. The Cold War destroyed this notion by splitting the Security Council, along with much of the world, into two parts whose mutual hostility overrides and obscures their common interests. The Council became an example of the old story of the fruitless desire and pursuit of the whole: the main parts would not make a whole except in very exceptional circumstances such as the Suez crisis of 1956 or the Congo crisis of 1960 – and then only uneasily and very briefly. And more than 20 years ago. This is a situation external to the Security Council, which may change one day. But until it does the Council is doomed to go on debating without possible recourse to the ultimate sanction vested in it by Chapter VII and so without any effective power to intervene, as a Council, in situations which constitute a threat to the peace, a breach of the peace or an act of aggression.

This has not come about because states, great and small, cherish their power to make war. The super powers in particular are profoundly concerned to avoid war with one another but they regard this as their own business, not the Council's. They have too a shared interest in preventing or circumscribing some wars by other states but this shared interest does not, in the prevailing circumstances, lead to concerted action – at any rate not normally or openly and so not by way of the Security Council. The Council gets left out.

The Council tends also to be excluded from areas where either super power is playing a major role. This limitation on its initiative was laid bare as long ago as 1956 when the USSR put Hungary out of bounds to the UN during the revolt of that year and the consequent Soviet invasion. It was no less evident throughout the Vietnam War which was waged by the United States until the United States was constrained – not by the UN – to stop waging it. In the even more protracted and politically more dangerous Middle East crises the Security Council has been a forum for anti-Israeli polemic and propaganda but has been prevented by the American veto from taking any practical steps which might be harmful to Israel. In this straitjacket the Council has won no laurels.

The second external restraint on the Council's effectiveness in enforcing the peace is different because, unlike the Cold War, it will in no circumstances go away. This second obstacle to collective action is the invention of nuclear weapons. The Council was given the right to use armed force at the very moment when a new kind of armed force was brought into the world – an armoury which, beyond a peradventure, the Council will never be allowed to use. The Charter was signed just six weeks before the bomb was dropped on Hiroshima. Ever since that day the force which the Security Council might conjure up to scare or chastise a deviant state is the kind of force which has become more and more unimpressive. The Council will never in the foreseeable future be empowered to levy a nuclear force; and a non-nuclear force is a sanction of declining efficacy. The invention of nuclear weapons has downgraded not only the non-nuclear state but also the United Nations as a peace-enforcement body. The UN's capacity in this field has been, and will continue to be, progressively restricted because the Security Council is not within the nuclear circle. The UN is a non-nuclear, pre-nuclear body.

ALLY FOR THE INDIVIDUAL

What I have said so far concerns the balance of power between the state and some collective wider than the state. But that is far short of the end of the matter. If the collective is no more than the state writ large, what shall it profit the individual if the one or the other prevail? The issue is barren unless it embraces a human purpose over and beyond the delectation of political scientists.

The Charter of the UN is an attempt, by states, to regulate the behaviour of states. Why is that desirable? Because, without some such regulation, a state may let loose unacceptable damage. What makes the damage unacceptable? The destruction or maiming of one state by another is an insufficient answer. The real answer is twofold. On the one hand it lies in the purely material concern of the state for itself. The damage it lets loose may recoil, the state may inflict on itself more harm than initially it bargained for or even more harm than it manages to inflict on an enemy. In other words, there is an unpredictability about the consequences of unbridled state action which causes states to wish, in their own interests, to regulate it.

But the larger part of the answer lies not in the interests of the state as an entity but in those of individuals. Although the UN is an association of states and statesmen, its ultimate purpose is to protect and succour individuals. It is easy to forget about individuals when considering international organisations, easy but wrong. The individual has a long history of conflict with the state which has acquired over the centuries the power to require individuals to sacrifice their lives at its behest and the power to restrict their freedoms at its discretion. An international organisation is a possible ally for the individual in moderating the state's capacity to demand this sacrifice and impose these restrictions. Normally the citizens acquiesce. Some revolt, but for the majority this is too heroic a stand in circumstances in which the rights and wrongs of the cause invoked are usually tangled. The state has worked itself into a position where it can ask too much too unquestioningly. The duties of the citizen to the state have been elevated into a loyalty which often rides roughshod over the duties of the state to the individual. In part – but only in part – the balance may be redressed by the state itself recognising and entrenching individual rights – as, for example, the right of the conscientious objector not to obey the summons to fight. But this is barely adequate since it limits the practice of a state without limiting its power to change its practice. The individual who is unfortunate enough to live in the wrong state remains at risk or worse.

His complementary remedy lies in an international system capable of putting curbs on the state from the outside: curbs on its domestic behaviour and curbs on its freedom to resort to war. I come back to Chapter VII.

The Charter endowed the Security Council with two separate functions. On the one hand, and apart from Chapter VII, the Council is a meeting place for statesmen in the tradition of the European concert; an adjunct to the business of diplomacy; an international or, more properly, an interstate convenience; a preventive and prophylactic facility which members may make use of, if they choose. Chapter VII looks in a different direction. It is the Charter's attempt to create a more or less automotive international organ and one moreover not shackled by Article 2.7 on domestic jurisdiction. The limitations are obvious. The Council is not greater than its parts; it can be kept inactive by a majority of them or even, in some cases, by one of them. None the less Chapter VII is significant. It challenges the apotheosis of the sovereign state. Because it does so without a commensurate redistribution of power away from the state, it adumbrates without effecting a constitutional revolution and so has remained without practical effect in world affairs.

The sovereign state has been Europe's solution to the problem of articulating a planet which is at once too big to be treated as a single entity and yet at the same time so contracted by the technological innovations of the past few centuries as to have all areas in permanent and often hostile contact with one another. And this European solution, grounded in the triumph of the secular state over religious and ideological claims to universal authority, has been copied all over the world. Even China is today such a state rather than the universal empire of its own earlier imaginings.

Law follows the flag. International lawyers were not always of the opinion that the geographically discrete state is so far paramount that no interference in its internal affairs is proper, however ill it conducts these affairs. Lawyers used to entertain the notion of a right of intervention, more particularly a right of humanitarian intervention. But the growth of the power, prestige and self-sufficiency of the state pushed this right into desuetude and disregard, so that it seemed natural in our own day for the Charter of the UN to declare in its first breath – in Article 2 – that there shall be no interference in the internal affairs of a member state. Strictly applied this provision amounts to a licence to the state, in effect to its government, to do what it likes within its borders without protest of chastisement from outside: to exercise, therefore, lordship over its citizens and denizens subject only to their power themselves to regulate the state's control over them.

But extremes beget their own modifications. There is a different tradition which cannot stomach this supremacy of the state over the individual; and the stronger the state the more urgent the case for redressing the balance between state and individual and, necessarily from the nature of the case, for doing so from outside the state. Hence the attempt after the Second World War to affirm the existence in law of crimes against humanity cognizable by an international tribunal. Hence the adoption in 1948, unanimously, of the set of aspirations and admonitions called the Universal Declaration of Human Rights. Hence, in the same vein, the establishment of the European Court of Human Rights and the Helsinki Agreements of 1975. And hence, finally, the whittling down of Article 2.7 itself in the case of apartheid which the UN has insisted on treating as a broader then domestic issue.

This slackening of the letter of the Charter has been partly a consequence of the outnumbering of white faces by black at the UN since the 1960s, but it is no less a consequence of a wider non-racial and human revulsion against the injustices and above all the inhumanities in practice of apartheid: a human response not a purely formal one. Article 2.7 has been eroded or evaded by concern for the rights and the plight of individuals. Theoretically and constitutionally, intervention in the internal affairs of a sovereign state remains taboo; that is the basis of the entire international system created by the Charter. But there are limits to the rule: the one, explicit, exempts from its operation threats to the peace, etc., as formulated in Chapter vii; the other, an infraction rather than an express exception, bends the rule in the face of gross affronts to the individual.

There is an affinity between these two cases. The victims of war and of inhumanity are the same – that is to say, they are individuals. Chapter vii of the Charter does not impinge directly on situations involving the invasion of human rights; it does not give the Council the right, let alone the power, to enter the lists on behalf of a maltreated individual. But obliquely Chapter vii bears on the conflict between the individual and the state because it posits a curb on the omnicompetent state; not, it is true, a curb on the state's disregard of human rights but a curb on its disturbance of the peace; and so a curb. This concordance between international authority and individual rights serves as a reminder that the United Nations, although created by statesmen, was also acclaimed by people. At the heart of this popular acclaim there was a desire to demote the over-mighty state which in the popular view is the maker of wars besides having arrogated to itself oppressive control over those within its borders.

Once upon a time, as they say in fairy stories, the citizens were the state. They not only constituted it; they ran it. They could do this if they were few, and the ideal came near to realisation in some ancient Greek cities, Athens being the most famous. Rome was at one point a city of that kind but the Romans took to using citizenship as a gift which they showered on all Italy and ultimately far beyond, so that on the one thousandth anniversary of the foundation of the city its chief magistrate, by then the emperor, was Philip the Arab. Citizenship so dispersed gave the individual citizen less and less say. His duties were his chief characteristic, his rights easily overlooked.

Then the Roman state – like a number of states today – fell to pieces under the pressures of insubordinate armies, runaway inflation, overtaxation for unproductive purposes, and rampant bribery and corruption. But the individual profited little from this attenuation of the power of the state to command his obedience. Having lost on the swings he now lost on the roundabouts, for the weak state was as useless to him as the strong state was menacing. The collapse of the Roman state fortified, not the individual, but the church, and for several centuries the church made even more exorbitant claims on his loyalty, his labours, his purse and even his mind in return for promises in the shape of post-mortem cheques. The revival and triumph of the secular state over the universal church in the later Middle Ages restored the dominant power of the state over the individual; and so far no new universalist power has emerged to challenge this supremacy of the states. The state is the paramount entity in the world and has increased the paramount power within its borders which it may exercise for good or evil. This power is often frightening, as is the vast increase in the state's capacity to inflict damage and suffering by war. The fears are felt and the damage is suffered by individuals. They want life to be kinder. The ultimate justification for an international system is that it may contribute to the security of individuals, in particular by asserting some control over the state. That is the link between modern international systems and the historic struggle of the individual to find forms of political organisation which do him more good than harm; which work for him.

CONCLUSIONS

I conclude with three observations.

First, continuing the theme of the over-mighty state, there are distinct notions for curtailing the power of the state. They may be called the universalist and the concert.

Universalism assumes a higher power and higher authority. It has taken two competing forms, secular and religious. The Roman Empire never occupied the whole world or even the whole of Europe. The medieval Holy Roman Empire, or more accurately Germano-Roman Empire, was an insubstantial version of a misleading dream: a claim, not a fact. Religious claims to universal dominion are equally empty. No religion – and certainly not Christianity – has ever embraced more than a fraction of mankind. The idea that wars between states can be prevented by a universal power was and is baseless.

These two ideals of a secular and a religious imperium cocooned the political thought of medieval Europe from the fifth century AD to the fifteenth. As they cleared away, the brilliant mind of Erasmus advanced the alternative proposition that the peace might be kept by a concert of Christian princes who would work together to that end. That idea is still with us. The European concert of the nineteenth century is part of its progeny and so are the Council of the League of Nations and the Security Council of the UN. The princes, now governments, are – unlike the medieval imperium – real. So far so good. But their concord remains elusive.

Secondly, the founders of the United Nations presupposed two broad categories of international dispute: those which can be settled without war and those which are leading to war. The Charter tries to deal with the latter by collective action up to and including the threat of collective war. But the classification does not fit the facts. There are indeed two categories into which nearly all postwar disputes can be fitted but they are not the categories envisaged by those who drafted Chapters VI and VII of the Charter. The history of the world since 1945 shows that it is nearer the truth to classify international disputes as those which can be settled without war and those which are left unsettled.

It is significant that the Security Council has been most active in this second class of unresolvable dispute and, through its peace-keeping missions, has contributed not to settling but to freezing them. This is a substantial, if provisional, service. But it emphasises the fact, disappointing to many observers, that the Security Council does not occupy the commanding heights of the international scene. Nor can it. It is highly improbable that the Council can win, within a generation at least, that influence over events with which some of its authors hoped to endow it.

My third conclusion is this. The Security Council is like a child of whom its parents expect too much. It is doomed to disappoint, to carry the cross of exaggerated expectations. The key to this disillusion is Chapter vii. Whereas Chapter vi is at the service of states, Chapter vii proposes to coerce a state.

There is nothing unusual about the coercion of one state by another. This is a natural consequence of the unequal distribution of power among states, particularly among states which are neighbours. Major powers interfere all the time, negatively or positively, in the affairs of lesser states within their reach: the power of the state spills over its borders. In the world since 1945 the dominance of Eastern Europe by the USSR has been a fact and this dominance takes the form of overt coercion whenever the Kremlin judges that to be desirable and covert manipulation the rest of the time. So too the United States can, when it chooses, dominate and steer events in much of Latin America.

But Chapter vii introduces a kind of coercion which is unusual and largely unacceptable. The Council itself has no power. Where a major state exercises power it does so by virtue of possessing it, but the Security Council may exercise power only through consensus. Within the ambit of Chapter vii the Council derives its authority from consensus but is required to exercise it by deploying power. This is an ill-assorted formula. Moreover, the consensus required to release the power includes the voices of states which neither have power in themselves nor the sharpened concern and responsibility which come from being neighbours of the designated delinquent. Their title to intervene is, by current standards, ambiguous. This ambiguity is a characteristic trait of the present stage in the development of an international system; and it is the most potent restraint on the effectiveness of the Security Council and so on the repute of the United Nations among statesmen and in the eyes of people.

3 The Secretary-General: a Comparative Analysis

ALAN JAMES

A notable feature of the past 100 years has been the growth of international organisations, by which I mean interstate organisations. Each of them has an executive head, often though by no means always given the title of secretary-general. All these secretaries-general will, almost in the nature of things, be more than mere bureaucrats, being involved in the political matters with which their organisations deal. It would, of course, be possible to look in isolation at the political role of the Secretary-General of the United Nations, which is the main focus of this chapter. But such an analysis might gain somewhat in strength if it is approached in the context of a general examination of the political influence of secretaries-general. This route might also, as an intellectual exercise, be more worthwhile. Accordingly, before looking at the factors which affect what the UN Secretary-General can do in international politics, I shall scamper around the whole organisational building, stopping briefly at the doors of some of his numerous peers.

My theme is that what any secretary-general can do is chiefly a function of the nature of his organisation. Clearly, an examination of this proposition requires that international organisations be divided into categories, and this is what I shall do first. I shall then draw some deductions about what one might expect of the secretaries-general in each category, and see whether these expectations are fulfilled. I shall go on to consider the strength of this organisational factor with regard to the UN Secretary-General, and compare it with other factors which might have a bearing on his personal role.

THEORY

I propose to divide international organisations into four types. I am not, of course, claiming that this is the only way of categorising them. Nor do

31

I think that any one organisation always falls neatly into one category. All I am doing is to suggest that it may sometimes be useful to look at organisations in this way.

The criterion for my analysis is operational. I am asking what is it that, characteristically, organisations do, what is the essential nature of their activity? First, there are *promotional organisations*, ones which are set up to encourage improvements in certain limited areas of national life. They are supplied with a defined goal, and have to do what they can to push states in that direction. Towards this end they often urge the acceptance of specific standards and programmes. A number of the UN's specialised agencies fall into this category, such as the International Labour Organisation and the World Health Organisation. So do some other UN bodies, such as its regional economic commissions and the UN Conference on Trade and Development (UNCTAD).

Secondly, there are *allocative organisations*. These control the distribution among states of certain resources. They may also have connected supervisory functions. The main financial agencies of the UN system fall in here – the World Bank and the International Monetary Fund – as does the UN's Development Programme. The proposed international regime for the deep sea bed is another and potentially very important instance of an allocative organisation.

Next come *regulatory organisations*. In these cases states may already be cooperating on a particular issue and set up an organisation to make their arrangements less cumbersome. Or an organisation may be established because it is a necessary means of achieving multilateral cooperation in a specific area. In either event such organisations, once set up, are directly concerned with continuing interstate activity. Examples include two of the oldest international organisations: the River Danube Commission and the Universal Postal Union. A fairly recent example – but one dealing with an ancient activity – is the International Maritime Organisation (formerly called the Inter-governmental Maritime Consultative Organisation). The North Atlantic Treaty Organisation and some other modern alliances also fall into this category.

Finally, there are *consultative organisations*. Their purpose is to provide a framework for regular discussion of the relevant issues of the day. Such discussion may aim at little more than an exchange of views; or it may hope to reach common ground; or it may be intended to put pressure on one or more of the member states, snapping at their heels in either warning or encouragement. In any event such organisations are responding to the problems and crises of the changing international situation. This means that the matters they deal with will often be of considerable sensitivity. One thinks here of organisations such as the Arab League and the Organisation of African Unity, the Commonwealth and the United Nations.

What then might one expect by way of activity and initiative from the secretaries-general of each type of organisation? It might be supposed that promotional organisations would give opportunities for prominent or even strong secretaries-general. Having been established to advance a particular cause it is to be expected that their executive heads would see it as their duty to press for movement towards the stated goal. Moreover, the member states, while not always liking such activity, might be expected to permit it, at least up to a fairly generous point. After all, they have set the thing up. And not much harm comes just from noises of an encouraging kind especially if, as may here often be the case, they relate to areas of no great political sensitivity.

Allocative organisations might be expected to have a rather different type of secretary-general. Any organisation which is in the business of distributing resources is necessarily going to place a lot of power in the hands of its executive head. Decisions will often need to be taken and fresh political instructions cannot constantly be sought. Thus the secretary-general of this type of organisation, more than of any other, might be a man having external authority. However, this authority will have to be exercised within very definite limits. States are not going to give resources to an international organisation and leave the secretary-general to dish them out as he chooses. He will have to keep within the established policies. Thus, while the secretary-general may be both important and visible, this will be on account of what he has to dispose of and not because of his bold initiatives and calls for action. Reliability will be what this type of secretary-general might be expected to exhibit rather than flamboyance: the bowler hat and the rolled umbrella rather than an open-necked shirt and sandals.

A third pattern might be expected from the secretaries-general of regulatory organisations. For here, on the face of it, is the least exciting of all secretary-generalships. The organisation will be lubricating a continuing interstate activity, so that the secretary-general may be expected to play a subordinate role. Moreover, if this activity is of a day-to-day, relatively humdrum kind, the secretary-general will have little opportunity to make even a marginal appearance on the international stage. And if the organisation's work is of greater political moment, he will be expected to know his place. In either event, there will be no missionary or patron role for him. It might therefore be supposed that

regulatory organisations will have secretaries-general of the faceless civil
servant type: sometimes seen, perhaps, but seldom heard.

Yet another series of speculations emerges when one thinks about the
part which the secretary-general of a consultative organisation might
play. On account of the issues with which the organisation deals, its
executive head will often be on the verge of or even involved in headline-
making events. But here he meets a dilemma. For on the one hand the
sensitivity of the subject matter means that he does well to tread warily.
States may from time to time appreciate his support, but they will be
very resentful of interference which they do not like. And the secretary-
general knows that if he loses the confidence of a large or important
section of the membership he will no longer be able to do his job
successfully. But on the other hand many consultative organisations are
based on a call for good international behaviour, and the secretary-
general is seen as standing for the values which his organisation
proclaims. It follows that he has an obligation, in some situations, to
speak out in defence of the organisation's principles and, at least by
implication, in criticism of some members.

However, it might be supposed that generally speaking caution will
win the day. Political martyrdom usually offers little by way either of
appeal or utility. But even caution is no guarantee of a quiet life. For,
with the best will in the world, the secretary-general of a consultative
organisation may sometimes find himself in situations where whatever
he does is going to be regarded by some as improper. It might therefore
be expected that such officials will usually be doubly cautious but will
none the less run the occupational risk of finding themselves in sharp-
edged controversy.

PRACTICE – GENERALLY

I will now offer some very sketchy evidence to see whether there might be
anything in these prognostications. I suggested that promotional
organisations might be expected to give scope for strong secretaries-
general. And it does happen that two of the three most dynamic
secretaries-general in the history of international organisation have
served promotional bodies. The first is Albert Thomas who, from 1920
to 1932, was the first Director of the International Labour Office, the
secretariat of the International Labour Organisation. This hugely
energetic and talented man determined to make the new organisation a

vehicle for the promotion of social justice. Accordingly, he took on the role of leader and was accepted as such by the various organs of the ILO. Of course, his personality had a very positive bearing on the part he was able to play. But it was the nature of the organisation which made room for such a large man.

A second example of a promotional organisation giving scope to a strong secretary-general is Raoul Prebisch, who, as the first Executive Secretary of the UN Economic Commission for Latin America (ECLA), imbued it with a zeal for reform and a willingness in this cause to espouse unorthodox ideas. Later he became first Secretary-General of the UN Conference on Trade and Development (UNCTAD) and gave it a sharp bite as a pressure group on behalf of the world's poorer nations.

It may not be a coincidence that a number of other secretaries-general who are well known for their leadership have served promotional organisations. Mention might be made, for example, of Gunnar Myrdal at the UN Economic Commission for Europe, Marcolino Gomes Candau, who was Director-General of the World Health Organisation for 20 years, and David Morse, who for an even longer period carried on Albert Thomas's work at the ILO.

With regard to allocative organisations my *a priori* suggestion was that their secretaries-general would be fairly visible but would be unlikely to place a strong individual stamp on their office. I fancy there may be something in this. Certainly the successive Presidents of the World Bank – by convention always an American – are easily identifiable. But while, for example, one associates Robert Macnamara with a campaign for Third World development, one does not get the impression that the President has a significant influence on overall policy. Press comment on the 1981 appointment of Alden Winship Clausen was to the effect that he would not make much difference to the World Bank's operations.

The Managing Director of the International Monetary Fund seems to be in the same position. The importance of the Fund brings him to the notice of the public and in financial circles his words are given close attention. But none the less it does not appear that even men of the calibre of Per Jacobsson and Pierre-Paul Schweitzer are able to control the Fund's general direction or turn the tide of opinion among its Executive Directors on specific issues of importance. And when Schweitzer offended the United States he found that the way to his reelection was barred.

Another allocative organisation, the UN Development Programme, underlines the point. It administers and coordinates most of the technical assistance provided through the UN system and it is not hard to identify one or two of those who have been closely associated with it. The names of Paul Hoffman and David Owen spring to mind. But they do so as administrators who were dedicated to the cause of development rather than as people who generally or on specific occasions altered the course on which their organisation was set.

I move on to regulatory organisations. Here, so far as technical organisations are concerned, my mind is singularly unencumbered by the names of any secretaries-general, which endorses my initial suggestion that the executive heads of these bodies might keep a very low profile. Who is at the top of the International Telecommunication Union? What even are the names of the 20 or so fisheries commissions which have been set up during the present century? Like refuse collection, we would soon notice the lack of such arrangements, but they do not seem to be much influenced in a positive way by their secretaries-general. This impression finds support in a recent study of four organisations of the kind I have called regulatory. It reports that their secretariats do not play a significant role in either delineating problems, shaping data or drafting resolutions.[1]

With regard to military organisations (which I class as regulatory), the prominence of the matters which concern them means that the student is easily aware of the identities and public activities of their secretaries-general. But this emphatically does not mean that they play a notable political role. The Secretary-General of NATO, for example, although he presides at all the organisation's meetings, whatever the level, is by no means on a par with the ambassadors and foreign ministers of the member states. Generally he eschews controversial interventions, and that he does well to do so is shown by the experience of the one Secretary-General who was more assertive. This was Paul-Henri Spaak, who took office in 1957 as NATO's second Secretary-General. He did not get far and within four years had resigned in disappointment. From his point of view it was particularly unfortunate that the then President of France, de Gaulle, had very different ideas about what NATO's (or for that matter any other international organisation's) Secretary-General should do. But even without this obstacle it is unlikely that Spaak would have been much more successful. In the sensitive area covered by NATO, no member state relishes frank advice from the organisation's leading official.

What of the secretaries-general of consultative organisations? Do they bear out my forecast that, while being politically active, they might try to be so in an uncontroversial way, and have good reason for taking this approach? It does seem to be so, although I shall be led to modify my initial suggestion in one respect.

One does not hear very much about the Secretary-General of the Organisation of American States (OAS). Certainly in this organisation's earlier years (it was established in 1948) he was sat upon very firmly when he used his annual report as a vehicle for comment on current issues. Thus his reports became mere factual accounts of what the organisation had done. Evidently none of the members wanted advice from an official. This may have been due on the one hand to the dominance in the OAS of the United States and on the other to the maturity of its Latin American members.

In the case of the Organisation of African Unity (OAU), by contrast, it was probably the very newness of the members which led to the same result. Lacking administrative or policy traditions of their own, they would not have wanted these deficiencies to be rubbed in by even a mildly assertive executive head. Thus the OAU's 1963 Charter designated him as the organisation's 'administrative secretary-general'. In itself this would not stop him from playing a prominent role, provided the members were willing. But such willingness has not yet been forthcoming. And when one Secretary-General did step out of line he soon found himself without a job. This was Nzo Ekangaki, a young Cameroonian, who celebrated his appointment as the OAU's second Secretary-General by playing a pivotal role in the improvement of Africa's position in relation to the European Economic Community. But then, in 1974, he took it upon himself (so it was claimed) to hire the international company, Lonrho, as a consultant to the OAU. The members, not liking Lonrho's colonialist connections, jibbed, and discovered earlier irregularities in Ekangaki's conduct. He found it prudent to resign, having served only half his four-year term.

Disputes are by no means lacking in the Arab world, so on the face of it there should be scope for the Secretary-General of the Arab League to exercise a mediatory influence among its members. And in fact he has often tried to do so, both with and without a specific mandate. Of course, not every inter-Arab dispute is suitable for this treatment, and he always has to move cautiously. But he is said to have played a significant role.

The Secretary-General of the Commonwealth, too, has been politically active in various ways, and this despite the handicap of starting in 1965 with the injunction that 'The Secretariat should not arrogate to itself executive functions.' He has, from time to time, elicited warning shots across the bows from some member states, not least Britain, especially during the early days of his office. And he knows, too, that there are limits to how far he can go. 'Secretaries should stick to taking minutes',[2] growled New Zealand's Prime Minister at the 1981 Heads of Government Meeting. But generally the Secretary-General has not given offence, despite quite considerable private political activity. Together with the experience of the Arab League this suggests a modification to the general proposition I advanced about the secretaries-general of consultative organisations. It is that where the organisation's ethos sets much store by at least an appearance of agreement and harmony, the secretary-general may, in private, be able to press the members rather more strongly than is the case in bodies of a more variegated kind.

PRACTICE–THE UN

What of the United Nations, which, for the purpose in hand, can be classed as a consultative organisation? It is not, of course, without other aspects. Reference has already been made to its Development Programme as allocative in nature. And on certain issues the UN assumes the mantle of a promotional agency, with regard, for example, to colonialism, white racism and economic development. But in the peace and security field, which is where, if anywhere, the Secretary-General is going to make a name for himself, the UN is overwhelmingly consultative in character. Moreover, it has no in-built bias towards outward unity. It discusses the high political issues of the day, and tries to chivy erring states in this direction or that. It is an area in which the uninformed public might expect the Secretary-General to play a prominent role. But the nature of the Organisation suggests that he will not be allowed much freedom.

So far four men have come and gone as UN Secretary-General. The first was Trygve Lie of Norway, who held the position from 1946 to 1953. After his resignation Dag Hammarskjöld of Sweden was appointed, and continued in office until his death in 1961. He was succeeded by U Thant of Burma, who served two five-year terms and then thankfully stood down. His successor was an Austrian, Kurt Waldheim, who took up office on 1 January 1972 and also served two five-year terms. He was willing, indeed keen, to carry on. But a key member of the Organisation, China, thought otherwise and a Peruvian, Javier Pérez de Cuéllar, took up office at the beginning of 1982.

Viewed overall, the Secretary-Generalship of the UN has not established a tradition of far-reaching personal intervention in matters of great importance. A partial exception to this statement is the second Secretary-General, Hammarskjöld, who for a number of years had what many regard as a brilliant record in this respect. But eventually he went too far, coming up very rudely against the limitations of his job. It is also the case that his predecessor, Lie, tried to assert himself as a semi-independent force on the international scene, but his efforts in this direction were almost wholly without success. The last two Secretaries-General, Thant and Waldheim, played a self-effacing role. This is not to say they were passive and unimaginative, only that they neither sought nor had thrust upon them personal interventions of a positive and headline-grabbing kind.

This is largely the sort of record which, I have suggested, one might expect of the secretaries-general of a consultative organisation. It therefore supports my general argument about the controlling influence of the nature of the organisation on what a secretary-general can do. And the general argument adds to the conviction carried by any particular claim to this effect. However, I have so far been looking only at this one, organisational, factor. It could be that there are more important factors producing the same result. Alternatively, it could be that the correlation I have tentatively identified reflects nothing but coincidence. In other words, my argument about the significance of an organisation's character might have little or no explanatory value.

I will therefore go on to look at this possibility by examining the relevance of other factors which, it can plausibly be argued, influence a secretary-general's role. They are first, the nature of his office; secondly, the circumstances in which he operates; and, thirdly, his personality. This more detailed examination will be conducted only in respect of one secretary-generalship, that of the United Nations.

Office

What, first, about the formal nature of this office? Could this be the factor which chiefly accounts for the relatively limited political role of the UN's Secretaries-General? I think not, for several reasons. First, in strictly formal terms, this is a fixed factor, as the provisions of the Charter regarding the Secretary-General have been unchanged throughout the UN's history. Accordingly, if the Charter had a controlling influence one would expect each Secretary-General to have had a broadly similar experience of office. But in fact there have been three different types: one, Lie, unsuccessfully assertive; another,

Hammarskjöld, making, for most of his time, a considerable international mark; and the other two, Thant and Waldheim, playing it cool and having relatively quiet terms.

The constitutional provisions regarding an office, however, are interpreted and developed in practice, so that its nature cannot be wholly understood just by looking at the original formulation. Subsequent developments can, of course, work both ways. But in the practice of the UN what has happened to the office of Secretary-General has been some expansion rather than diminution, and this took place during the first two incumbencies. Lie may not have had a very successful term, but the interpretation he stamped on his office was clearly expansionist. Hammarskjöld reinforced this development and, through his successes, put it on a much sounder footing. Accordingly, if the nature of the office was the controlling factor, one would expect Thant to have played at least as prominent a role as his predecessors. But this was not so. Nor did the fourth Secretary-General, Waldheim, pick up where the second, Hammarskjöld, had left off, and this was not due to any constitutional retreat during Thant's term.

Yet another factor points in the same direction. By and large the UN Secretary-Generalship has not established a tradition of significant political activism. If the performance of the incumbents is controlled by the nature of their office, one would assume that the provisions of the Charter on this point are, if not restrictive, at least discouraging in tone, offering no enticements for substantial personal intervention. But this is not the case. For as well as some routine statements about the job, the Secretary-General is given the right, in Article 99, to bring any threatening matter to the Security Council's attention. This provision was intended to have and has been seen on all sides as having considerable importance. This is not so much on account of the specific power it bestows (in fact it has only been invoked on two occasions), as in the fact that it provides the Secretary-General with a political base, offering a justification for quiet enquiries and public activities in a highly sensitive area. On this ground he can claim that he is expected, indeed obliged, to be not just an administrator but also something in the nature of an independent political actor.

But the public record is not generally in accord with the expectations to which Article 99 might well give rise. The Secretaries-General have not created many waves in the international pond. This fact, together with my previous points, suggests very strongly that there is no direct correlation between the legal basis of the office of Secretary-General and the performance in office of its various holders. The legal basis *is* important, but as a *basis* for the job and not as a guide to how far the Secretary-General will actually go.

Circumstance

The second factor which might account for the UN Secretary-General's political limits and opportunities is circumstance. There is, of course, a sense in which he is almost always its creature, as he cannot create situations which are suitable for his intervention. But what I have in mind here is the claim that some historical periods are more likely than others to be encouraging or restricting. It is a point which is not unfamiliar but one rarely finds it spelt out with much precision. This is understandable, for imposing periods on history is a dubious business, as is the construction of hypotheses about their significance. But I will offer some tentative suggestions.

It might be supposed that when relations between the chief members of an organisation are bad there is not going to be much scope for an active role for the secretary-general. Not much is likely to be specifically left to his discretion in respect of high political matters, nor are interventions on his own initiative likely to find favour. Contrariwise, when relations are good, the members might be expected to have relatively little use for the secretary-general: they can make their own arrangements without his emollient assistance. It is when relations are at an in-between stage that the secretary-general is perhaps most likely to come into his own. For at such times the leading member states may be sufficiently at one to agree on desired goals but insufficiently close to achieve them without assistance. Similarly, they may welcome diplomatic nudges in a pacific direction.

How do these ideas stand up? They get off to a good start in that Lie was in office at a time of deteriorating and then bad East–West relations. The Cold War threw its shadow over almost everything the UN touched. It is not surprising, therefore, that his attempts to play a positive role so often got him into hot water. During Hammarskjöld's incumbency things were, with the death of Stalin, somewhat improved. It might therefore be supposed that he would have more leeway than Lie. In fact he became extremely active, more so indeed than the circumstances argument suggests. However, while this is compatible with the hypothesis, the experience of the next two Secretaries-General throws considerable doubt upon it. For it was only during Thant's tenure, after

the Cuban missile crisis of 1962, that *détente* properly got under way, and
it never developed to the degree of harmony which, I have suggested,
might enable the member states to dispense with the political services of
the Secretary-General. Accordingly, this argument leads one to expect a
substantial measure of personal initiative from Thant and Waldheim,
which in fact was not forthcoming. I therefore conclude, cautiously – on
account of the argument's rather uncertain foundation – that the general
circumstances of a period do not have an overriding influence on the
amount of personal intervention in which the UN Secretary-General is
able to engage.

Personality

What, thirdly, about the influence of personality? This factor is
undoubtedly of great importance in all walks of life. It is, therefore,
perhaps not surprising that the UN's ability to play a prominent role is
widely assumed to be dependent on having a talented and thrusting man
at the top. This is particularly noticeable when an election is being held
for the Secretary-Generalship. At this time commentators regularly
demand a man of zeal and resourcefulness so that the UN can assume a
sharper and more significant international profile. Not everyone nowadays subscribes to the view that history is the history of great men. But
many appear to think that the history of the UN is to a large extent the
history of weak ones.

There is a fair amount of evidence which appears to support this view.
The last Secretary-General, Waldheim, was very much a diplomat of the
old school: polished and courteous, conscious of protocol, ever polite,
always correct. These qualities made him an ambassador before he was
40, and he went on to become his country's foreign minister before
becoming UN Secretary-General. Here the adjective often applied to
him was 'colourless'. He had a successful but unspectacular incumbency
which was perhaps what one might have expected, for he was a successful
but unspectacular man.

Waldheim's predecessor, Thant, also provides support for the personality argument. He was a calm, quiet and assured man, which was
often ascribed to his Buddhism. The time of his appointment was one of
crisis and turbulence for the UN, so his lack-lustre qualities then had
some appeal. But they soon began to pall. Passivity was the characteristic
with which he was closely identified, and states and commentators

discovered that they wanted something more. Especially was this so after his controversial withdrawal of the UN Emergency Force from Egypt in May 1967 at the request of President Nasser. A rain of criticism, even vilification, fell about his head. This was unjustified on several grounds, not least the fact that states were simply using Thant as a scapegoat for their own failure to stop the war in the Middle East which soon followed. Be that as it may, by the end of his term Thant was belittled on almost every side, and the fact that the UN had not had a particularly sparkling time during his tenure was plausibly linked with his outwardly dull personality.

The case for personality finds further and powerful support of a different kind in the career as Secretary-General of Dag Hammarskjöld. I referred earlier to Thomas and Prebisch being two of the three most dynamic secretaries-general whom international organisation has seen. Hammarskjöld is the other member of my trio. The least known on appointment of all the UN's Secretaries-General he has, so far as success and reputation are concerned, come to overshadow them all. Intellectually speaking, too, he was head and shoulders above the others, and he expressed his concern for practical action by the UN in a superbly subtle and inventive way. First he won his spurs by successfully negotiating for the release of some American airmen imprisoned in China (the Communist government of which was at that time excluded from the UN). Then he was given far-reaching responsibilities in connection with the establishment and operation of the UN Emergency Force which was sent to Egypt at the time of the Suez crisis. This was in 1956. Two years later he played a fairly independent role in relation to the UN Observer Group which had been sent to Lebanon. He followed this with some independent moves in Laos, and then in 1960 urged the UN to involve itself in the crisis which had hit the fledgling state of the Congo (now Zaire). The organisation responded, and again more or less 'left it to Dag'. Peace-keeping, as it has come to be called, had been born.

However, already there had been some rumblings of dissatisfaction with Hammarskjöld's tendency to go his own way. And now in the Congo he soon gave serious offence. The UN Force acted in a manner which worked against the interests of the left-wing premier, Lumumba, and this led to the famous, or infamous, shoe-banging protest in the General Assembly by Mr Khrushchev. The Soviet leader demanded that the Secretary-Generalship become a troika, a three-headed office manned by representatives of the West, East and the neutralist states. Hammarskjöld defended himself, and received much support. But Britain, too, was worried about the way things were going in the Congo, and France, under de Gaulle, had principled objections to a prominent role for the organisation and, especially, its Secretary-General.

At the time of his death in September 1961, therefore, Hammarskjöld was well past the peak of his usefulness to the UN. No Secretary-General can make much of a contribution if he is actively distrusted by one of the Organisation's most important members. And this fall from grace was not despite his thrustful and imaginative personality. It was because of it. To a large extent Hammarskjöld went his own way, and found that the UN would not follow him. As authority in the UN rests, ultimately (and not so ultimately), with the member states and not with the Secretary-General, he was on a very shaky limb. He was *not*, superficial appearances to the contrary, the UN's leader.

Hammarskjöld's experience, therefore, gives a severe knock to the idea that personality is the all important factor in a Secretary-General's success or failure in high political matters. And the tenure of the UN's first Secretary-General also suggests that there are serious deficiencies in this idea. Trygve Lie, like Hammarskjöld, was a member of his government at the time of his appointment as Secretary-General. But whereas Hammarskjöld had previously been an academic and a civil servant, Lie had been a trade union negotiator and a politician. Given this background it is not surprising that there was a certain brashness about his style. He certainly looked forward to being a strong Secretary-General, and tried to make himself what he called a force for peace. Unfortunately, what peace requires is by no means obvious and almost invariably controversial. And Lie tended to favour the Soviet rather than the American interpretation, which did him no good in the eyes of the UN's host country. He had got off to a bad start in 1946 by publicly favouring the case being put by the Soviet Union in the dispute over the presence of Soviet troops in Northern Iran. This led to an acrimonious exchange with the US representative in the delegates' lounge. But he was not deterred. Later on he upset the West by criticising regional defence pacts when NATO was being negotiated, played what America regarded as an unhelpful role in the Berlin crisis, and campaigned for the seating of China's new Communist regime.

As it happened, the United States did not bear Lie great ill will on account of these moves. But when, in June 1950, he condemned the invasion of South Korea by the North, he lost all his good will with the Soviet Union. That country declared him *persona non grata* and refused to have any official dealings with him, referring to him as the person currently fulfilling the functions of Secretary-General. Lie hung on for a few years (given the fact that the UN was fighting in Korea he could hardly do other), but it was an unsatisfactory situation and he resigned in 1953.

Here, then, was a strong personality who was particularly unsuccessful as Secretary-General. Together with the argument advanced in connection with Hammarskjöld, it suggests that the case for personality as the controlling factor in determining what a Secretary-General can do is inadequate. In turn this suggests that little credence can be put in the claim that if the third and fourth Secretaries-General had been more forceful men the UN would have been much more successful in the 1960s and 1970s. Certainly personality has an influence on how a Secretary-General reacts to a situation and hence on his success in dealing with it. But it is not the overriding element among those on which success depends.

I therefore return to the argument with which I started both the chapter as a whole and its second, UN, half: that the role which the UN (or any) Secretary-General is able to play in international relations is primarily dependent on the character of his organisation. Other factors will certainly have an influence, and I have drawn attention to the three which occur to me. But I believe the overriding consideration is the nature of the UN itself, as, for this purpose, a consultative body. In this area the member states just do not want a publicly-thrustful Secretary-General. As Lie has been quoted as saying: 'everything is in order so long as I agree with a particular government, but as soon as I don't – "Aren't we paying you? Aren't you a servant of the governments? You are an administrator, why do you talk!".'[3] Hammarskjöld, too, eventually came up against the resistance of sovereign states to being seriously inconvenienced by an organisation of which they were members. Thant took, on the whole, a less provocative line, which meant that he got on quite well with the members, and lasted to the end of his second five-year term. But they tired of him and on one matter – the withdrawal of the UN peace-keeping force from the Egyptian–Israeli border – got cross with him. The United States, too, was very displeased by his attitude to the Vietnam War. So there was no question of him continuing in office beyond 1971. Waldheim rarely put a foot wrong so far as states were concerned, which is why most of the major powers were willing to see him reelected for an unprecedented third term. This did not happen, but it is very significant that his successor is very much in the Waldheim mould. In fact, it is arguable that most states now have a more realistic understanding of the kind of role the UN Secretary-General can usefully play – a limited one – and that this view is likely to be increasingly shared by future candidates for the office.

HAMMARSKJÖLD: A SPECIAL CASE

Before concluding, however, it is necessary to look at what may be thought to be a fairly substantial loose end hanging from my general argument about the primary importance of the organisational factor. It concerns Dag Hammarskjöld's achievement as the UN's second Secretary-General. I have suggested that eventually he came up against the UN's consultative character, against the fact that some important members felt that they were insufficiently involved in the key consultations. But the loose end concerns the earlier period of Hammarskjöld's almost triumphal progress. Why, to put it harshly, was he allowed to get away with so much for so long? Partly, without doubt, it was a matter of personality. But I believe that it was also due to circumstances which were very specific to the time at which he was in office, and which therefore do not provide a basis for generalisation about the possible role of the UN, or any, Secretary-General.

What I have in mind is not the argument which often used to be met, that Hammarskjöld was able to capitalise on the winding down of empire. Most of the issues with which he was closely involved were not, in fact, ones which had to do with the ending of colonialism, properly so-called. And many more new states have been created since Hammarskjöld's death than during his period in office. What does largely account for Hammarskjöld's extraordinary role is the concept of momentum, together with some tardiness on the part of states to take in the full political implications of the new concept of peace-keeping.

At the time of Suez, Hammarskjöld was instrumental in getting Britain and France out of a jam. They, and others, were enormously relieved. Moreover, Hammarskjöld had operated with great flair and assurance. For these two reasons he was encouraged to continue in this vein, and it was discovered that he needed little encouragement. He proceeded to build on his own success, creating a momentum which could only be stopped at considerable political cost. At the same time states took a little while to get to grips with the fact that peace-keeping was, although a secondary activity, one with considerable implications and consequences in the realm of high politics. It took a major crisis – in the Congo – to get them to grasp the nettle which they themselves had sown. Conveniently for the West, it was the Soviet Union who took the major anti-Hammarskjöldian line. But the Western states were not always happy with the way things were going, and must have been glad that this unpopular dirty work had been done for them.

Subsequent Secretaries-General have had to operate under

Hammarskjöld's considerable shadow. Moreover, it has been inflated beyond its due measure. For a long time this led, even in some official quarters, to unrealistic expectations about the amount of political influence the UN Secretary-General is able to exert. Only now are things beginning to get back in proportion with Hammarskjöld being seen as the exception and not the norm. Of course, many observers still find this conclusion unpalatable. Some do so because they espouse the ill-thought-out idea that the UN Secretary-General operates on a higher moral plane than states, that he somehow represents the superior interests of the global community. Such people rarely consider either the general implications of this claim or whether they would be willing to defer to the Secretary-General if he spoke out against the interests of their own state. They are in fact just indulging in woolly internationalism.

The reality is that the UN is the sort of organisation in which a powerful Secretary-General is rarely welcome, and therefore unusual. For it is the member states who determine how much rope the Secretary-General is to have, and customarily the allowance is not large. In this the UN simply reflects the basic fact that at the political level the world is, for better or ill, overwhelmingly made up of sovereign states. This condition is likely to continue for at least as far as we can see into the future.

NOTES AND REFERENCES

1. Robert I. McLaren, *Civil Servants and Public Policy: A Comparative Study of International Secretariats* (Waterloo, Ont.: Wilfrid Laurier University Press, 1980).
2. *The Times*, 6 October 1981.
3. S. M. Schwebel, *The Secretary-General of the United Nations* (Cambridge, Mass.: Harvard University Press, 1952) p. 165.

4 The UN and International Security*

SIR ANTHONY PARSONS

The UN, in my experience, is an organisation which excites one of three emotions amongst the British people. The vast majority are indifferent to and ignorant of the UN. Those who are conscious of its existence are usually either passionately opposed to it, or equally passionately devoted to it. The former category regard it as a collection of more-or-less harmless, but overpaid, international windbags, nattering on endlessly about their pet obsessions with no regard for what is happening in the real world outside: at best, an expensive waste of time and effort, at worst a vehicle for the benefit of the Soviet Union and its allies to the detriment of the Western world. The devotees of the UN take the view that it should be the saviour of mankind and that it has failed to realise this potential only because of the lack of effort put into it by member states, particularly those of the Western world. I am, of course, speaking of the UN in its capacity as a factor in the maintenance of international peace and security. I do not think that there is any argument of principle about the value of many of its other functions, for example, the provision of aid and technical assistance, the care and protection of refugees, etc.

My own view of the UN falls between the two extremes that I have mentioned, and I could not, of course, be indifferent to an organisation with which I have been so closely connected for so many years. I believe that it is only possible to judge the UN if one understands it fully. It is necessary to recognise its limitations in order to appreciate its genuine capabilities and to strengthen its ability to manage effectively international crises.

* This chapter is based on the Twenty-Ninth Stevenson Memorial Lecture, delivered by Sir Anthony Parsons on 14 February 1983 at the London School of Economics. It was first published in *Millenium: Journal of International Studies*, Vol. 12, No. 2 (1983). The opinions expressed in the chapter are those of the author and do not necessarily represent those of the Foreign and Commonwealth Office or those of the British Government.

To do so, we must keep constantly in mind the nature of the origins of the United Nations and the far-reaching evolutionary changes that have taken place during the 35 years or so of the existence of the Organisation. These changes have transformed it into something far removed from the original conception of those who drafted the Charter, which became effective in 1945.

We perhaps tend to forget that the United Nations was a direct projection into peacetime of the wartime alliance. The intention of the founding fathers was that the United Nations should be a League of Nations with teeth: a world organisation that would have at its disposal the *coercive* means to deter and, if necessary, to punish, any future aggression. In a nutshell, the UN was to prevent the outbreak of a Third World War, a war even more appalling and destructive than the wars of 1914–18 and 1939–45, a war which might indeed bring about the destruction of mankind itself. The military articles of Chapter VII of the UN Charter were the heart of the matter. The UN was to have at its disposal a standing military organisation with a Chiefs of Staff Committee drawn from the five permanent members of the Security Council, namely the United States, the Soviet Union, Britain, France and China. With formidable military force on standby, it would be able to prevent the militarism of another Hitler or another Mussolini from plunging the world yet again into conflict.

A glance at the original membership is a good illustration of the fact that the UN was a direct child of the wartime alliance. Only states that had declared war on the Axis powers before the end of hostilities were allowed to join at the creation. It is curious nowadays to think that even such respectable and active UN member states as Sweden and Finland were debarred from founder membership because of their neutrality during the war. The core of the original 51 members was the Western Alliance and the Soviet Union. At the periphery were 20 Latin American states, many of which had rushed to declare war on the Axis powers in order to qualify for UN membership. It is also interesting to note that there were only three African founder member states – Liberia, Egypt and Ethiopia – and eight founder member states from Asia. Some of the Asian states, for example India, Syria and Lebanon, were still in effect under colonial or mandatory rule.

We all know what happened then. Within a short time after the end of the war and the creation of the United Nations, the wartime alliance collapsed and the Cold War set in, the situation with which we have had to live at varying temperatures ever since. As a result, the military articles of the Charter were never implemented. The whole military structure remained a dead letter. Thus the principal coercive instrument of the United Nations never progressed beyond the blueprint stage. I do not think that anyone envisages that this situation is liable to change in the foreseeable future.

This left the United Nations with a lesser coercive weapon, namely mandatory economic sanctions as envisaged in Chapter VII of the Charter. However, mandatory sanctions have not in practice proved to be an effective measure. It is arguable whether they hastened or delayed a solution to the problem of Southern Rhodesia; it is certain that they were not decisive. Equally, it cannot be said that the mandatory arms embargo applied by the United Nations against South Africa some years ago has weakened the military strength of the South African Republic. It is theoretically possible to envisage a state, isolated and totally dependent on overseas trade for its essential supplies, without any great power patron, which could be vulnerable to mandatory sanctions should it commit an act of aggression or threaten to do so. But, looking round the present trouble spots of the world, it is difficult to imagine such an eventuality. I think that many of the member states that advocate sanctions against this or that country would agree with me that their purpose is more punitive than coercive and that they would not necessarily expect the imposition of sanctions to have the effect envisaged in the Charter.

In summary, the fact that we have to face is that the United Nations has no effective means at its disposal to enforce compliance even with mandatory resolutions of the Security Council. With the exception of the Korean War, where the United Nations was able to take military enforcement action thanks to the absence of the Soviet Union from the Security Council at the crucial moment, the military structure laid down in the Charter has never come into being and is unlikely to be activated in the future. Economic sanctions have proved to be, at best, a very uncertain weapon. My conclusion, therefore, is that the first major evolution of the United Nations away from the design drawn up at San Francisco has been that the Organisation, from being a potential instrument of coercion and enforcement, has become an instrument of persuasion. Fundamental willingness on the part of contending parties to settle their disputes by peaceful means through the agency of the world organisation before or after armed conflict, has become an essential ingredient in any successful United Nations action. This is something that, at least for the time being, we have to accept and to make the best of.

The second major evolution in the nature of the United Nations came about through a process that is nowhere mentioned in the United

Nations Charter, namely decolonisation. I do not believe that the drafters at San Francisco contemplated in their wildest dreams that, in well under 40 years, the membership of the United Nations would have grown from 51 to the present total of 157. Casting my mind back to 1945, we all felt that the European empires would never be restored in their prewar form and that there would be a growing measure of independence for colonial and mandated territories. But I would have been locked up in a lunatic asylum if I had predicted in 1945 that the original African membership of the United Nations would have grown by 1980 from three to over 50; that the original Asian membership of eight would have grown to about 40; and that the emergent and developing countries of Asia, Africa and Latin America would come to comprise about 75 per cent of the total membership of the Organisation. Characterisations such as the 'Third World' and the 'Non-aligned Movement' were unknown in the diplomatic vocabulary of the 1940s.

We can now more or less take it for granted that the parliamentary conjuncture of the United Nations will remain roughly as it is for many years to come. We are close to the goal of 'universality'. If all existing disputes were solved, for example North and South Korea and Namibia, and if all those remaining dependent territories that could sustain full sovereign independence were to acquire it, the total membership of the United Nations would only increase by about another ten states. The pattern would still be a Third World majority of about 75 per cent with the remainder divided between the Western group and the Eastern Europeans with the former numerically greater than the latter.

This qualitative change in the membership over the past generation has produced proportionate effects in the preoccupations of the United Nations in regard to what we call international peace and security. At the creation, as I have suggested, everybody hoped that the United Nations would concentrate on the prevention of the outbreak of a Third World War. By a Third World War, people meant another global conflict probably originating in Central Europe. However, to the emergent Third World, the concept of 'international peace and security' means something quite different. To the Arabs and the Israelis, it means the prospect of conflict in the Middle East. To Vietnamese, Cambodians and others in South East Asia, it means the tragedy of Indo-China. To the sub-Saharan African states, it has meant the crises arising out of the continued existence of white minority regimes on the African continent. Hence, in United Nations terms, the confrontation between East and West in Central Europe has generally been conducted outside the UN, except for the disarmament debates of the General Assembly. Certainly

these are prolific and probably produce more resolutions than any other
topic under discussion on the United Nations agenda. But they have
regrettably produced little by way of practical results. The Security
Council on the other hand, the principal organ for the maintenance of
international peace and security and the main focus of this chapter, has
for many years been almost wholly preoccupied with Third World
problems, particularly those of the Middle East and Southern Africa. At
a guess, I would estimate that about 80 per cent of the 500 or so
resolutions hitherto adopted by the Security Council have been about
those two subjects, particularly the Middle East.

To sum up again at this point, the United Nations was founded as an
instrument of coercion designed to prevent the outbreak of another
world war in Central Europe. It has evolved into an instrument of
persuasion, preoccupied almost entirely with the post-decolonisation
crises of the Third World, particularly in the Middle East and Southern
Africa. The Security Council can draw up guidelines for the settlement of
disputes as it has done with Resolution 242 of 1967 on the Middle East,
and Resolution 435 of 1977 on Namibia. It can recommend various
means of reaching peaceful settlement as envisaged, for example, in
Article 33 of the Charter, namely negotiations, inquiry, mediation,
conciliation, etc. It can participate in these processes through subcommittees of its own creation and by other means. It has no lack of
mechanisms at its command. It has been proved, however, that the
Council has no means effectively to compel parties to disputes to obey its
resolutions. It can only hope to persuade.

For the remainder of this chapter I will concentrate on two aspects of
the pacific settlement of disputes that have developed within the United
Nations over the years. Neither of these instruments is mentioned in the
Charter, nor were they necessarily envisaged by the founder members.
They have evolved out of necessity as the Organisation itself has evolved
in the way I have described. I am referring first, to what has come to be
known as the 'good offices' of the Secretary-General, and secondly, to
United Nations peace-keeping forces – the Blue Berets.

The Secretary-General's good offices, that is to say the use of the
Secretary-General as a mediator between conflicting parties, either on
his own initiative or with a mandate from the Security Council or the
General Assembly, is the one form of confidential diplomacy available to
the United Nations. It has two virtues. First, its confidentiality enables
the parties in question to avoid public statements of their positions while
mediation is under way. This in itself helps to lower the temperature and
to create an atmosphere in which there is some hope of a peaceful

resolution of the dispute. It has the consequential effect of reducing the likelihood of armed conflict breaking out. Secondly, it is frequently easier for parties to a dispute to accept the Secretary-General as a mediator than it is for them to accept mediation from some third state or group of states. The latter more often than not creates difficulties where the dispute in question is sensitive in terms of the internal politics of the parties. But they can accept the Secretary-General as the chief executive of a world organisation of which they are themselves members.

Let me give two examples. In the late 1960s, when Britain announced that it was going to withdraw protection from the small states of the Persian Gulf, one of the outstanding problems was the Iranian historic claim to the islands of Bahrain. The then Shah of Iran realised that, when the British had departed, he would be faced with two difficult choices. He could either prosecute his claim by military force, thus seriously disturbing the stability of the area and destroying any hope of Iran building a reasonably stable relationship with the Arab world; or he could drop his claim, thus exposing himself to severe internal criticism from those elements that felt strongly that Bahrain was a part of Iran.

In brief, the three parties concerned, namely Britain, Iran and Bahrain, decided to have recourse to the good offices of the Secretary-General. After over one year of confidential diplomacy, all parties agreed that the Secretary-General should send a personal representative to Bahrain to ascertain the wishes of the people and that, if these wishes were confirmed by the Security Council, *all parties would accept the judgement*. The ascertainment took place and eventually the Security Council unanimously adopted a resolution confirming the desire of the people of Bahrain to be *members of an independent Arab state*. Iran felt itself able to accept this judgement, coming as it did from the international community as a whole via the Secretary-General and ultimately the Security Council. I was personally involved in this exercise and have always believed that it would have been impossible to find an alternative agency which could have produced so satisfactory a result to a problem which seriously threatened peace and security in an important and explosive region of the world.

A second example is the saga of the Vietnamese boat people in 1979. There was at that time an uncontrolled mass exodus of people of Chinese origin from Vietnam, which was creating not only severe humanitarian problems, but also an atmosphere of general tension in Southeast Asia. Bilateral pressure on the government of Vietnam proved fruitless. In August of that year, the Secretary-General called a conference of all interested parties in Geneva. The Vietnamese government felt able to accept the outcome of this conference, coming as it did from the international community under the aegis of the Secretary-General. As a result, the flow of refugees was controlled and arrangements were made that went some way towards solving the humanitarian problems and also towards reducing the tension that the exodus had created.

Of course the Secretary-General is not always successful – we must always remember that we are talking about persuasion, and sometimes people cannot be persuaded. For example, in the Falklands crisis last year, the Secretary-General was accepted by the parties to use his good offices to bring about the implementation of a mandatory resolution of the Security Council – Resolution 502 – which, lacking the coercive means, the Council had no way to implement. In spite of his extremely dedicated, vigorous and skilful efforts, the Secretary-General failed to bring about the desired result, although I believe that he came closer to doing so than any of the other mediators who had been in the field previously. Equally, the Secretary-General has been using his good offices for many years over the Cyprus dispute without visible results. However, in that case, the fact that he has been engaged with the problem for so long has helped to reduce the temperature: the parties have, generally speaking, moderated their public statements, and the risk of further armed conflict has been diminished.

United Nations peace-keeping is another story of success and failure. It is important to understand that UN peace-keeping forces, whether observers or formed units, are not intended to enforce solutions to problems. They can only be deployed with the consent of the parties and are yet another instrument of persuasion. Their objective is to defuse crises either before or after armed conflict has taken place and, by acting as a buffer between both sides, to create an atmosphere in which peaceful negotiations can begin for a resolution of the underlying problem. If the parties fail to take advantage of this breathing space and if the problem either remains unsolved or further armed conflict breaks out, the peace-keeping forces themselves cannot be blamed. For all the failures, the most recent and vivid one being the inability of UNIFIL to check the Israelis' invasion of Lebanon last summer, I believe that, had it not been for UN peace-keeping forces, many people now alive would be dead, many disputes would be in a higher state of tension than they are, and the world as a whole would be a far more dangerous place than it is even now. Let me give you two examples, both cases where I believe that UN peace-keeping operations were indispensable.

The first is, in fact, the first time that UN peace-keeping forces were deployed, i.e., after the Anglo-French invasion of Egypt in 1956 following the Israeli attack on Sinai. It was clear to the British and French governments from the international reaction to the Suez affair that they would have to withdraw. However, for a multitude of reasons, they could not have done so unilaterally. There were internal political considerations to be taken into account. Who would ensure that the Suez Canal would be reopened? What troops would replace them? Would conflict be resumed between Israel and Egypt? But it was possible from all these points of view for the British and French governments to be seen to accede to a resolution of the UN that proposed that the Anglo-French forces should be replaced by United Nations forces. This happened, the British and French withdrew, and the UN forces moved in to reopen the canal and to act as a buffer between the Egyptian and Israeli armies. As a result, ten years of peace ensued in the troubled region of the Middle East. It was broken, as we all know, when the Egyptian President obliged the UN force, there only with the consent of the parties, to withdraw in 1967. But the UN can scarcely be blamed for the fact that parties and their friends and allies failed to take advantage of that ten-year breathing space to bring about some composition of their differences.

My second example concerns precisely the same area. At the end of the Yom Kippur War of October 1973, there was a situation of the most appalling danger to global peace. At the northern end of the Suez Canal Egyptian forces had crossed into the Sinai. At the southern end, Israeli forces had crossed the canal into the Egyptian heartland, isolating the Egyptian Third Army. Fighting was still continuing and there was a confused situation with no clear line of demarcation between the warring parties, and no prospect of a ceasefire. The Soviet Union put airborne forces on alert to fly to the area on the Egyptian side. The United States followed suit by alerting its own airborne forces in Western Europe. The world came close to a naked confrontation between the super powers on a battlefield. Neither side could find a way to climb down. At the last moment, they used the Security Council of the United Nations as a ladder from which to dismount from their high horses. A Security Council resolution was adopted which led to the immediate deployment, within 24 hours, of a UN peace-keeping force into the area. There was a ceasefire and the UN forces took up positions as a buffer between the Egyptian and Israeli forces. Simultaneously, an analogous operation was taking place to separate Syrian and Israeli forces on the Golan Heights. The tension declined, the immediate danger passed, and an atmosphere was recreated in which peaceful negotiations could take place. On this occasion the peaceful negotiations were at least partially successful and the UN peace-keeping force was able to withdraw when the Camp David agreements brought about the peace treaty between Egypt and Israel leading to Israeli evacuation of Sinai.

In both cases, I cannot think of any other agency which could have brought about the same result. There is, of course, no doubt that the United Nations is passing through a severe crisis. It has experienced a number of failures in the last year or so. As I have said, UNIFIL did not prove to be an effective deterrent to the Israeli invasion of Lebanon. The Secretary-General was unable to bring about a peaceful Argentine withdrawal from the Falklands. For the moment, the Security Council has been bypassed in the negotiations to bring about a peaceful solution of the problem of Namibia (see chapter 11). These events and others combined to create a general atmosphere of pessimism regarding the United Nations as an effective instrument to maintain or to restore international peace and security.

In this chapter, by drawing attention to some of the successes of the United Nations, I have tried to redress this balance: not in a spirit of starry-eyed optimism, but by trying to clarify the reasons for the limitations of the power of the United Nations, and at the same time to demonstrate how it can act effectively as an instrument of persuasion.

Is there any way in which its persuasive powers can be strengthened? I have only one major suggestion to make. It is too often the case that the United Nations is brought into play after a crisis has reached the point of no return, i.e., to pick up the pieces after armed conflict has already broken out..The Gulf war between Iran and Iraq is a good case in point. Any intelligent person reading his newspapers in the summer of 1980 could have guessed that serious tension was developing between Iran and Iraq and that armed conflict was a probability. For various reasons, no member state contemplated having recourse to the Security Council until after the war had started, by which time it was too late. If the Security Council had been convened, say a month before the conflict broke out, and if it had summoned say the foreign ministers of Iran and Iraq to New York to explain to the Council in public what the causes of the growing tension were, this act alone might have made it more difficult for either side to unleash its armed forces. Even though a positive resolution might not have been possible in New York, the very fact that the crisis was under public international scrutiny might have had a deterrent effect.

Thus the Security Council should be prepared to take preemptive action more frequently before disputes reach a point where peaceful solutions become impossible. The problem is that, for one reason or another, individual member states of the Security Council always seem to be reluctant to take the initiative to call the Council in advance of a crisis reaching danger point. This may sound like passing the buck, but I think that the Secretary-General should be prepared to make more frequent use of Article 99 of the Charter which authorises him 'to bring to the attention of the Security Council any matter which in his opinion may threaten the maintenance of international peace and security'.

The Secretary-General has to be very careful before invoking Article 99. If by doing so he sails across the bows of either of the super powers or of the Non-aligned group in the Council, he can find himself in serious trouble. But I still believe that he is the only person who is in practice likely to initiate regular preemptive action by the Council. One prerequisite is that the Secretary-General should have his own sources of information about crisis areas. At present, he has to rely for the most part on the public media, which, with great respect, can be both inaccurate and lacking comprehensiveness. Apart from the public media, he has to depend on reports given to him by member states which are more often than not prejudiced from the point of view of their individual national interests. He does, of course, sometimes have technical UN representatives on the spot, United Nations Development Programme resident representatives and so on. There also may be a peace-keeping force already *in situ* which can provide him with information. However, in the majority of cases he is dependent on other people to provide him with the information on which to make his own assessment.

My tentative suggestion, which would not cost much money, is that consideration should be given to the establishment of UN political presences in the major trouble spots of the world. These would constitute 'UN Ambassadors' whose duty it would be to report directly to the Secretary-General. Their reporting would be confined to assessments of the degree of tension in regional disputes and the danger of the tension rising to the point of conflict. Armed with his own sources of information, the Secretary-General would be in a stronger position to argue with any recalcitrant member of the Security Council that he was justified in invoking Article 99 and calling a meeting of the Security Council in a specific instance.

The present Secretary-General, as we have seen from his Annual Report for 1982, is deeply aware of the dangerous condition of today's world. The above suggestion is just one of perhaps several ways in which I believe that the ability of the United Nations to anticipate and to defuse crises might be strengthened.

CONCLUSION

I end this chapter where I began. It is wrong to write off the United Nations simply because it cannot do what its founding fathers set out to enable it to achieve. Just because, as the poet R. S. Thomas puts it 'the star's bridle is hung too high' we should not cease to aspire to them. In the meantime, we should continue to make the best of things in the lower foothills of our journey.

I have tried to indicate how the United Nations has evolved in its function regarding international peace and security into the early 1980s. I would not expect to see any radical change in the decade before us. A fundamental increase in the capability of the United Nations would require a degree of reconciliation between East and West which is difficult to imagine in present circumstances. But I do not think that there will be a decline. The world needs the United Nations as an instrument of last resort in dangerous crisis, and the Third World needs it more than anyone else. My guess, therefore, is that it will continue over the next few years roughly as it has during recent years. It will have its successes; it will have its failures. Its main preoccupation will continue to be the security problems which bedevil the Third World, particularly in Asia and Africa. I hope I have said enough in this essay to demonstrate my belief that, were the Organisation to collapse, the world would be a far more dangerous place than it already is.

5 The UN and the Falklands Crisis

J. E. SPENCE

For the student of the United Nations, the Falklands crisis offers a valuable case study of the strengths and weaknesses of that organisation as an agency for promoting the peaceful settlement of disputes through its role as a 'third party' concerned to act impartially in mediation of a conflict between two member states. At first sight the failure of the · United Nations, despite several resolutions of the Security Council and the 'good offices' of the Secretary-General, to avert the outbreak of armed hostilities between Britain and Argentina in late April 1982 and, once begun, to achieve a ceasefire appears a confirmation of its weaknesses rather than a vindication of its strengths as an independent and effective crisis manager. Thus in the Falklands dispute – it could be argued – the UN did little more than mirror the conflict in an institutionalised setting, providing through the mechanism of the Security Council a propaganda forum for the warring parties and their supporters and exercising little, if any, influence on the course of the dispute and its eventual outcome.

There is a measure of truth in this pessimistic assessment, but it obscures some interesting and significant aspects of the UN's role throughout the crisis, all of which deserve analysis if a more balanced judgement is to be made. This chapter attempts such a judgement by focusing on the style and content of the diplomacy that occurred at the UN in the April–June 1982 period.[1] The argument is that despite the clear evidence of failure to resolve conflict short of war, there was a very real sense in which the UN revealed itself as more than simply the sum of its parts, aspiring, though not always succeeding, to play the role of an independent actor whose authority, status and resulting political influence could not be ignored or brushed aside by national decision-makers.

Until April 1982 and the start of a two-month period of intense diplomatic activity (both private and public, within and outside the framework of the Security Council), UN involvement in the dispute between Britain and Argentina over the future status of the Falkland Islands had been intermittent. In 1948 the Argentinian government turned down a proposal for adjudication of the issue by the International Court of Justice.[2] This 'tacitly acknowledged'[3] legal weakness proved no great disadvantage in the heady atmosphere of the 1950s and 1960s when the ideological appeal of anti-colonialism ensured massive majorities in the General Assembly for resolutions pressing for the decolonisation of dependent territories. In the specific context of the Falklands, Resolution 2065 passed in December 1965, following Argentina's reference of the dispute to the UN 'Committee of 24' on decolonisation called on Britain and Argentina to 'proceed without delay with negotiation . . . with a view to finding a peaceful solution to the problem'.[4] The substance of this resolution was repeated in 1973 and 1976 with Britain abstaining on the first two occasions and voting against on the last. During this period support for the Argentinian claim was forthcoming at two meetings (1976 and 1979) of the Non-aligned Movement; on both occasions 'Argentina . . . obtained a single sentence in the Political Declaration endorsing Argentinian claims to sovereignty over the Malvinas.'[5]

This sporadic concern shown by the UN suggests that the Falklands issue never acquired the saliency characteristic of other more dramatic disputes such as those arising from, e.g. the status of Namibia or the future of Rhodesia. Indeed this relative indifference at the level of international organisation was reflected in the low priority given to the Falklands by successive British governments. Bilateral discussions took place in the mid-1960s, in 1970–1 (when a communication agreement resulted), and were resumed on several occasions, usually at junior ministerial level, during the remainder of the decade. Further meetings were held in February 1981 and February 1982, but on each occasion the efforts of individual ministers and civil servants to reach some accommodation with their Argentinian counterparts foundered on the hostility of the islanders to any change in their status and the unwillingness of governments to brave the well-orchestrated and vociferous opposition of the sizeable Falklands lobby in the House of Commons. In any case the threat of military intervention by Argentina seemed remote and beyond serious consideration; Argentinian pressure on the issue was interpreted as designed solely to distract, however briefly, the population from the burdens of economic and social distress.

THE ROLE OF THE SECURITY COUNCIL

The dilatory interest shown by both the UN and Britain in a resolution of the Falklands issue largely explains the profound surprise, indeed shock, that greeted the news of invasion on 2 April in both London and at UN headquarters in New York. Yet the shortcomings of British diplomacy in the years preceding the crisis were quickly compensated by the skill with which support was generated for the British position.[6] It is worth noting that even at this early stage, the Secretary-General Javier Pérez de Cuéllar and Ambassador Kamanda Wa Kamanda of Zaire, President of the Security Council, were involved in an informal third party role. On 1 April, following an abortive attempt by the United States delegate, Mrs Jeanne Kirkpatrick, to arrange a private discussion between Ambassador Eduardo Rocco of Argentina and the British representative, Sir Anthony Parsons (a foretaste of what was to come by way of public mediation through the 'good offices' of Alexander Haig, the Secretary of State), the Secretary-General appealed to both governments to show restraint in their handling of the crisis. Sir Anthony, aware by now that an invasion of the Falklands was only hours away, asked, in private session of the Security Council, for a public session of the Council. This was granted and a presidential appeal for restraint was adopted.[7]

The debate that began on 3 April makes instructive reading for the student of 'public' conference diplomacy. Both parties to the dispute invoked principle in support of their case: for the Argentinian delegate, the need to assert the territorial integrity of his country justified the invasion of the Falklands; Las Malvinas had always been Argentinian territory and his government was simply recovering what had been 'seized by the British by an illegitimate act of force in 1833'.[8] The right of self-determination could not apply to the inhabitants of the Falklands since the 1833 'illegitimate act of force' by the United Kingdom 'had been followed by the expulsion of Argentinian nationals and their replacement by a tiny number of citizens from the colonial power . . . which makes inapplicable to the dispute the principle of self-determination'.[9] For Sir Anthony this argument was unacceptable: the inhabitants were 'people of mainly British origin . . . the United Kingdom had exercised sovereignty over the Falkland Islands since early in the 19th century'.[10]

The result of the debate was – at first sight – a surprising victory for the British-sponsored Resolution 502 which (i) condemned the Argentinian invasion of the islands; (ii) demanded an immediate withdrawal of Argentinian forces; and (iii) called on both parties to find a diplomatic solution to the dispute. Ten of the fifteen states on the Council voted for the resolution, and significantly their number included four Third World countries – Guyana, Uganda, Togo and Zaire. Panama voted against, while the Soviet Union, Poland, China and Spain abstained.

This resolution set the parameters for much of what followed in diplomatic (and to a degree military) terms over the next ten weeks. It provided a constitutional rubric for the UN's role as a third party. The consensus represented by Resolution 502 was more than just an *ad hoc* expression of the views of those states which happened at that time to be members of the Security Council. It established – in a very real sense – a normative standard backed by the authority of the Organisation as a whole by which subsequent actions of the two protagonists would be judged. Resolution 502 set, therefore, constraints which neither Britain nor Argentina could lightly ignore in the flurry of discussion that subsequently ensued both at the UN and elsewhere in the search for a negotiated settlement.

The importance of Resolution 502 justifies some analysis of the motives and subsequent actions of those who supported it (and those who by abstaining did not in effect approve) and of Britain and Argentina in particular. Both the latter had henceforth to conduct their diplomatic and military strategies in the knowledge that the British view that aggression had taken place had been vindicated and indeed legitimised by the UN via the invocation of Chapter VII of the Charter (actions with respect to threats to the peace).

More significantly, Britain could now have recourse to Article 51 (the inherent right of individual or collective self-defence) to justify the use of force to recover what was rightfully hers; hence the taskforce ' . . . appeared blessed with UN approval'.[11]

There can be no doubt that Resolution 502 represented a major diplomatic and political defeat for the Argentinian government. The junta had wrongly assumed, as Sir Anthony himself has pointed out, that a former

imperial power [could not] prevail diplomatically in the UN over an issue of decolonisation against a member or members of the Non-Aligned Movement whose cause in the South Atlantic had been espoused by successive Non-Aligned summits . . . They were wrong: they had underestimated the depth of antipathy of virtually the whole membership to the use of force to settle political disputes whatever the merits of the case.[12]

Costa Mendes, the junta's foreign minister, had advised that there was little prospect of Britain mobilising the necessary votes for an adverse vote against his government's action.[13] Even if it did, the Russians, who enjoyed close economic relations with Argentina, would use their veto in the unlikely event that Britain could persuade the Council to meet and debate the issue. (This was only one of several major blunders including the more fundamental misreading of the British domestic mood and Mrs Thatcher's determination to take the most vigorous diplomatic and military measures to restore the islands to British sovereignty.) Costa Mendes was not present when the Security Council debate began, leaving the crucial opening statement for his government to the newly-arrived Eduardo Rocco. The result was that neither had the time to lobby for support in advance of the final vote on Resolution 502. By contrast, Sir Anthony Parsons succeeded brilliantly in this respect: we cannot at this stage know what diplomatic bargains, if any, were struck, but Hastings and Jenkins make a fair guess at what was probably involved: 'At times like this a diplomat must draw on every resource at his disposal – an old favour done, a personal contact kept in good repair, a trade deal or cultural exchange in the offing, perhaps simple friendship.'[14]

Especially significant and perhaps surprising was the voting behaviour of the Third World membership of the Security Council. No doubt – as Hastings and Jenkins suggest – France leaned on Togo to support the resolution. Guyana likewise sided with Britain, perhaps bearing in mind the encouragement that defeat of the resolution would give Venezuela in their border dispute. Jordan's vote swung Britain's way only after a personal appeal from Mrs Thatcher to King Hussein, while Uganda was allegedly impressed with the argument that Argentinian action was straightforward aggression.[15] As for the Russian abstention, we may only speculate that despite dependence on Argentinian foodstuffs and traditional support for 'anti-colonial' causes, little, if anything, was directly at stake in the crisis for Soviet interests. It is one thing to buy grain and meat from a Fascist dictatorship, quite another to be seen openly supporting its 'militaristic' adventures. Perhaps, too, there was some satisfaction to be gained from a crisis which would at the very least – however temporarily – weaken NATO through the withdrawal of British forces to the South Atlantic and at best go sour and perhaps bring down a profoundly hostile Conservative government.

The three weeks following the passing of Resolution 502 on 3 April witnessed a combination of diplomatic and military manoeuvring. The speedy and effective despatch of the taskforce gave Britain two major advantages: first (and here the length of time it took the taskforce to reach the Falklands was important), it enabled the government to match the threat of violence if negotiations failed with a diplomatic posture suggesting willingness to reach a settlement on the basis of Resolution 502; secondly, it spurred on the variety of attempts at third party negotiation made by Alexander Haig, the Peruvian President and the Secretary-General of the UN. Had the taskforce not been despatched, had Britain been content to trust to diplomacy alone – its own and those of third parties – the probable outcome would probably have followed 'the pattern of so many events of which the Security Council was seized – a violent change in the *status quo* followed by an interminable negotiation leaving the altered situation unredressed: the Middle East, Afghanistan, South East Asia being good examples'.[16] On the other hand, the significance of Resolution 502 lay in the fact that both Britain and Argentina were obliged by its terms to give at least an appearance of serious negotiation, responding in good faith to the various proposals put forward for a settlement. From Britain's perspective, in particular, it was important to maintain the consensus so painstakingly built up in the Security Council, but at the same time resist 'any subsequent demand that Britain stall or recall the taskforce'[17] before being given the clearest possible evidence that Argentina was willing to withdraw its forces from the islands on terms consistent with Britain's massive military and diplomatic commitment to achieve that end.

THE ROLE OF THE SECRETARY-GENERAL

What role did the UN, and in particular the Secretary-General, play during the first month of the crisis? Following the passage of Resolution 502, Alan James's definition of what one might currently and in general terms expect of a Secretary-General is helpful in analysing the particular strategy followed by Pérez de Cuéllar:

> initiatives . . . which are both striking and generally acceptable are going to be uncommon; . . . a good deal of his most fruitful activity will take place behind the scenes. What is needed, therefore, is a man who moves skilfully at this last level; who is willing, when necessary, to act on his own; but who recognises the limits within which he must operate and does not find unduly frustrating.[18]

Throughout April, de Cuéllar was content to leave the task of mediation in the hands of Alexander Haig. (The latter had proposed a plan calling for mutual withdrawal of Argentinian and British forces; a tripartite administration involving the United States, Britain and Argentina; and negotiations in due course over the key issue of sovereignty.) Indeed, the Secretary-General had little choice in the matter; he was not at this stage empowered to act as mediator and the invocation of his authority under Article 99 of the Charter might well have upset the delicate balance of agreement represented by Resolution 502 – especially in view of the traditional Russian antipathy to an 'activist' role for the Secretary-General. There was little he could do – even if he had been so inclined – to stop the United States from assuming the role of mediator, a task for which it might have seemed eminently well qualified, given its close ties with both parties and the influence deriving from its standing as a super power. (That the Haig initiative failed in circumstances damaging to American prestige – in the sense that both parties resented American intrusion – cannot be regarded as the fault of the Secretary-General.)

Hence the latter pursued a course of quiet diplomacy, establishing a taskforce under a deputy to prepare contingency plans in the event of Haig's failure and offering on 19 April both parties to the dispute a 'list of the ways in which the UN might be able to help bring about a negotiated settlement'.[19] Similarly, towards the end of April, as the taskforce neared the islands and the likelihood of war increased, the Secretary-General, together with the President of the Security Council, resisted calls from a variety of sources for a reconvening of the Council on the grounds that this could only damage the Haig mission's chances of success.

By the end of the month, however, fighting had broken out between the two sides and this effectively wrecked any prospect of success for the Haig proposals. The occupation of South Georgia on 25 April, the bombing of airfields at Goose Green and Port Stanley, and the sinking of the *Belgrano* (2 May) led the Secretary-General to assume a formal, public role as mediator. He proposed a 'set of ideas' to both delegations which included 'the concepts of mutual withdrawal, the commencement of diplomatic negotiation . . . , the lifting of sanctions in the exclusion zones, and the establishment of transitional arrangements in the Falklands pending the outcome of diplomatic negotiations'.[20]

At this point, however, the coalition in the Security Council began to show signs of breaking up. The Irish delegate tried to recall the Council and there followed a series of 'informal consultations' in which Sir Anthony Parsons emphasised that Britain's military action could not cease unless there was clear evidence on the part of Argentina of an intention to withdraw from the islands. The Council agreed to support the Secretary-General's initiatives, and a period of intense negotiation under his auspices continued until 19 May. This involved some 30 separate meetings with the two sides and telephone appeals to both Mrs Thatcher and General Galtieri. Sir Anthony has described elsewhere the detailed course of these negotiations, and it is significant that both he and the Secretary-General (in his report to the Council on 21 May),[21] agree that a solution at one stage appeared reasonably close. The sticking point was the unwillingness of the parties to agree on the precise nature of the interim administration, the time-frame for subsequent negotiations over the islands' future, 'certain aspects of mutual withdrawal of forces', and the 'geographic area to be covered by the terms of the interim agreement'.[22]

There is evidence that the Secretary-General's efforts were also complicated by the peace proposals put forward in May by yet another 'third party', namely Belaunde Terry, the President of Peru. These did not depart substantially from the original plan put forward by Haig, and aroused a favourable response in London largely, according to Hastings and Jenkins, because the sinking of the *Sheffield* seemed to cast doubt on the taskforce's capacity to capture the Falklands.[23] By contrast the loss of the *Sheffield* encouraged the junta to reject the Peruvian plan and put its faith in the continued negotiations via the Secretary-General in the hope of winning greater concessions from the British. According to Hastings and Jenkins, 'of all Costa Mendes' errors of judgement, this was the most disastrous. Had he picked up Belaunde that Thursday he would have gained more than he could have dreamed possible in February, and might have saved his government's life.'[24] But the discussions at the UN – as we have already noted – came to nothing, and it is hard to disagree with the view that the three-week period of diplomatic negotiation (2–21 May) was 'bedevilled by the conflicting ambitions of the various peace makers'.[25]

Two more debates of the Security Council followed the Secretary-General's admission on 20 May of his failure to reach a settlement. The first began on 21 May and lasted five days. Despite the efforts of the Irish delegation to move acceptance of a ceasefire and resumption of negotiations, the Council – largely at the prompting of the non-aligned representatives – passed a resolution (505) mandating the Secretary-General to negotiate a ceasefire. By that time, Britain had landed its forces at San Carlos Bay; three British ships had been sunk and sixteen Argentinian aircraft destroyed. This was hardly a propitious atmosphere for continued negotiation, and on 2 June the Secretary-General once again had to report the failure of his mission. The second debate in the Security Council went less well for Britain (2–4 June). Again a ceasefire was proposed, and the result was a resolution which Britain and the United States felt impelled to veto, although Mrs Kirkpatrick subsequently recorded an abstention, much to the astonishment of her fellow delegates! This debate effectively ended the UN's role in the crisis, though the Secretary-General made one last attempt to avert 'a final battle for Port Stanley, but without success'.[26]

CONCLUSIONS

What conclusions can be drawn from this brief and inevitably selective account of the UN's role as a third party in the Falklands crisis? Does the record suggest yet another abject failure by the Organisation to add to those which have bedevilled its history since 1945? Paradoxically, it could be argued that the UN has emerged strengthened rather than weakened from its trial by ordeal in the Falklands. It is true that some six weeks of intense third party diplomacy – both private and public – failed to prevent the outbreak of war. But – and this is the point to stress – the members of the Organisation did in fact engage in a debate which, although at times clouded in ideological rhetoric, seriously addressed the crucial issue of aggression by a member state, and in the process established a diplomatic consensus which held for much of the period under review. This consensus – as this chapter has tried to show – was the product of both 'open' and 'secret' diplomacy carried on within and outside the formal confines of the Security Council: nor was this diplomacy limited to its membership. (Some 50 delegations spoke, for example, in the debate in the third week of May which led to Resolution 505.) As Sir Anthony Parsons points out,

> The Falklands debates were lively, serious and full of meaning . . . tactical errors and omissions in debate and in private consultations could cost support and forfeit votes . . . This was in vivid contrast to the sterilities of debate on the subjects which mainly preoccupy the Security Council . . . The Falklands debate had a pristine quality which I had not previously encountered.[27]

Secondly, and rather surprisingly in view of the massive support Argentina had received in the 1960s and 1970s arising from General

Assembly 'anti-colonial' resolutions, the Security Council, by adopting Resolution 502, clearly and decisively rejected the doctrine that 'colonialism equals permanent aggression'. Instead priority was given to the principle of self-determination; hence aggression against a people of British stock, however small in numbers, appeared so obvious a violation of law and morality that few states outside Latin America could be found to defend it. For once the terms of the UN Charter, especially Chapter VII, could apply without that ambiguity about the meaning of 'aggression' that had so often shrouded previous debates on the subject, and made difficult the assignation of responsibility for its use against another state. In other words, the Goa precedent of 1961 appeared well and truly buried, the result perhaps of states (especially those in the Third World) learning from the experience of the last twenty years. This period, as Peter Willets points out, has witnessed several disturbing violations of the principle of self-determination in places as far apart as East Timor, Namibia and the West Bank of Israel.[28]

Thirdly, the fact that both protagonists clearly regarded the Security Council as a body before which defence and justification of their policies was required suggests that the UN, in contrast to the relatively passive role it was forced to adopt in the Cuban missile crisis of 1962, was more than simply a marginal actor operating on the sidelines of the crisis. In particular both parties to the dispute were constrained by Resolution 502 and acted with caution and due consideration of the effects of their actions on those whose diplomatic support was crucial. Here Britain was obviously more successful (indeed success at the UN made the task of winning support from the EEC easier in the sense that Britain's European allies could be seen, like Britain, to be on the side of the constitutional angels), but it must be stressed, however, that diplomatic victory for Britain in the first Security Council debate in effect meant the acceptance of 'an international jurisdiction'[29] over her subsequent actions. Resolution 502 was clearly to Britain's advantage, but Mrs Thatcher's government had perforce to be seen to be acting within the political and constitutional limits it imposed. That Britain was able to maintain a UN consensus for the greater part of the crisis is a tribute to its diplomatic skills, but also a recognition that every effort had to be made to maintain the Organisation's goodwill and its backing for British action.

And if the prize of diplomatic advantage was not to be put at risk, both parties had to accept limitations on their military conduct as well. Thus Britain did not attack the Argentinian mainland, though bombing the airfields and destroying airborne missile capability had obvious military utility. This idea was quickly scotched by the British Attorney-General who argued that 'an attack on the mainland would be construed as falling outside the framework of Article 51 of the United Nations Charter empowering Britain to act in her own self-defence'.[30] Similarly, the Argentinian takeover of the Falklands was conducted with a degree of restraint: no preliminary bombardment of Port Stanley took place, and the British defenders (despite offering a courageous resistance) were captured without loss of life and subsequently treated with a decent respect for the laws of war. Nor did the junta at any stage attempt to use the sizeable local British community as hostages; indeed any attempt at internment would have been politically counterproductive and a useful propaganda weapon in the hands of their British opponents.

Finally, we come to the position of the Secretary-General. Could Pérez de Cuéllar have done more in his role as mediator? This, to my mind, is doubtful. After all, if the efforts of a super power personified in Alexander Haig could not succeed, what prospect was there for the representative of an international organisation possessed of moral authority but lacking the political bargaining power of his American counterpart? Indeed it could be argued that the 'even-handed' approach initially adopted by Haig was the prime cause of his ultimate failure. As Philip Windsor remarks, 'the British were convinced that [President Reagan] was betraying an ally, the Argentinians that he was on the side of the British'.[31] Had the US government come down firmly on one side or the other, as in the Suez crisis of 1956, a compromise might have been reached in advance of the outbreak of hostilities. In these circumstances – admittedly highly speculative – the Secretary-General's initiatives might have been deployed with more chance of success on the analogy of the role played by Dag Hammarskjöld in 1956.

Accepting that the Secretary-General, and by definition the United Nations, failed in their attempt at third party mediation in the Falklands crisis, does not preclude acknowledgement of what, in fact, was achieved. After all, the conflict between Britain and Argentina was peculiarly intractable in the sense that although both sides appeared to be fighting for limited objectives (the Argentinians to hold what the use of force had achieved, and the British for a return to the *status quo ante*), major issues of principle were involved: self-determination and resistance to unprovoked aggression versus territorial integrity, itself the product of a sense of unfulfilled historic destiny and decades of national aspiration.

Thus, although the war was ostensibly fought to decide who was to exercise sovereignty over the islands, the assertion by each party of separate and conflicting principles complicated the efforts of the mediators to persuade them to 'split the difference' and 'share' sovereignty on a tripartite basis. Thus for Britain aggression could not be seen to pay, especially as the Conservative government had made much of this principle in defending its decision to send the taskforce. Even a modest foothold for Argentina in some transitional post-settlement administration under UN overall control was ultimately unacceptable to the extent that a continued Argentinian presence would have demonstrated that aggression did, in fact, produce a favourable change in the *status quo*. Similarly, for Argentina, withdrawal from the islands, even with a guarantee of future participation in their administration, was an outcome hardly commensurate with the expenditure of military effort and the boastful promises made to the Argentinian people before and during the crisis.

What this analysis suggests is that from the start the crisis was not amenable to management through the mediation of third parties. As Phil Williams perceptively argues, the three preconditions for successful crisis management were absent in the Falklands case.[32] First, unlike the super powers in their confrontations over Cuba, Berlin and the Middle East, for example, neither Britain nor Argentina was constrained by the 'fear of war': any military conflict between them was bound to be limited to the conventional sphere and fought out in a remote and geographically confined area. Thus one major incentive to manage the crisis was missing, and this in turn reduced the moral appeal of the various proposals for compromise. (War was not, after all, unthinkable in this particular instance.) Secondly, the work of mediation was undermined by the high degree of misperception on both sides before and during the crisis about each other's intentions, together with the absence of 'guidelines' for coping with crises analogous to those developed in a rough and ready way by the super powers over a period of 30 years. Thirdly, domestic pressures on both countries reduced the flexibility of decision-makers in their reaction to the solutions offered by third parties. 'Backing down was not a realistic option in domestic political terms.'[33] In other words, by the time the crisis broke the interests of both parties were symmetrical – a condition which, on the evidence of crises elsewhere, makes the task of management unusually difficult, if not altogether impossible. As Williams comments: 'the balance of interests in crises tends to determine the balance of resolve, and with both governments attaching high values to the stakes, the conflict became virtually impossible to deal with in a way that did not involve a trial of military strength'.[34]

If Williams is correct in his analysis, then it is hardly surprising that the UN failed to avert war over the Falklands. Yet in a variety of ways – as this chapter has tried to show – the UN played a not insignificant role, particularly in acting as a restraining influence on the protagonists. This is not a trivial achievement, nor is it necessarily guaranteed to survive the future. What it does suggest is that the UN can from time to time – depending on the issue, the attitudes of the states involved, and a variety of other variables – appear to be 'more than the sum of its parts'. In the Falklands crisis this was no mean thing.

NOTES AND REFERENCES

1. The author is grateful to Ms Patricia Farquhar, Librarian at the UN Information Centre in London, and Dr Peter Willetts of the City University for their kind assistance in the preparation of this chapter.
2. J. Pearce, 'The Falkland Islands Dispute', *The World Today*, 38 (1982) 161.
3. Ibid., 161.
4. P. Willetts, 'Latin America, the United Nations and the Non-Aligned Movement' in *Latin America and Caribbean Contemporary Research*, II, 1982–3 (New York: Holmes & Meier, 1984).
5. Ibid.
6. Sir Anthony Parsons, 'The Falklands Crisis in the United Nations, 31 March–14 June 1982', *International Affairs*, 59 (1983) 169–78. This is an invaluable source for discussion of all the key issues involved and my debt to it will be obvious.
7. Ibid., 169–70.
8. Ibid., 170.
9. *United Nations Security Council*: provisional record of meeting held on 2 April 1982, S/PV2345, 17.
10. Ibid., 3–5.
11. Max Hastings and Simon Jenkins, *The Battle for the Falklands* (London: Pan Books, 1983) p. 204. This is the most detailed account of the crisis available and the author acknowledges his debt to both authors.
12. Parsons, 'The Falklands Crisis', 178.
13. Philip Windsor, 'Diplomatic Dimensions of the Falklands Crisis', *Millennium: Journal of International Studies*, 12 (1983) 90. This point is made explicitly in an earlier draft of this paper which the author very kindly allowed me to see.
14. Hastings and Jenkins, *Battle for the Falklands*, p. 122.
15. Ibid., pp. 122–3.
16. Parsons, 'The Falklands Crisis', 172.
17. Hastings and Jenkins, *Battle for the Falklands*, p. 122.
18. Alan James, 'Kurt Waldheim: Diplomats' Diplomat', *The Yearbook of World Affairs*, 37 (1983) 94.
19. Parsons, 'The Falklands Crisis', 172.
20. Ibid., 173.

21. Thus on 11 May the Argentinian delegation seemingly made a 'major concession': the question of sovereignty would not be prejudged in Argentina's favour at the outset of negotiations under the Security Council's auspices. See Parsons, ibid., 173.
22. *Report of the Secretary-General*, 4.
23. Hastings and Jenkins, *Battle for the Falklands*, p. 197.
24. Ibid., p. 197.
25. Ibid., p. 194.
26. Parsons, 'The Falklands Crisis', 177.
27. Ibid., 177.
28. Willetts, 'Latin America', 8 where the lack of widespread support for Argentina's position among the non-aligned movement is explained in detail.
29. Windsor, 'Diplomatic Dimensions', 195.
30. Hastings and Jenkins, *Battle for the Falklands*, p. 190.
31. Windsor, 'Diplomatic Dimensions', 93.
32. Phil Williams, 'Miscalculation, Crisis Management and the Falklands Conflict', *The World Today*, 39 (1983) 147.
33. Ibid., 148.
34. Ibid., 148.

Part II
Multilateral Diplomacy

6 The General Assembly Reconsidered

MAURICE KEENS-SOPER

THE ATTACK ON 'SECRET' DIPLOMACY

At the Paris Peace Conference of 1919 it seemed plain that the diplomatic system of Europe had failed and that, left unreformed, its rudimentary institutions for the conduct of international politics would fail again. Force and the threat of war, long considered indispensable instruments of policy, now threatened to destroy not only those engaged in their use but the civilisation of which the states of Europe and their worldwide ramifications were the political expression. States, it was therefore determined, must henceforth bind themselves to one another in promises of permanent peacetime association to find less terminal ways to contain their conflicts, adjust their interests and civilise their affairs. War however was only the most haphazard of a whole repertoire of discredited practices. The malign calculus of the balance of power, the privileged position of the 'great powers', their divisive alliances and immoral arms races were equally implicated in failure. But most fundamental of all, the institution through which all these were related was held responsible for the catastrophe. Almost overnight diplomacy became '*secret* diplomacy' and that expression, in what had been proclaimed the century of the common man, a term of damning criticism. Diplomacy was seen to be the art of circumscribing anarchy and had led to chaos. 'If you want Peace, prepare for War' was no longer acceptable to the millions who had been mobilised with promises of a lasting as well as victorious peace. To be permanent, the peace had to be *organised*. Something better – more orderly and rational – had to be constructed. The reform of the diplomatic system of Europe entailed the reform of diplomacy.

To the American President, Woodrow Wilson, who provided the political and moral impetus for the creation of the League of Nations, 'secret diplomacy' epitomised the corrupt practices of an aristocratic activity wedded to despotic government. His vision of the League was of an association of states, who in practising self-government internally, would bring to the external relations of states the evident virtues of democracy. The method by which diplomacy was to be purged of its secrecy was to establish it in a novel organisational setting where its activities would, like democracy itself, be subject to public scrutiny. The provenance of this belief in the benefits of 'open covenants openly arrived at' is of more than antiquarian interest because it provides the ultimate justification for the creation of an assembly as an essential part of international organisation. The United Nations operates in a world unlike that of the League, but because the former was in most important respects a 'second try', modelled on the ideas and experience of the latter, it is to the League that one is led in the search for answers to questions of a conceptual kind. At San Francisco, where in 1945 the Charter of the United Nations was negotiated and signed by some 50 states, there was little discussion whether a General Assembly should form part of the organisation. The issue was taken for granted and discussion concerned the powers and position of the assembly and not its existence.

THE LIBERAL THEORY OF 'OPEN' DIPLOMACY

At the centre of belief in the merits of 'open' diplomacy is a doctrine of political responsibility. It asserts that authority differs from the arbitrariness of mere power when it is derived from, and is accountable for its exercise to, the 'consent of the governed'. This precept, developed within the civil associations of Europe to justify a shift in their principles of legitimacy from the 'descending' theory of monarchical to the 'ascending' theory of popular right, is of course the voice and theme of Liberalism. Radical within the diverse historical traditions of a single civilisation, its attempted application to the external relations of the generality of states was more so. In this view the guarantee of responsibility lay in the *manifest* exercise of authority, because the public – presumed to be 'interested', rational, attentive, informed, organised but above all free – would have it so. 'Open diplomacy' would be to international relations what the principle of 'no taxation without representation' was to liberal democracy. It would foster peaceful conduct between states for the same reasons that free, open and representative institutions were the organisation of civil peace. The 'light of reason' and the powers of human artifice were presumed creative and pacific, so that where states had nothing to hide from one another it followed they would come to realise they also had little to fear.

In liberal-democratic thought the source of conflict, including war, is neither evil nor ingrained wilfulness but rather a combination of sloth and ignorance. These generate misunderstandings and from these stem our woes. From this condition release is however possible. It is to be found neither in God nor our Fates but within ourselves. In general terms this remedial activity is known as education and it requires three distinctive undertakings: a recognition of the importance of knowledge and the need to assemble 'all the relevant facts'; a willingness to engage in thorough discussion based upon the evidence; and a further willingness to accept conclusions based upon the two engagements just mentioned. The distinctly modern, liberal-democratic, twist to this conception, in its application to civil and international affairs, is that this set of commitments which conducts one from ignorance via enlightenment to contentment has to occur in a suitably endowed public space. Under these conditions systematic discussion would result in the ability to deal with more than symptoms of conflict and their temporary adjustment. A collaborative and sustained effort to 'get to the bottom of things' and unearth that most fugitive of modern logical categories, that of 'underlying causes', would indicate a sound method for the 'solution of problems' and create a fraternal sense of common purpose into the bargain. In this manner the deliberations of diplomats gathered in public assembly would develop a new kind of *esprit de corps* based upon more than professional solidarity. The habit of working together on an organised and thorough footing would equip diplomats to tackle issues before they became dangerous and threatened war. 'Open diplomacy' unlike 'secret diplomacy' would become a preventative social science replacing a precarious and irresponsible art. Though representatives of governments, men so engaged would emerge from their inherited provincialisms to act as connectors between what David Jones calls 'the known-site' and the 'world-floor'.[1] In short an assembly would be an academy in which knowledge and open discourse would engender trust – a notoriously opaque quality and the one most immediate to political association. Diplomats would enter the assembly ignorant of everything but the arguments of *raison d'état* to graduate as citizens of one world, reasonable men embodying 'the reason of the whole'. Though seldom made explicit, some such would seem to be the presuppositions of a public assembly of states and of its putative connection with the reform of international relations.

THE DEGENERATION INTO PROPAGANDA

Whereas in conferences of old the public might be allowed to observe the formal opening and closing sessions, the General Assembly of the United Nations has public galleries and fixed amenities for the news media and, with rare exceptions, it meets in public. Its staple method of work is to deliberate not across or around a conference table but through 'debate'. In the early days of the League it was imagined that the Assembly would meet every few years or so, leaving the regular and important 'executive' business to the smaller and more influential Council. Very soon, however, the Assembly came to meet for three weeks every year at the League's headquarters in Geneva, where after a general debate lasting a week it divided up into committees. The General Assembly of the United Nations now meets for three months every autumn in New York. It may also meet in emergency session and increasingly convenes special sessions for the consideration of single topics such as disarmament, development or Namibia. Most of the 157 states now members of the UN keep permanent diplomatic missions in New York, so that when one adds to this list the international agencies – WHO, ILO, FAO and so on – non-states, non-member states, would-be states and representatives of regional international organisations who may take part in some of the work of the General Assembly, midtown Manhattan is a busy place in the American autumn.

Within the crowded atmosphere of a concentrated agenda the observer at the United Nations is reminded of how, in becoming one world of many states, two of diplomacy's most precious resources – political space in which to buffer conflicts and time in which to cultivate accord – have been eroded. The principle of 'interest' which used to select and discipline the gatherings of diplomats has given way to the more egalitarian and combustible presumption that an issue of interest to some is of rightful concern to all – whether or not it affects the peace of the world. Whatever else this produces it gives 'distinguished delegates', as diplomats are called, plenty to talk about. Indeed, as one moves between the animated conversation of the delegates' lounge overlooking East River and the half-familiar because half-parliamentary setting of the Assembly chamber one is held by a sense of confusion. The Charter and the Assembly's own 'rules of procedure' tell one something but they do not reveal the assumptions upon which what greets one's ears and eyes are said to be taking place. It is not at all obvious how an assembly of sovereign states foregathered in a deliberative chamber and intentionally appearing as a parliamentary, even legislative, body is to safeguard the peace, resolve disputes and conduct common welfare activities when the principle upon which the organisation is based – the equality of independent states – means that none can be bound without its consent. Between states the basis of cooperation is voluntary. Agreement is reached through negotiation. Hence the importance of diplomacy as the condition and 'prime consequence of independent statehood. The attempt to bind states against their will produces either resentment, stalemate or 'the dice of war', whereas within a parliamentary order matters go differently. An issue raised in debate is resolved through votes in such a way that those 'defeated' by a majority authorise their own submission. In his *Speech to the Electors of Bristol* Edmund Burke put the matter thus:

> Parliament is not a congress of ambassadors from different and hostile interests, which interests each must maintain, against other agents and advocates; but Parliament is a deliberative assembly of one nation, with one interest, that of the whole – where not local purposes, not local prejudices, ought to guide, but the general good, resulting from the general reason of the whole.[2]

In the absence of any comparable 'reason of the whole' between member states, the League of Nations wisely required unanimity in votes on all but procedural questions. The United Nations altered this practice so that in the Security Council a majority of nine of the fifteen members can 'decide', providing all the permanent members are in agreement. In the General Assembly a two-thirds majority is needed to carry resolutions on 'important' issues. But the question remains. What are the practical consequences of an assembly that 'debates', tables resolutions and ultimately votes, when it cannot legislate, when its majorities, no matter how large, cannot bind, and when its 'recommendations' must therefore lack authority when they do not attract consent?

Following the example of the League, the General Assembly of the United Nations begins each session with a general debate which lasts about a month. In 1982 some 129 heads of state, heads of government, foreign ministers and ambassadors addressed one another and the world from the podium of the Assembly. Haig and Gromyko were followed by spokesmen from Britain and France, China, the Democratic People's Republic of Yemen, San Tome, the Seychelles and so on, revealing between them and at great length much of interest to themselves but little in the way of the collaborative virtues anticipated by liberal thought. In every case reason was in the service not of an enlightened global community but of national interests, and since these are subject to little annual change speeches were tedious and repetitious as well as self-justificatory.

The general debate is however a public event in two senses. It is the showpiece of the annual session and allows world leaders to find occasion – in secret or at least in private – to confer without making an event of their doing so. However little may be gleaned from the general debate, it is only the prologue to the Assembly's work. This largely takes place in the seven committees of the whole, into which it divides to tackle an agenda which in 1982 contained 150 items.

Each committee receives a cluster of items and is known by its general character. The first committee deals with disarmament, the 'special political committee' with 'political', the second with economic and social, the third with human rights, the fourth with decolonisation, the fifth and sixth with budgetary and legal items. Each committee has over the years developed a style of its own. The disarmament committee seems to ramble more than the budgetary and legal committees, whose distinguishing features seem to be fastidious acrimony and professional cuteness, respectively. By and large, however, the committees all obey a similar pattern. There is usually a general debate in each committee covering the area of business, followed by debate on groups of agenda items, many of which are regular fixtures. The pace quickens, if that is the word, when a resolution is tabled and its sponsors begin lobbying delegates, in the committee chambers, in the lounges, wherever flesh can be pressed and ears bent. Diplomats are to be seen winning support for a formulation that may differ only by a shade, a word, from the previous year's condemnation of 'the Zionist entity' of Israel or 'the illegal and criminal regime of South Africa' and yet this activity may make all the difference to whether a country will vote for, against or abstain. What difference these votes make to the world is less certain. We are in the world of what Geoffrey Goodwin has called 'voting power politics', where all that is not tactics is irrelevant. When each committee has debated and discussed, tabled resolutions, bargained over amendments and finally responded to the roll-call, its work goes to the plenary session of the Assembly where as likely as not the issue will be further debated and again voted upon. This is not the inescapable rhetoric of 'open diplomacy'. This is diplomacy become rhetoric.

The General Assembly can only 'recommend' so the official purpose of votes is to express what 'diplomatic consensus' exists. The larger the majorities the wider the area of agreement, but since the 'equality of states' is a legal fact that ignores power and reputation there is much decoding of the outcome to discover how particular states have cast their votes. Votes may garnish but they do not banish the calculus of power in the eyes of those who wield or fear it. Any member state can place an item on the agenda and table a resolution, and therefore what is debated and to what effect is determined by the composition of the Assembly. The central and most signal fact about the General Assembly is that its affairs are now governed by a loosely organised grouping of Third World countries who can, when they act together, assure a two-thirds majority on any issue they choose. What do these reliable majorities of African, Asian and Latin American states indicate? Are they the expression of individual, separately considered national interests fitfully juxtaposed? Or do the resolutions they pass contain something political and even moral of a kind that transcends both national frontiers and mathematics?

The answers to these questions are to be found less in the numbers or identity of votes cast for resolutions than in the responses of those states named in resolutions and who naturally enough – unless the resolution is so general as to be harmless as well as useless – have voted against it. It is the position and attitude of minorities that determine the authority of a non-legislative assembly. The General Assembly has no powers and its authority is entirely persuasive. If, in the opinion of those from whom compliance is sought, it lacks this authority the Assembly has failed to make the only point it is equipped to make. Since it cannot 'impose' obligations it must carry conviction. Even so it is far from clear in what reasonable sense any majority of states can claim, irrespective of size, population, economic and political standing, to voice 'the reason of the whole' simply by virtue of being able to manage votes in an assembly whose decisions are determined by largely unrepresentative governments.

We are here, I think, in the full confusion, perhaps deliberately contrived, of a diplomatic system seeking reform by falling into traps set by its own rhetoric and hoping thereby to persuade itself – and thence the world – that it is creating a responsible order. The attempt to use parliamentary-sounding utterances to transform an association of states into an international community, to make words and rules devices that can lead events and merge interests, shows either an extraordinary faith in the powers of artifice and reason or suggests that reason itself is here the borrowed voice of another faith.

That so much of the proceedings of the General Assembly are uneventful and seem to be contained within a logic of their own quite marvellously divorced from outside events, has little however to do with constitutional artifice. 'Distinguished delegates' who, morning and afternoon, sit listening on headphones while from behind glass-fronted visors translators are busy in the five working languages of the Organisation, are not waiting impatiently to catch Mr Speaker's eye. They are not waiting to urge, argue with, inform and persuade their colleagues. Their audience, and therefore their purpose, lies elsewhere. Except for the spasmodic appearance of crocodiles of mute visitors being shown around by the well-manicured lady mythologues in UN blue, the public galleries are empty. Yet although usually deserted it is to the 'public gallery' that delegates speak. It is because this symbol of openness exists, because its business is public, is translated, published, put on record and selectively used by governments and the largely state-controlled press agencies, that the General Assembly is the sort of place it is.

Speaking thus for the record, to announce government policy or to address their own domestic audience, this is neither 'open diplomacy', enlightened discussion, nor part of the pressure group and interest politics of parliamentary life by which success is indirectly sought. This is something unique: a version of power politics in which words are related only to other words, including the obligation to maintain on all occasions the perfect accord between the position of one's own government and the principles and purposes of the United Nations Charter. In the absence of serious dialectical clinch, where words are invested with meaning as well as passion because they are related to actions which can in turn be influenced by words, the Assembly is a chamber whose prevailing voice is that of propaganda. Where the only thing its members have in common is the readiness to deplore 'empty rhetoric' and the need for all to discover 'a common political will' one is however beyond rhetoric. Rhetoric was once not a term of abuse but an honoured part of public life where powers of persuasion were considered a valued art affecting events. Rhetoric, like an authentic deliberative assembly, is the expression of a single community where however much reason and passion serve particular interests it is ultimately for the benefit of Burke's 'one interest, that of the whole'. This is not the case with propaganda which seeks to control and overwhelm rather than persuade, and whose closed certainties therefore equip it to mark but not bridge divisions. Rhetoric belongs to education, propaganda to indoctrination. Diplomacy, which seeks to educate states in their mutual interests, is therefore incompatible with propaganda. The trouble is that because the General Assembly is a gathering of 'different and hostile interests' it ensures that rhetoric is turned into propaganda.

A stock rejoinder to this complaint is to assert that even though the babel of propagandists seeking voting combinations may be a far cry from the initial conception of the General Assembly, this may tell us only that it is performing an essential service in allowing power politics to find its voice. The voice may be crude and bullying, full of cant and casuistry, but that would not have surprised Machiavelli and should not perhaps disturb us. If what comes out of the General Assembly reveals more about the reign of will and passion at the centre of 'national interest' than it does about the part played by reason and artifice, that in itself might be thought to be educational. The voice of the Assembly may be strident and painful to those raised in the traditions of which the Charter is an expression, but it is part of that tradition to accept that there is seldom smoke without fire. Western countries may not like what they hear in the General Assembly, particularly as so much of it is directed at them by the ex-colonial Third World in a mangled and resentful version of their own political and moral inheritance, but it is in their own long-term interest to listen and learn the lessons. The General Assembly may not have been designed as an agency of this kind but it is a sign of life that organisations created for one purpose are adapted for others.

This kind of argument is favoured by so-called 'realists' who, in claiming to see through the UN, detect a lesson in the extent to which Liberalism has been hoisted by its wantonly misplaced faith in reason. If not the midwife of a world community, the General Assembly is in this view nevertheless a faithful account of the present configuration of world politics. The fallacy at work here should be instructive. A mirror or barometer tells the truth and in that sense is neutral. The General Assembly is not a neutral reflection of power politics but its oddest constituent. It is controlled by Third World countries who are not interested in merely signalling to the world what is on their minds. They want action they cannot perform themselves and see the General Assembly as an instrument. In giving voice to demands through majorities in the Assembly these countries are seeking to exercise influence which in other respects they lack. And if the 'demands' become a catalogue of vengeful accusations, the result of exhortation may well be less rather than more sympathy. Indignation and propaganda work only where those who rely upon them either control those they wish to influence, or, where their audience is not captive, it remains responsive. Declaimed annually from a podium, rage may provide a vent but it is as likely to create fresh frustrations. To raise an issue, such as the rights of the Palestinians to their own state, to have it regularly on the agenda, to debate it at length and to win massive majorities in support of resolutions condemning Israel – and then to find all this entirely ignored, is an education in the futility of deliberation. Propaganda cannot make words more effective where those at whom they are directed have the means to ignore them. Nor is it surprising that the Soviet Union, which has little interest in the efficacy of 'open discussion' and no conception of the political freedom upon which it rests, is adept at articulating the frustrations to which Third World countries often condemn themselves.

Among those who recognise the truth of this dilemma is another kind of realist who is often to be found among diplomats at the General Assembly. Admitting the irrelevance of its bluster the Assembly is none the less justified because of what it allows to occur outside the formal sessions in 'the corridors' of the building and wherever delegates can meet and speak in confidence. This view accepts with varying degrees of complacency the argument that however wasteful, what is said 'for public consumption' has the merit of allowing, and even acting as a spur to, 'serious negotiation' 'in private'. Why it should be thought that states that are repeatedly subjected to the concerted assaults of propaganda should be more amenable to negotiations than would otherwise be the case is not always made clear, but it seems to rest upon the assumption that words are instruments whose bluntness may be compensated for by number and repetition. (Whether effective or not, this argument contains a view of language that is ultimately incompatible with diplomacy, the art *par excellence* of the tactful and precise use of words.)

The extreme version of this view succeeds in turning the entire justification of the General Assembly on its head. Here it is valued not for anything that is said in public or for its role as an inducement to negotiate elsewhere, but solely for its use as a guise behind whose antics diplomats can discuss whatever they choose. There is no doubt that the UN is used like this and the regular sessions of the Assembly do provide an opportunity for confidential talks, but those who seek to justify the General Assembly on these grounds do not always seem to realise how much they are thereby admitting. It is not that 'secret diplomacy' is reinstated in the lounges, restaurants, bars, theatres, nightclubs and whore-houses of Manhattan as a way of furthering the official business on the agenda of the Assembly. That would be entirely unexceptionable because compatible with, and indispensable to, its professed purposes. It suggests on the contrary that the entire agenda, the sessions of the committees, their 'debates', resolutions and votes are a voluminous sham whose sole merit is the conduct of an ideological fraud on the publics of the world for the convenience of governments. A public assembly designed to educate and increase confidence in the conduct of international relations is thus justified because it allows the old corrupt activities of 'secret diplomacy' to carry on, not as before, honestly or at least discreetly, but under cover of liberal-democratic notions.

If the General Assembly therefore provides a firm framework for inherent contradictions, some of these are to be found illustrated in the demand by the Third World for a New International Economic Order. Because of the way it has been publicly framed, the North-South dialogue has largely taken the form of those demanding 'justice' declaring that their plight derives from the legacy and greed of those from whom more aid is to come. Through report after report it is 'Western imperialism' and its 'economic stranglehold' that is depicted as the villain of the piece. Leaving on one side the dubious historical and economic theories upon which this view rests – it is an amalgam of LSE Fabianism stiffened with Marxism and a sniff of racialism – it is the results of this campaign, or rather their absence, that are striking. Based upon righteous indignation, the attempt to cajole and shame Western countries has succeeded only in generating expectations. The issue is not whether the 'Third World' is hard done by but how to develop effective cooperation that will succeed in closing a gap that is growing. And it is by no means clear that the United Nations is the kind of setting in which these issues can be handled. All that seems to happen is that the issue, like all others at the UN, is invested with such intense political feeling that it cannot reach beyond polemics. The demand for 'global negoti-ations' at the UN fosters illusions as well as frustrations. It provides countries with inefficient as well as unrepresentative regimes with ready excuses for ignoring their fundamental problems by shifting blame onto outside shoulders and, since governments are the principal channels for aid, adds to these ills at the same time as justifying the increasing politicisation of life. For those interested in political liberty as well as justice this is a disturbing prospect.

Some comfort is taken for all the effort expended on development at the UN by the Cancun meeting of 24 heads of states representing the North–South issue and which included the Secretary-General of the United Nations. Had it not been for the continuous furore raised by the developing countries, the argument goes, Cancun would not have taken place. Apart from the fact that little was achieved at Cancun, what this omits is that in order to be able to meet informally, away from the press and publicity, a limited number of political leaders had to find somewhere outside the United Nations to hold talks.

For Third World countries the General Assembly is therefore an anvil upon which power and privilege are to be browbeaten into their images of right and justice. It is perhaps worth outlining how some Western countries seem to be responding. The French are resignedly contemptuous and treat the General Assembly, and indeed the UN, as a huge and hideously disfigured body which only the Anglo-Saxon liberal imagination in its most cynical and self-flagellatory mood could have inflicted upon itself and the world. The British and West Germans do their best to ignore the bluster and decode the propaganda, finding ways of lowering the temperature and fostering working relations 'behind the scenes'. This they achieve to some effect and with dignity. The USA veers from a pained sense of being neither appreciated nor understood, to an abrasive determination to match slander with riposte. And then there are the Swedes, the darlings of the Third World, whose good works are matched only by their glutinous smugness. Of the Soviet Union and its satellites it may be noted that for them, like other political and diplomatic institutions, the UN is a battlefield where words are weapons in the inevitable struggle in which they are the predestined ultimate victors. Because it has a settled idea of what is at issue, Soviet conduct is, however, professional and measured. Having for most of the Cold War been a beleaguered minority it now has the ear of many Third World countries, though the occupation of Afghanistan led many of them to vote in favour of resolutions sharply critical of Soviet policy. The Chinese, having spent much of their first decade in the UN keeping quiet, are now beginning to assert themselves. Soviet hegemony is the constant theme of a country which wishes to be seen by the Third World as one of them and not as a great power.

SUMMARY SO FAR

Events have thus falsified the assumptions upon which the General Assembly was reared. First of all there is no such thing as 'secret diplomacy'. The expression is a pleonasm based upon a misconception. Its rapid acceptance as a truism reflected the conditions of war and the ability of rhetoric to substitute myth for analysis. Diplomacy is a confidential art because those very public and mutually fearful bodies – states – will not conduct their public business in the open. They cannot afford to deprive themselves of the ability to compromise without losing face, and the attempt to oblige them to 'come clean' results in greater dishonesty as well as additional frustrations. Since there is no such thing as 'secret diplomacy' it could not therefore have been responsible for the Great War. That was caused less by the failure of the diplomatic system than the determination of one of its members, Germany, to destroy the balance of power upon which it rested. Neither diplomacy nor four years of military stalemate was able to prevent this and when the diplomatic system was restored by a new Atlantic power it did so persuaded that only the internationalisation of its own historical experience could redeem it. The 'empty rhetoric' of the General Assembly can be traced to the successful – and rhetorical – attack upon 'secret diplomacy'.

In the second place there is no such present entity which can answer to the name of an international community of which the General Assembly is the expression, embodiment, discovery, forcing-house or promise. Belief that in seeking, for example, to exorcise the evil of apartheid or to vindicate Palestinian rights the General Assembly is impregnating the diplomatic system with sentiments of solidarity ignores the difference between destruction and the divisive energies it unleashes, and creation, which so far as politics is concerned has to induce trust if it is to civilise conflict and issue in community. As David Jones says:

> so is the honey-root of known-site
> bitter fruit for world-floor.

Finally, and for similar reasons, there is no such thing as 'world public opinion'. With the development of mass communications and the inexorable expansion of government into every aspect of civil life there is little prospect for the creation or expression of opinion that is not, in crucial respects, the creature of state control. Yet more dismal is the thought that were it to exist there is little enough reason to presume that a world public opinion would be enlightened.

Since there is no such thing as 'open diplomacy', states must have the means of treating with one another in such confidence that they are able to speak the same language. The basis of that common language is interest. Secrecy may guarantee neither responsibility nor success, but confidentiality does at least reduce the quantum of what Orwell called 'humbug'. The end result of humbug is cynicism, a condition fatal equally to diplomacy and to political liberty. The complete rupture between word and deed largely favours those who assert power as the only form of effective action.

HOW TO RECONSIDER THE GENERAL ASSEMBLY

If the General Assembly is flawed both as a 'piece of multilateral diplomatic machinery' and as the deliberative assembly of an incipient global community, can one find for it a role and an accompanying justification, or should one cut one's losses and curtail the corrupting practices of a failed enterprise? That choice does not exist for reasons which Dag Hammarskjöld, a great servant of the United Nations and an advocate of 'quiet diplomacy', pointed out many years ago: the General Assembly is perhaps the one place in the world where the weak, the poor and the aggrieved can feel at home as part of it. If this is true then Western countries have sound reasons of self-interest in finding answers to its failings. The issue is therefore how to reconsider the General Assembly so that it can serve rather than subvert the peaceful conduct of international relations. It requires a standpoint critical of, but not necessarily hostile to, both the rationalist postulates upon which the Assembly rests and the self-styled 'realism' of its more recent critics. This, in outline only, I propose to offer by way of conclusion.

Political reality is so diffuse, hostile and intractable that before we can mobilise it as power or give it reasoned direction we have to give it shape and humanise it. This we do through metaphor and we do it all the time without thinking about it. Imagination outstrips calculation and subordinates even passion to its creations. The authority of metaphor, the power of the 'as if', is part of what Hegel called 'the cunning of reason', of the way reason tricks both calculation and passion into the position of its agents. The 'League of Nations' and the 'United Nations' are structures of reason and power only in so far as they succeed first as structures of metaphor. The 'Security Council' and the 'General Assembly' were ploys of fantasy seeking to represent and to bind a mixture of experience and leaps of faith. In particular the General Assembly was created in the image of a deliberative chamber and furnished with everything except the indispensable ballast of a common historical experience. Too precocious for the time, the metaphor of what Senator Vandenburg – the man who sold the United Nations to the American public – called 'the town-meeting of to-morrow's world' collapsed under the strain of 'the Cold War' and 'the Iron Curtain'.

Nevertheless, historically and as a matter of political interest, the most important fact about the General Assembly is that it was created as a gesture: a gesture made by the great powers to preserve their standing, to embody their own political ideas and to appease the demands of new, middle-ranking and small states. In conception it was a gesture in which gestures were to be made. Discussion not decision was to characterise its activities. Those who conceived the idea of an international organisation with a deliberative assembly perhaps failed to give sufficient prominence to the idea that an assembly depends in turn upon the idea of a *stage*, of a public space upon which gestures – utterance and movement – are enacted. In the most literal sense an assembly is a representative occasion, a public space upon which are brought together – *re-presented* – spokesmen who direct their utterances at one another but also to an audience.

In contrast a conference of diplomats, meeting around a green baize table and protected by closed doors and a 'news blackout' is an un-public, un-stage-like occasion. It makes good sense to understand the General Assembly as a sideshow which has come, over the years, to upstage the Security Council because it has been acted upon and transformed by actors with a will to be heard. Instinctively many Third World countries (though not, for reasons I do not understand, the Arabs) have grasped some of this in spite of the fact that before they appeared 'on the scene' the United States had, throughout the 1950s, abused the Assembly as a revivalist meeting-hall to rally the West. Roundheads of both non-conformist and Marxist persuasions are probably too blunt in their seriousness not to misconstrue a stage as an anvil.

For if the 'as if' of the General Assembly turns upon the 'as if' of the stage and thus opens up, as I think it does, possibilities compatible with its origins and present complexion, it also carries with it conditions and restraints. Metaphors can only familiarise with meaning because they also, like blinkers, impose discipline. The stage is no more a free-for-all where anything can be said any-old-how than Westminster is a roofed-in Hyde Park Corner. A stage can only 'work' when it succeeds in dramatising and until recently this was so well understood that it did not need saying. At the fag end of a century whose greatest revolutions have been in communications, we increasingly share a world rendered more immediate without it becoming more familiar. As David Jones foresaw:

So can all virtue curdle in transit
so vice may be virtue uprooted.

Drama is therefore essential to our grasp of events because it strikes a picture of completeness within which we are offered meaning. As a stage, an assembly can be effective only where, in bringing the world before it, in presenting the world to its public, the dramatic enactment of issues succeeds in moving its audiences. If this is so then it has very limited place for merely 'letting off steam'. An audience can only be moved by will and assertion where there is art and discrimination. The true wager of an assembly that neither legislates nor controls an executive and is not the embodiment of a community is that it exerts itself by attracting attention. The point of debate has little to do with the laboured business of concocting majorities behind ineffectual resolutions and everything to do with creating interest by dramatising events. Whatever authority the Assembly is capable of lies there: in the power of its utterances to command attention. 'Fanaticism', according to Santayana, 'consists in redoubling your efforts when you have forgotten your aim'. It consists also in repeating yourself when you have misconceived your metaphor. As a result the General Assembly is threatened by its own antics: it is either a bore or a bureaucratic embarrassment, and from both audiences turn away.

Although any issue can be dramatised, not every public space is a stage, and not every sort of public utterance makes good theatre. The tedium of the Assembly has little to do with the performing talents of delegates who, as 'representative' figures, have been schooled as public personages. It has something to do with the architecture of the chambers. Half conference rooms, half debating forums, those responsible for their layout seem not to have known which way the world was going and to have settled for a mixture of metaphors. The true fault lies of course in the scripts. These it is that are terminal to the dramatic possibilities of the General Assembly. Why there are not more suicides among the gifted translators one does not know, but the public and the newsmen get the message and keep away. A stage can carry any 'message' as long as it is not so flogged to death that it produces empty seats. Theatres and 'people's assemblies' are deadly in totalitarian regimes because they are such profoundly dishonest places, and although the Assembly is a place where anything can be said, little of importance and less of truth is.

'Processions that lack high stilts', Yeats tells us, 'have nothing that catches the eye.' Assemblies that foment propaganda condemn themselves. The spectre that haunts the United Nations is not that of a world in agony wrestling with its fate but of men stalemated in the futility of their proceedings. Those inclined to find it merely quaint that one might mourn the forests of trees axed and pulped to print what is said on 42nd Street, might examine what has become of human rights in the United Nations. I am referring not only to the spectacle of Israel, the people of the holocaust, branded in the General Assembly as a racist entity, but

more generally to the habit of using 'human rights' to debase the
vocabulary of Western values, to gut them of all meaning, by their
cynical deployment in the daily propaganda of 'voting power politics'.
But instead of bemoaning this as unlikely to produce good theatre or
make for lively debate, one needs to be reminded of two things. Because
'human rights' are the most sensitive of issues between a government
and its citizens they go to the heart of sovereignty. For the United
Nations to 'promote' human rights when it is an organisation of states is
therefore a recipe for conflict. It raises an issue to debase it. 'Debating'
human rights does not, however, leave matters where they are merely
because states ignore what is said in criticism and concentrate upon their
own virtues. The cant generated in 'debate' is itself an assault on the
values in question. The moral of George Orwell's masterpiece is that
'humbug' is a killer. One reads in *1984* that 'The purpose of *Newspeak*
was not only to promote a medium of expression for the world-view and
mental habits proper to the devotees of *Ingsoc*, but *to make all other
modes of thought impossible.*'[3]

In any case the point is that not everything can be expressed on stage
and become drama. Hate, unbridled passion and truths diminished by
repetition have no place there; they cannot be contained upon a stage
without issuing in violence or boredom; they cannot be used to defend
right and justice in an assembly without doing violence to reasoned
discourse; and they cannot therefore be made compatible with an
international organisation designed to foster accord. It is those who
demand radical action who must learn this lesson, if they are to derive
any satisfaction from the General Assembly. The great issues as they
should appear at the United Nations – liberty, justice, peace, race, cities
and nature – have to be staged in such a way that those from whom action
is sought are enabled to 'bow' to an authority they can embrace without
loss of dignity. That requires reason, will and organisation, but first of
all it needs imagination and art. It needs, as Edmund Burke described it:

> . . . all the pleasing illusions which make power gentle and obedience
> liberal . . . all the decent drapery of life . . . all the superadded ideas,
> furnished from the wardrobe of a moral imagination, which the heart
> owns and the understanding ratifies, *as necessary to cover the defects
> of our naked, shivering nature, and to raise it to dignity in our own
> estimation.*[4]

In its history, European diplomacy surrounded itself with spectacle.
Congresses were festive occasions. Ambassadors strutted with their

sovereign's pride. Swords were drawn, wars threatened, in defence of rank. At the United Nations diplomats enter their chambers modestly and sit business-like at desks according to their names in the alphabetical order of the English language. But states still need an opportunity to show off their existence, especially when there is often little else they can do. The General Assembly is an important stage because it allows those who sought independence to proclaim their dignity and attest to the fact that preservation of their independence remains their essential reason of state.

The mistake of modern international organisation has been to try to do more than surround negotiations with a stage upon which states can appear. The mistake has been to pretend to stage the negotiations themselves in pursuit of notions incompatible with the character of a diplomatic system. Instead of being content to give periodic point to the outcome of the painstaking business of diplomacy the liberal-democratic imagination decided to create an assembly, without appreciating that it was also creating a theatre in which more or less the same play would be on show. The play bears little relation to the real action which goes on either quite outside the United Nations or offstage and 'behind the scenes' where diplomacy has always taken place.

Those who created the United Nations were aware of this because the negotiations which were publicly brought to a head with the signing of the Charter in the Opera House of San Francisco were negotiated by professionals deliberating in private. It is time to return to that order of priorities and redress the balance between the discredited public activities of the General Assembly and its usefulness as a gathering of diplomats. The public spectacle of the Assembly could serve a much-needed purpose in dramatising issues which it is not equipped to resolve. But this role needs to be subordinate and disciplined so that it can be an expression of, and not a substitute for, serious negotiations. What the Assembly lacks in powers might be compensated for in meaning.

NOTES AND REFERENCES

1. David Jones, *The Tribune's Visitation* (London: Fulcrum Press, 1969).

> As wine of the country
>   sweet if drawn from wood
> near to the living wood
>   that bore the grape
>   sours if taken far

so can all virtue curdle in transit
so vice may be virtue uprooted
so is the honey-root of known-site
    bitter fruit for world-floor.

2. B. W. Hill (ed), *Edmund Burke on Government, Politics and Society* (London: Fontana, 1975) p. 156.
3. George Orwell, *1984* (Harmondsworth: Penguin, 1948) p. 198. Emphasis added.
4. Edmund Burke, *Reflections on the Revolution in France* (London: Dent, 1964) p. 74. Emphasis added.

7 Permanent Missions in New York[1]

E. R. APPATHURAI

Writing in 1963, Professor Thomas Hovet stated that 'the key to any understanding of the United Nations is a recognition of the role the Organisation plays as an instrument of diplomacy. As a diplomatic instrument, the United Nations is in some sense a permanent international conference. Representatives of 110 nations are in almost continual attendance at the headquarters in Manhattan and their very presence provides a ready atmosphere for constant diplomatic negotiations.'[2] If Hovet was correct then, he is even more correct 20 years later. One indication that this is so is the fact that of the 158 member states of the United Nations no less than 154 have established permanent missions at New York.[3] Even those few remaining states which have not become members of the United Nations have, for the most part, established permanent observer missions. These include the two Koreas, the Holy See, Monaco and Switzerland.

The importance of representation at United Nations headquarters on a permanent basis has been recognised even by other groups of 'substate' status such as the PLO and SWAPO which also maintain observer missions at New York. Some intergovernmental organisations such as the Asian-African Legal Consultative Committee, Council for Mutual Economic Assistance, European Economic Community, Latin-American Economic System, League of Arab States, Organisation of African Unity and Organisation of the Islamic Conference, have received 'standing invitations' to participate in the sessions and work of the General Assembly as observers and to maintain offices at headquarters. To this list must be added the 'liaison offices' maintained at New York by the specialised agencies of the United Nations itself. The myriad of mutually interacting policy influences generated by all these groups and institutions in their work with the principal organs and other

94

bodies of the Organisation bear ample witness to the claim that the United Nations has remained both an instrument and a centre of diplomatic activity since its creation.

This chapter deals with the permanent missions which the Organisation's member states maintain at New York and principally with the diplomatic activities which they undertake in the interaction of governments with the United Nations. Permanent missions are seen here as the focal points of such interaction, transmitting policy influences from governments to the Organisation and vice versa, but not necessarily in the role of passive transmission belts. Their capacity for influencing policy varies widely, however, reflecting in the Organisation the realities of military, political and economic power on the world scene in general.

THE EVOLUTION AND FUNCTIONS OF PERMANENT MISSIONS

Before considering the elements which affect the relative influence and effectiveness of the permanent missions it might be useful to note some salient features in regard to their evolution, and the functions which they perform. The phenomenon of permanent delegations to international organisations had already appeared during the days of the League of Nations although, as Walters states, 'the system of permanent delegations was of no serious consequence in League history'.[4] Permanent representation then was embryonic in nature, with the great powers of the time, Japan excepted, operating exclusively out of their capitals and the lesser powers struggling on the slippery slopes of Secretariat hostility (the Secretariat feared an intermediary between itself and the national capitals) to establish a meaningful presence at Geneva for their delegations. Though in the first two years of the life of the United Nations its member governments were themselves groping for a formula to regulate their relations with the Organisation, the presence of missions in New York was never questioned by the Secretariat. Additionally, but for some mild hesitation on the part of the British,[5] the great powers were in the forefront of the movement to establish permanent missions. The status of these missions was legitimised by General Assembly Resolution 257 (III) of 3 December 1948.

The evolution of permanent missions may be seen in another development as well. Since the inception of the Organisation, the date on which a state was admitted to membership in the United Nations and the date on which it established its permanent mission have become progressively more synchronised. While between 1945 and 1955 over half of the new members took up to three years to establish permanent missions, after 1955 two-thirds of the new members took only up to three months to do so.[6] On 23 September 1983, St Christopher and Nevis, which was admitted to the Organisation as its 158th member, had its permanent representative, Ambassador William Valentine Herbert, present his credentials to the Secretary-General on the very same day, although this is not to say that that is necessarily the current practice.

A variety of reasons have prompted governments to establish permanent missions. One is the sheer growth in the number of states on the world scene. The presence of their representatives in one place makes it easier for them to follow developments, trends and opinions at the global level as they are reflected in the Organisation. Another reason is the perceived need on the part of member governments to participate in the deliberations and activities of the United Nations more actively than through simple membership in it. Some governments have desired high visibility for their newly acquired political independence. On the other hand, some governments have wished to have low visibility for their unilateral actions which they would like to process through, and in the name of, the Organisation. A few governments have sought to prevent the internationalisation of domestic issues which might result in their being raised by other states in the Organisation. Some governments have felt that the United Nations as an international organisation, especially if it has an active Secretary-General, has the potential of assuming a dynamic of its own over which they would need to keep a 'watching brief'. Yet others have felt the need to support the Organisation as the only means through which they could have their voices heard, benefit from the vast data bank in the Secretariat and the expertise of the officials there, or interact with the big powers on the principle of the sovereign equality of states. For one or more of these reasons, governments have tended to follow their admission to the Organisation with the establishment of permanent missions at New York.

An almost unending series of meetings which takes place at the United Nations on every conceivable subject between sessions of the General Assembly has also prompted governments to establish permanent missions. For the small and new states, their only opportunity to follow the proceedings of such meetings is by using, however inadequately, the members of the permanent missions. Even the big powers who are adequately staffed and who often send specialists to these meetings need to be advised on the attitudes of other representatives and be alerted to potential difficulties in the negotiating process. A distinguishing feature of this process is that none of the member governments, however powerful in the traditional sense, is in complete control of the situation once an issue is brought into the Organisation. The countermoves of opponents, their changing attitudes and positions, the procedures of the various bodies of the Organisation, the necessity to avoid pyrrhic victories and the 'tyranny of time' all impose limitations on the successful practice of this process which permanent mission personnel, as resident diplomats and with varying degrees of expertise and effectiveness, seek to mitigate.

Governments have valued the utility of permanent missions also for the conduct of their bilateral diplomacy. This is discussed in Part III of this book.

Yet another reason for governments establishing permanent missions concerns their participation in the annual sessions of the General Assembly. The mission does much of the preparatory work including the introduction of new agenda items and the handling of old issues. During the sessions, apart from providing information about the city of New York and generally about the procedures and practices of the Organisation, the permanent mission becomes the base of operations for national representation in the Assembly. Its communications facilities, including its codes, are used for transmission and receipt of messages affecting the work of the national delegation. More importantly, permanent mission personnel also bear an important share of the negotiating responsibility.

Finally, of course, there is the fact that the Security Council is, officially, in permanent session. While there are only 15 member states who constitute the Council at any given time, many of the issues dealt with in the Council either seriously and directly affect or are of interest to other states as well. The negotiation of the security interests of states results in round-the-clock, behind-the-scenes consultations and bargaining which goes well beyond the confines of the Council's limited membership. Besides, the ten non-permanent seats rotate, which means not only that other states have to be prepared to take their seats in the Council but they must also be prepared for the prior negotiations as to which country will fill a particular vacancy. Although Article 28.1 of the Charter states only that 'each member of the Security Council shall [for the purposes of the Council] be represented at all times at the seat of the Organisation', it is easy to see why states which are not members of the Security Council themselves have a need for the establishment of permanent missions.

THE INFLUENCE OF THE 'PARLIAMENTARY' SETTING

Permanent missions resemble traditional embassies in the functions which they perform, namely, representation, negotiation, information-gathering, public relations and the promotion of friendly relations. However, since they carry out these functions in a different setting, the tasks which they perform are quite distinct from those of traditional diplomats.

The 'setting' in which permanent representatives function is 'parliamentary diplomacy' as described by Dean Rusk:

> What might be called parliamentary diplomacy is a type of multi-lateral negotiation which involves at least four factors: First, a continuing organization with interest and responsibilities which are broader than the specific items that happen to appear upon the agenda at any particular time – in other words, more than a traditional international conference called to cover specific agenda. Second, regular public debate exposed to the media of mass communication and in touch, therefore, with public opinions around the globe. Third, rules of procedure which govern the process of debate and which are themselves subject to tactical manipulation to advance or oppose a point of view. And lastly, formal conclusions, ordinarily expressed in resolution, which are reached by majority votes of some description, on a simple or two-thirds majority or based upon a financial contribution or economic stake – some with and some without a veto. Typically, we are talking about the United Nations and its related organizations, although not exclusively so, because the same type of organization is growing up in other parts of the international scene.[7]

The setting in which a traditional ambassador functions is a foreign capital. He is concerned with explaining, defending and pursuing the foreign policy of his government in its relations with the country of accreditation. Since he is engaged in bilateral, not multilateral par-liamentary diplomacy, none of the characteristics which Rusk outlined applies in his case. Nor is he obliged to bring the same perspectives to his work as the permanent representative. Since the permanent represen-tative functions in a multinational and highly visible context, he has to pay even more attention than the traditional ambassador to the image which his country projects abroad.

The parliamentary diplomatic setting impinges also upon the nature of the issues which involve a permanent representative. While a traditional ambassador addresses himself to specific issues between his own government and that of his accreditation, the questions with which a permanent representative deals are often of a generalised nature which have a worldwide relevance, if not applicability, such as international security, global welfare and development. While undoubtedly a major concern of the permanent representative is the pursuance of his government's interests in and through the Organisation, it is also true that a considerable amount of the consultations which take place among permanent representatives are not limited to the immediate direct gains of one's own government but for the purpose of seeking a consensus on general issues.

A distinctive quality of the permanent mission is that it assumes different statuses and roles in the making of decisions on international questions. At the home end, it is regarded as an outpost of the government. At the United Nations, however, the members of permanent missions, though formally functioning as representatives of their governments, may and do often become, in a sense, a part of the Organisation. The clearest instance of this is their participation in the work of the Security Council which is, in effect, a council of 15 permanent representatives. Members of permanent missions also assume elective offices in other organs, committees and commissions of the United Nations. In such instances they become a part of the Organisation in the decision-making machinery of the Organisation. The traditional ambassador is never able to become part of the decision-making machinery of the state to which he is accredited.

Parliamentary diplomacy offers greater opportunity for officials below the level of head of mission to carry out their duties with more authority than is permitted by their governments to the traditional diplomats at that level. As a corollary of this, there is also a greater informality in the relationships among diplomats in the Organisation. A number of items on the agenda of the representative organs call for exchanges of information and analyses of data among the diplomats at the seat of the Organisation. Because such exercises cut across routine diplomatic ranks and titles, there is less rank consciousness (although this is not altogether absent, especially among the diplomats of new states), less protocol and more informality in the relationships of senior personnel such as the heads of missions with their junior colleagues. This applies both within a mission and across missions, heightened by the fact that junior officials are often experts in their respective issue areas, contributing significantly, in their own right, to the making of policy in the United Nations.

Finally, the division of responsibility in the making of national policy is less clear-cut in multilateral diplomacy than in bilateral diplomacy. In the latter case the government is able to make policy almost entirely on the strength of its own resources. In the case of the former, the issues which are dealt with in the representative organs are multinational in character and, almost invariably, there is less information on them at many capitals than at New York. Governments are thus largely dependent upon their missions for much of the information necessary for the making of policy, particularly where it concerns the attitudes of other governments and the possible patterns of voting on given issues. Since issues in multilateral diplomacy become the subject of partisan debate, and disposal in terms of the aggregated interests of the other members of the Organisation, it is through a dialogue with permanent missions that governments can develop a national policy. This involves even the decision whether or not to place a question before the Organisation.

THE LOCI OF INTERACTION

In the performance of their tasks the permanent representatives have at least five loci in, and with which, they interact – the formal meetings of the Organisation, the group to which their governments belong, the Secretariat of the United Nations, the world's press and electronic media and, of course, their home governments. In the meetings of the Organisation the permanent representatives promote their governmental policies; they make speeches in open sessions, draft resolutions, sponsor and oppose resolutions, canvass electoral support for their candidacy for office in the institutions of the United Nations, and cast votes on behalf of their governments.

During the General Assembly sessions, members of national delegations, those from home as well as those permanently resident in New York, undertake private negotiations, but the role of the permanent missions is not insignificant. All delegations include some or all diplomatic members of permanent missions. It is among these persons that consultations took place during the earlier stages of preparing for the Assembly, and among them that commitments were made and understandings reached in regard to the resolutions under discussion in the Assembly. For this reason this nucleus of permanent mission personnel also plays an important part in negotiating any differences that may arise during the course of debate, including changes in agreements earlier reached. Since these officials are continuously resident at New York and develop personal relationships among themselves, the task of private negotiation is easier for them than for national delegates who arrive for short periods, particularly as the pace of action in the parliamentary process and unexpected developments in the Assembly leave little time for consultations with home governments.

The impact of personal relationships on policy matters is difficult to measure but the value in cultivating good personal relationships is more easily seen when such relationships are absent than when they are present. A permanent representative who seeks to have his colleagues support a proposal in which he is interested may not succeed, on grounds of personal friendship, in persuading them to change their instructions, since such changes require authorisation by governments which may or may not be cooperative. But the maintenance of good personal relationships by the individual permanent representative with his colleagues often constrains the latter to make the best effort possible to accommodate his wishes within the framework of their own instructions. It is in the 'squaring' of other people's wishes with one's own instructions that personal relationships play a role. Where good personal relationships exist, permanent representatives make a positive effort to accommodate the requests of other permanent representatives in an effort to be helpful. Some of the bigger states have special 'liaison officers' in their permanent missions to keep in constant touch with members of other delegations, to ascertain their thinking on given issues through the vicissitudes of Assembly debate. These officers keep and revise their own tabulations of possible voting positions. If some delegations cannot be depended upon for the final vote, attempts are made to persuade them.

Several methods of persuasion are used by permanent missions to move reluctant delegations.[8] Warnings are issued of possible adverse consequences to their governments if they persist in their line of action. Log-rolling arrangements are made: 'I'll vote for you this time if you will vote for me next time.' Appeals to group solidarity are undertaken. Direct threats to cut off aid are held out. Appeals are made to the principles of the Charter. If all this fails, a permanent mission may recommend to its government that bilateral diplomatic action be taken in the national capitals of those 'deviant' delegations to try to arrange for suitable instructions to be issued to them. In all this negotiation the aim of the liaison officers is to see if they can possibly get the 'doubtful' delegations to vote with their own government's position on given issues. Alternatively, the effort is to ensure that a delegation abstains from voting instead of casting a negative vote. If it will prove embarrassing for a representative to be at the Assembly and abstain, he may even be persuaded to stay away from the Assembly meeting.

One of the most important developments which has taken place in the Organisation, apart from the 'common law development'[9] of the permanent missions themselves, is the growth of the group system. It is in the group system that much of the Organisation's politics is played out. Groups are the contemporary energising force of the United Nations, the 'stuff of [UN] politics'.

Groups in the headquarters of the Organisation at New York are made up of clusterings of the permanent missions of states which are members of these groups. The states are those of certain geographic regions which have either a similar historical, cultural and economic background, or shared ideological values, in some cases a mixture of both, and which by virtue of such affinities concert their diplomatic activity in the Organisation for common purposes. A group, being an informal consultative body is not mentioned in the Charter of the United Nations although it has acquired a semi-official character by virtue of the use to which it is put by the United Nations for the orderly conduct of its business.

There are five geographic groups recognised in the practice of the Organisation. These are the African group (50 states), the Asian group (40 states), the Eastern European group (11 states), the Latin American group (33 states), and the Western European 'and others' group (22 states) which is so called because it includes Canada, Australia and New Zealand. For several years the Secretary-General has resorted to meetings with the chairpersons of the geographic groups for conveying messages to, or for consulting with, the members of the respective groups.[10]

While the main groups are formed along geographic lines, there are also subgroups within these main groups, which are formed on the basis of the specialised interests of states. Some examples of these are the Nordic group, the ASEAN group, the European Community, the Arab group and the Organisation of the Islamic Conference. In addition to these are the larger umbrella groups such as the non-aligned group and the Afro-Asian group and also, on a functional basis, the Group of 77.

Permanent mission personnel spend much of their time moving from meeting to meeting in this multiplicity of groups which is the forum where they negotiate agreements on elections in the UN, as well as common policy positions and tactics to be adopted in its representative organs. In elections it is now the accepted position that nominees of one group for office in the UN will not be contested by others in the same group (there are always exceptions to this) as well as by nominees of other groups. The group system has advanced so far that there is an intergroup understanding to this effect. In substantive questions each group, with the exception of the Western European group,[11] attempts to hammer out an agreed group position. Draft resolutions are first brought into the groups, debated, modified and accepted by group consensus or rejected. Once accepted, the majority of the members of the group may be expected to vote in its favour in the representative organs. Thus the impact of the group on policy-making in the United Nations is great. It is also considerable at the national capitals of African, Asian and Latin American countries which often instruct their representatives to support the group consensus. The following statement by an ambassador of one of the leading states in the African group is typical of the practice of 80 per cent of the members of that group: 'The group plays a very important role in the decision-making. If the position of my government and that of the group vary, I inform my government of the difference and would ask if it still wants to keep its position. Very often the government switches to the group position.'[12] The desire of these governments not to isolate themselves in the group to which they belong is one motive for such instruction. In addition, the reliance on group consensus results from the incapacity in the foreign offices of many of these states to undertake independent study on UN matters.

For the representatives of the smaller states in the UN, the group serves as a forum for the exchange of ideas and mutual education. It also provides added strength. It is largely through group support that the permanent representatives of small states can hope to place their own objectives or interests on the Organisation's agenda. As one permanent representative observed: 'If we decide on things in common we are given more attention. There are big powers with small votes and small powers with big votes. No matter what the US and USSR think, they cannot ignore us. Group formation gives this balance.'[13] While this might be an overstatement where the serious interests of the super powers are concerned, in several other matters that have come up for discussion in the UN, small states have acquired a more significant role through their groups than their size and power in international politics would permit.

The third locus of interaction for the permanent representatives is the Secretariat at the Organisation's headquarters. A senior official on the 38th floor stated that 'consultations with the permanent missions are the

Secretary-General's daily bread. He may spend 80 per cent of his day with the permanent missions and the rest of it with Secretariat officials.'[14] Dag Hammarsjköld, when he was Secretary-General, witnessed to the usefulness to him of the permanent missions:

> In my experience I have found several arrangements of value to enable the Secretary-General to obtain what might be regarded as representative opinion of the Organization in respect of political issues faced by him. One such arrangement might be described as the institution of the permanent missions to the United Nations through which the member states have enabled the Secretary-General to carry on frequent consultations safeguarded by private diplomacy.[15]

Some of the consultations which the Secretary-General conducts may concern material arrangements regarding the obligations which given states have undertaken in respect of specific issues such as, for example, peace-keeping. Questions of finance may bring the Secretary-General and the permanent representatives, especially of the major donors, into consultations with each other and these consultations may be initiated by either side. At times permanent representatives have complained to the Secretary-General about some Secretariat initiative or activity, or about appointments made or not made to the Secretariat. One official in New York remarked that in the case of some countries, 'behind every successful applicant for appointment to the Secretariat stands a permanent representative!' Consultations have also been initiated with the Secretary-General by permanent representatives in an effort to ascertain his views or through him the views and attitudes of other governments on given issues or to state to him their own national positions on these issues, including the politics of elections to high offices in the Organisation. In times of crisis, groups of 'like-minded' permanent representatives have met with the Secretary-General to make suggestions for the resolution of the problems.

At another level, a member of a mission may contact a Secretariat official in a substantive department for assistance in the formulation of a resolution. On occasion a Secretariat official may encourage an initiative undertaken by a mission or attempt to discourage one that might either fail or, if passed, be impossible to implement. Sometimes the Secretariat can be helpful in breaking a deadlock by making a compromise proposal. The extent to which this happens depends on the willingness of the Secretariat official to tread on rather sensitive ground and the relations of the official with the member of the mission concerned.

The fourth locus of interaction for permanent missions is the world's media which are represented in the Organisation, and which turn the United Nations into a valuable information centre for all permanent missions. Often they are useful to many permanent representatives who are less informed than they of developments even within the Organisation. Besides, world news is constantly received in the Organisation and discussions among the press corps and permanent missions are helpful in speedily sorting out the reactions of governments to such news. The task of gathering information in the United Nations is not easy if it is to be undertaken solely by the scrutiny of the documentation issuing from the Organisation. The vastness of such documentation is well known. Consequently, most members of permanent missions spend at least a portion of their day in the UN building in order to 'gossip' in the good sense of the word.

Permanent missions interact with the world's media also through their public relations departments, which bring much psychological acumen, careful preparation and drafting skill to bear on their press releases and official handouts. If, for instance, a government's representative assumes posture X in public debate with the full realisation that what will ultimately be achievable through private negotiation is only X minus Y, he is not disappointed when the final result turns out to be X – Y. But his own public and those other interested publics in other parts of the world are not privy either to the representative's private assessments of the question or of the non-public negotiations conducted in regard to it. Consequently their expectations continue to remain at the level raised by the contents of the representative's initial public speech. The problem of presenting the final outcome as constituting not a retreat on the part of the representative but as an effective exercise of leadership by him in a new direction, or in some other explanation designed not to tarnish the public image of the representative's government, is the task of the department of public relations.

The timing of a representative's speeches in the United Nations is another important question to which the department of public relations is sensitive. A speech delivered on a Friday afternoon may capture the headlines for a whole weekend. Accordingly, negotiations must be conducted with other delegations in the Organisation in order to secure an advantageous position in the roster of speakers.

The fifth locus of interaction for the permanent representative is his home government, to which he must report and make recommendations. The reporting function is of great importance in the making of policy at home. The permanent representative reports on the views of the members of his group, his discussions with individual ambassadors both within and outside his own group, his contacts with the members of the press corps and non-governmental organisations at New York and his consultations with the Secretariat on the implementation by it of United Nations resolutions passed in these sessions of the Assembly or the Councils of the Organisation. He also reports on the discussions which take place between assembly sessions in the various *ad hoc* bodies and functional commissions established by the United Nations, some of which are of several years' standing. Reporting is a continuous process, since at no time of the year is the UN free of meetings held by these bodies.

CONCLUSION

Although all permanent missions perform the same functions, they exhibit a wide range of differences in their resources, styles of decision-making and their capabilities for influence within the Organisation and in their governments. For instance, while the United States mission carried five members of ambassadorial rank in its staff of 48 in March 1983, and the Soviet had two ambassadors in its staff of 109, the mission of Equatorial Guinea had one member of ambassadorial rank (the permanent representative) in its staff of two, and the Maldive Islands in its mission of two did not have even an ambassador but only a third secretary and an attaché.

Moreover, since the 'voting weight' of a permanent representative inside the Organisation is not matched by the 'political wieght' of his country in world politics, the result of such imbalance is mutual frustration. The more developed states resent the time and effort spent on issues they refuse to support and which, therefore, at least for the present, remain without consequence. The less developed states, for their part, resent the fact that they are unable, and the developed states unwilling, to implement what they regard as the wishes of the majority as reflected in the resolutions passed.

These difficulties faced by the UN do not, however, stem from the activities of the permanent missions. Rather, they are the result of the inequalities in power relations, and the uneven levels of social and economic development among the states in the world. As Marie-Claude Smouts has pointed out, the new states have also challenged the code of norms and system of values upon which the United Nations was created as being Western, mercantile, Christian and imperialist.[16] The difficulties which the Organisation faces seem to have much to do with the redefinition of its norms and values, to make them universally more acceptable. Let us hope, without too much confidence, that the permanent missions which provide a forum for constant interaction among states in their mutual education and the making of policy on international issues can concert their diplomacy towards the amelioration of the imbalances on the world scene which complicate their tasks within the Organisation.

NOTES AND REFERENCES

1. In the preparation of this chapter I have received assistance from several permanent representatives and Secretariat officials at New York who found time to meet with me. I am also indebted to Miss Anne Winslow, former editor-in-chief of the Carnegie Endowment for International Peace, from whose criticism and advice I have once again benefited and to Mr Issa Ben Yacine Diallo, the principal officer in the Executive Office of the Secretary-General, for the many hours of his precious time spent in discussions with me. I am grateful to Bruylant, Brussels, for permission to use material from my earlier study on this subject. I acknowledge as mine any errors of fact and judgement in the present chapter.
2. Thomas Hovet, Jr, 'United Nations Diplomacy', *Journal of International Affairs*, vol. 17, no. 1 (1963) 29.
3. The following states do not maintain permanent missions at UN headquarters as of September 1983: Belize, Comoros, Solomon Islands, Vanuatu.
4. F. P. Walters, *A History of the League of Nations* (Toronto: OUP, 1967) p. 199. For a full discussion of the role of the permanent delegations to the League of Nations see the chapter by Victor Ghebali, pp. 25–122 in Volume I of the four volumes published by the Carnegie Endowment for International Peace entitled *Les Missions Permanentes auprès des Organisations Internationales* (Brussels: Bruylant, 1971). Also see P. B. Potter, 'Permanent Delegations to the League of Nations', *American Political Science Review*, vol. xxv, no. 1 (February 1931) 21–4 and Harold Tobin, 'The Problem of Permanent Representation at the League of Nations', *Political Science Quarterly*, vol. xlvii, no. 4 (December 1933) 481–512.
5. See P. B. Russell and J. E. Muther, *A History of the United Nations Charter* (Washington D.C.: The Brookings Institution, 1958) p. 445, where they write: 'The only other procedural issue requiring debate was the American proposal to keep the Security Council in continuous session. Great Britain did not oppose the principle, but was afraid that it would result in men of second-rate capacity becoming permanent representatives whereas the need was for responsible Cabinet Ministers to attend important sessions.'
6. For a statistical statement of this phenomenon and a fuller study on the

permanent missions to the United Nations see my work published in 1975 by the Carnegie Endowment for International Peace as Volume III of *Les Missions Permanentes auprès des Organisations Internationales*.

7. Dean Rusk, 'Parliamentary Diplomacy – Debate vs. Negotiations', *World Affairs Interpreter* (Summer 1955) 121–2.

8. For an understanding of negotiating tactics in the General Assembly see S. M. Finger, *Your Man at the UN* (New York and London: New York University Press, 1980) pp. 29–36. See also D. G. Bishop, 'The US Mission and Corridor Diplomacy' in Gerard J. Mangone (ed), *The Administration of United States Policy through the United Nations* (New York: Oceana Publications, 1967) especially pp. 57–66.

9. Dag Hammarskjöld, *Introduction to the Annual Report of the Secretary-General*, 14th Session (1959) p. 2.

10. At present, Turkey is a member both of the Asian and the 'Western European and others' group while the United States, except for electoral purposes, and South Africa and Israel, for different reasons, do not formally belong to any of the geographic groups.

11. In several interviews which this writer held with permanent representatives at New York in September 1983 it was pointed out that, although the Western European Group does not concert as a bloc for striking a common policy on issues before the Organisation, the representatives belonging to the EEC have recently followed the practice more and more of holding intensive consultations as a group on such issues.

12. Interview given to this writer at UN headquarters, New York.

13. Ditto.

14. Ditto.

15. See Wilder Foote (ed), *Servant of Peace: a Selection of the Speeches and Statements of Dag Hammarsjköld, Secretary-General of the United Nations, 1953–61* (New York: Harper & Row, 1962).

16. Marie-Claude Smouts, 'The Crisis of International Organisations', *Etúdes*, Monthly Review of the Pères de la Compagnie de Jésus (fevrier 1983) p. 170. Translation from French by this writer.

8 The Poverty of Multilateral Economic Diplomacy

SUSAN STRANGE

It would be easy to write as pessimistically about the economic side of the UN's activities as contributors to this book have written about its political organs. Many enthusiasts for international organisation now find themselves sunk in despair about the future prospects and are inclined to dismiss as utterly futile many of the goings-on at which UN delegates spend so much time and effort. Few doubt that the current scene in New York or Geneva or other places where the members foregather is depressing and the future prospect dim.

Almost a decade of North–South 'dialogue' (so-called) seems to have reached a point where neither side has any more to say to the other. North and South are like two people in a Harold Pinter play: there they both sit talking right past one another, repeating to themselves and for their own satisfaction the words and phrases they have already used to each other countless times before. After the clarion call of the Brandt Commission for a great new effort to tackle the fundamental problems of international economic disorder and discontent, there has followed a deathly silence. The heads of state have met at summits in Cancun, in Williamsburg and elsewhere, and we have heard yet another re-run of the Pinter dialogue of the deaf.

Nor does the rest of the scene before us present a very cheerful sight. After the last Multilateral Trade Negotiations the trend towards protectionism, state subsidies and discrimination of all kinds makes it very doubtful if yet another round of trade talks is even worth arranging. And meanwhile, although the IMF carries on with its annual shindigs, another dialogue of the deaf goes on between Europeans complaining bitterly about the imposition of high American interest rates and Americans increasingly resentful of Europe's free-riding on an expensive

American defence programme. The long-drawn-out UN negotiations on
the law of the sea (UNCLOS) have been hopelessly becalmed ever since
the present US administration came to power: even though they have
now said they will reopen the discussions, it is by no means certain that
the agreed text that took so long to negotiate can still serve as a basis for a
new maritime order. I could go on, but there is no need; after all the
special conferences and studies of the mid-1970s on population, on the
environment, on food and hunger, on water resources or whatever, there
is little sign of progress or achievement. The sense of having reached an
impasse, of being stuck at a dead end with no way out of it in sight seems
to be one shared by a great many people of many diverse opinions and
interests.

For example, a recent article in *South*, the magazine published by the
Third World Foundation in London, concluded that 'The late 1970s has
witnessed a slowing down of UN action comparable only to the pause
imposed by the Cold War . . . Most of the diagnoses of the UN's
shortcomings seem to overlook the fact that the large area of harmony
and automatic functioning has come up against its limits with the
demand for a new international economic order.'[1]

Many well-meaning and idealistic supporters of the UN idea feel cast
down, along with the writer of the *South* article, by the notion that the
United Nations and those of its agencies concerned with economic
matters have got themselves stuck up a blind alley and are making no
more progress. In this chapter, however, by looking beyond the
economic diplomacy conducted at the UN, I propose to offer a less
pessimistic interpretation. I shall argue first, that the atmosphere of
pessimism is encouraged and the outlook made to seem darker and more
depressing than necessary, by the curious persistence that has marked
the past decade or so in pursuing rather hopeless causes and in flogging
dead diplomatic horses. The reasons for this persistence seem to me to
call for some consideration and possibly explanation. And secondly I
shall argue that the supposed 'failures' of the UN in economic
diplomacy – that area of international relations which, after all, was
going to be one of the major respects in which it was going to improve
upon the old League of Nations – should be seen rather as the
reemergence, after a period of rather unusual (even unnatural) sup-
pression, of age-old disagreements about the basic issues of political
economy. It is not to be likened to reaching the end of a blind alley, the
exhaustion of goodwill and the running dry of the wells of the
international cooperative spirit. Rather, it is the rediscovery at long last
that the outcomes of the world economy, the determination of who-gets-

what between states, classes, generations and sexes is a rather more complex matter than the conduct of economic diplomacy through international organisations. It is the result of multiple bargaining within states, outside states as well as between states – and it has almost always been so.

It is the basic disagreement over priorities and over the relative importance of different social values (as well as disagreement over the distribution of those values) which lies behind all the dialogues of the deaf – East–West, North–South, transatlantic and transpacific – of which we are the impotent spectators. Delegations on either side disagree about ends long before they disagree about means. No wonder then that there is a sense of having reached an impasse.

THE ISSUES

Let us start therefore from first principles. Let us ask: what are the main issues that have to be bargained about, whether it is in the world economy, in a national political economy or even in a village or a family?

To my mind, there are four major goals or values which political authority (faced with the need to work and produce in order to live) has in some measure to seek and to pursue. The main issues relate either to how each value should be achieved, or to what relative priority should be assigned or to how they should be distributed.

The first value is wealth. Authority has to decide how wealth is to be produced, in what manner, or according to what mode of production the factors of land, labour, capital and knowledge are to be combined to produce goods and services for current or future use, and how much.

The second is order or security. Authority has to decide how violence is to be restrained and how the security necessary to the preservation of life and the production of wealth is to be obtained.

The third is equity or justice. Authority has to decide on the rules and the resource transfers necessary for the smooth functioning of society without internal discontent, strife and revolution. And it is obvious at this point that the quotient of equity – or perceived fairness in John Rawls's terms – needed by any society will vary inversely with the coerciveness with which authority is exercised, and also perhaps with the amounts both of wealth produced and security provided. People will put up with great injustices if the penalties of objection are severe and/or if authority is producing enough of other values.

The fourth and last value is of course the converse of the same coin: liberty or the freedom to choose. The authority that makes the rules has to allow some freedom even to slaves; how much will depend on how much consent it can either demand by force or win by its provision of wealth, security and justice.

Political theorists and philosophers will find all this very elementary and very crude. True, but the point I have to make is simply that all the basic political issues arising about the economic life of a society are really about the conflict – or trade-off to use the economists' term – between these four values. It is easy to see how this happens in the old, obsolete, billiard-ball state. Government has to decide whether society's predominant mode of production will be socialist or capitalist, whether the deciding voice will be that of the market or the planner. Government has to decide how to use the state's monopoly of violence to maintain order within and to deter disruption of order from without. It establishes the principles of justice through the law and through welfare policies and administers them. And it is the state which determines the limits of freedom of individuals, enterprises and political parties.

Today, however, the international economic order so-called no longer conforms to the billiard-ball model. Much of the production within states is international production directed by the managers of transnational corporations and even more has to operate in response to a world market quite beyond the control of the individual state. But though the power to decide the four major issues involving trade-offs between the basic values has escaped the control of individual states – if indeed they ever entirely had it – the issues themselves have not changed. They are still concerned with how much wealth is to be produced and by what means; how much security and order is to be provided, for whom and at what cost; how much distributive justice is necessary to ensure social stability and consensus; and how much freedom to choose can be permitted to individuals, and to political groups or economic enterprises.

It will be evident that in the present-day integrated world market economy – I refuse to use the misleading euphemism 'interdependent' – these issues are in part decided not only beyond the individual state but also beyond the combined control of all states. It is not only therefore interstate bargaining and negotiation that counts, but also bargaining in the market or between market operators and states. Think for example of current discussions in OPEC over the 'proper' price of a barrel of oil. Or consider recent developments in the tin market in which it appeared that the Tin Agreement negotiated between governments was being used by a group of producers (thought to be Malaysian) which first of all bought up forward so much tin that the price went to record heights, then forced it so low that the buffer stock manager under the Tin Agreement had to intervene to hold the floor price, thus reinforcing producer power in future negotiation. Here, in short, is an example of power politics played out on the floor of the London Metal Exchange.

It must also be evident that the outcome of this complex web of interstate, intrastate and intramarket bargaining will be differently judged according to the priority accorded to each of the four basic values. And this is why in studying international economic diplomacy – and using the term in the broad sense I have indicated – we cannot afford to look only at the judgements made of the outcome from any one point of view or within just one paradigm.

THE TYRANNY OF THE PARADIGMS

For it is value-judgements which, in the last resort, most sharply distinguish the three main paradigms of economic thought concerning the way the world economy ought to operate. These are the liberal/pluralist, the neo-marxist structuralist/dependency and the realist/mercantilist paradigms. Each, it will be noticed, has both an economic and a political kind of label. Each is based on a different interpretation of economic history and leads to different judgements about what is good and bad about the present state of the world. Each leads to different policy conclusions. It is this divergence, emerging gradually in the 1960s and more rapidly in the 1970s, which is reflected in the inconclusive debates in the United Nations, in GATT and UNCTAD, in the International Monetary Fund and the World Bank, and in many other associated agencies and conferences. Though all three paradigms express certain basic truths about economic life in a world system, each is also fatally flawed when it comes to offering practical and convincing advice on how members of the United Nations should escape from their apparent impasse.

Let me illustrate the point very briefly. The predominant paradigm in the study of economics is the liberal/pluralist view of the world economy. This makes the basic (but often unstated) assumption that the production of wealth is the first aim of national systems and of the international one. The paramount need for this purpose is to ensure the most efficient allocation of resources and the lowest-cost combination of factors of production. It makes the further assumption that an open world market economy with as few impediments to the free movement of capital and technology and free trade in goods and services will incidentally bias the system towards cooperation and away from conflict. In this view, the first 25 years of the UN system were years of substantial progress and achievement; the 1970s, by contrast, were years of standstill and even backsliding. Following the lead given by Richard Cooper's highly influential book *The Economics of Interdependence*[2] – that word again! – the pluralists have argued that the open world economy has added to the list of questions regarding trade and money on which states need to negotiate. Unless they do, they cannot enjoy the benefits of greater division of labour, lower costs of traded goods and services and wider markets that the open economy offers. It is from this paradigm that the concern of much American writing about 'regimes' mainly derives.

By contrast, the structuralist/radical paradigm judges the performance of the system in terms of distributive justice; this is far more important to this school than the system's performance in terms of efficiency in the production of wealth. The main criterion for judging international economic diplomacy, therefore, is how far it has been possible if not to achieve greater justice from the system then at least to assert a concern for the principle of economic justice, and to build a coalition of states united in pursuit of this goal. From this point of view, the demand for a New International Economic Order and the Charter of the Economic Rights and Duties of States is the international analogue to the Tennis Court Oath before the French Revolution.

Nor must we omit the realist/mercantilist (or economic nationalist) paradigm. In this view, the absence of any paramount authority or world government leaves the ultimate responsibility still – despite all the erosion of economic control – with the individual state. The national interest and the military and economic security of the state must still dictate policy and first priority should therefore be given to freedom of choice for the state. Thus, the record of economic diplomacy, whether in or out of the United Nations, must be judged by how far it has permitted individual national governments to pursue and secure whatever they regard as their national interest, whether this involves keeping high-cost farmers or high-cost steelworkers secure in their jobs or keeping up the price of oil or of tin or spending a third of the national income on defence.

And the truth is, as we all know only too well, that though this may not be the most respectable or the most admired view of the world, the realist/mercantilist paradigm is in fact the one in the light of which most governments, when they have any power to exercise, have acted. They have seen the United Nations and other international organisations as tools of foreign policy; they are there to be used, abused or ignored according to the shifting perceptions and directions of national foreign policy. Remember and compare the statements about the UN made in their more unbuttoned moments by General de Gaulle, Lord Home, Nikita Khrushchev or, now, President Reagan.

Bearing in mind these three highly divergent views of the world economy it would clearly be much easier to make an assessment of the record of the UN as a diplomatic forum if one were to adopt uncritically any one of the basic paradigms. I can think of many liberal economists who have done it, and many neo-Marxist or reformist *dependistas* who have done likewise. Nor is it hard to weigh up the balance sheet of the UN as negotiations there have contributed to or detracted from the nationalist interests of any particular state, be it the United States, the Soviet Union, Britain or Japan.

But if, as I do, one perceives that each of the paradigms has some validity, that there is something to be said for each of the values to which they attach such importance, then making a dispassionate assessment becomes much more difficult. Moreover, it seems to me that each paradigm contains a fatal flaw; each makes at least one false assumption which leads one to doubt whether the policy prescriptions that one might deduce from their balance-sheet of the record are either desirable or practicable.

Consider, for example, the liberal paradigm. That seems to make several doubtful assumptions. The most obvious is that efficiency is the most important criterion for political action, the creation of wealth the purpose of social organisation. The fallacy of that particular presumption is proclaimed by the domestic policies of every capitalist state from the United States to Switzerland, Japan or West Germany. It may of course suit their national interest to argue the need for an open world market economy and for the minimum regulation of those who operate in it, but in the long run the basic contention of the Brandt Commission cannot easily be brushed aside, that *some* attention to the distributive equity of the world economy is in the interests of the rich who wish to stay on top of the heap and do not want it either to collapse, explode or be turned upside down. The only problem – as with national politics – is to know how much equity must be worked into the system and how long is the long run. We are back therefore to my concept of the trade-off of values.

The second liberal fallacy is the understatement of the value of order or economic security to the system as a whole – a mistake never made, incidentally, by the patron saint of liberals, Adam Smith. Though he argued for the division of labour he was under no illusion about the prior necessity both of national defence and of sound money, neither of which were to be had without the intervention of authority with the market economy. In fact I think Adam Smith would have agreed with me that the record of the world market economy in the 1970s shows the greater importance for continued progress in the creation of wealth of maintaining sound, stable money than of removing barriers to free trade. The present recession has not been caused by the general abandonment of freer trade policies and the outbreak of trade wars between the major trading countries, although in 1973 many people feared that this would happen; it has been caused far more by the failure first to maintain the real value of the dollar as the main medium of exchange in international transactions and second the failure so to manage the transfer of wealth to the oil producers that it had neither deflationary nor inflationary consequences. In fact it has had both, and we have suffered both unemployment and inflation.

Indeed, there is a third fallacy specific to the pluralist wing of the liberal school if one may so characterise people like Kindleberger and other American advocates of international cooperation who agree with Richard Cooper that the solution to the inherent contradiction between an international political system divided into states and a world economy united by trade, investment and production lies in multilateral cooperation and the multiplication of international regimes. I propose to explain why I think this belief is fallacious when I return a little later to considering various proposals for reform of the UN system of economic diplomacy.

First, though, I shall briefly note the fallacies inherent in the other two diagnoses of our present predicament. It seems to me that the Third World or radical fallacy – or perhaps illusion is the better word – is that North–South bargaining is somehow like collective bargaining between management and labour, so that a better deal can be extracted by maintaining the solidarity of developing countries – just as a better wage agreement can be won by a union if there are no blacklegs. It sounds very plausible but the analogy only holds good – or so I believe – where relatively unimportant matters are being negotiated. In the first place, collective bargaining in industry takes place within a certain framework of enforced rules, whereas in the international economy there is no superior enforcing authority. Secondly, labour unions negotiate with two weapons – a carrot and a stick. They can promise to 'deliver' the labour necessary to continued production, or they can withhold that labour by striking. (The basic weakness of Solidarity in Poland was that it had control of the stick, but not the carrot: it could not deliver a disciplined and obedient labour force to the government or the army and therefore it could only bargain in the short run.) Internationally, the Third World association known as the Group of 77 is in an even worse situation for it has control neither of a carrot nor of a stick. It cannot promise to deliver (for instance) the investment guarantees industrialised countries would like. Nor can it organise an effective strike by withholding its cooperation in international production, international trade or international banking. Robert Mortimer's conclusion that 'Empowerment through solidarity has occurred' is directly followed by a significant qualification: 'The Third World', he writes, 'has demonstrated its potential as a collective actor . . . it has developed the foundations of organization and working routines that protect against some of the ravages of dispersion.'[3] It may be – and I would not deny it – that United States policy-makers will have to reckon with the coalition even though for some time it can hold the line against its demands – but only for long-run reasons of self-interest that relate to the fallacy of the realist or mercantilist paradigm.

Roughly speaking, the realist paradigm concludes that powerful states can ignore resolutions railroaded through the UN by Group of 77 majorities because votes are cheap and because 'Sticks and stones can break my bones but words can never hurt me.' What it ignores is the increasing disparity between the formal sovereignty accorded by admission to membership of the United Nations and the real freedom of a state to choose its policies and its destiny. The disparity is increased as the UN lets mini-states in as full members; for by inflating the number of formally sovereign states, it debases the coinage of its legitimation process. At the same time, real sovereignty for many small, weak or poor states is diluted as they come to depend more and more on the outside world for arms, for credit, technology and – in order to acquire these – also for markets in which to sell the products of their agriculture or industry. Yet it is not they but the rich and powerful who decide the terms of access to all of these things – or what is worse, fail to take decisions, or having taken a decision, then change their minds. The only alternative, of decoupling or opting out of the system and trying to go it alone, becomes less attractive with every year that passes as both the political risks and the economic costs of doing so mount up.

In the long run, this growing disparity between formal sovereignty at the UN and diminishing sovereignty (and increased uncertainty) in the world economy cannot help but produce increasing alienation and discontent with the asymmetry of 'interdependence'. Such disaffection is something that the United States government can ignore in a great many Third World countries, but perhaps not in certain strategically sensitive countries whose domestic politics cannot be allowed to get too unruly without damaging American security interests. US corporations and US banks, however, are in a different position. Very often they can no longer afford to behave with the nonchalance of Kennecott in Chile or Anglo-Iranian in Iran. And there are an increasing number of American industries where in defining the national interest according to realist principles, the United States is having increasingly to choose between the protectionism demanded by the small, the old or the inefficient and the flexibility and cooperativeness felt to be necessary by the large, the go-ahead and the competitive.

THE RECORD

It is time to make some assessment of the record, given that we cannot give exclusive rights to any of the contending schools of thought, each of which is both right and wrong. For reasons of space, tedium and truth I do not propose a catalogue of UN conventions, resolutions, recommendations or agreed codes of conduct. This would take too long; it would be too boring; and it would not reveal very much. Indeed, it might actively mislead, for as the GATT report on international trade in 1980–1 observed, even beneath agreement on formal rules it is possible for there to be increasing divergence of behaviour.

> While the rules of the GATT continue to exert considerable influence on policy conduct, there is no denying that infractions and circumventions of them have continued to multiply.
>   Little comfort can be drawn from the fact that relatively few overt and general measures of protection have been taken when it has to be admitted that measures in the 'grey area' which are often discriminatory have been growing in number and frequency. That there has not been more open violence to the rules is also partly explained by the increasing resort to privately agreed and officially tolerated if not promoted restraints on trade and competition.[4]

With the wish therefore to give a more realistic even if necessarily impressionistic representation of what is going on, I shall briefly suggest a few general trends in the diplomacy of economic negotiations in the UN system. I shall suggest that these trends add up between them to a situation which both gives us more hope than one can derive from simply looking at the diplomatic stalemates of the 1980s, and one which directs us to look beyond diplomacy within the United Nations for a better understanding of North–South relations and of developments in the international political economy.

The first general trend which I find most strongly marked in all sorts of negotiations is the refusal to give up, the determination to stick it out and to stay with the frustrating process of argument and disagreement on fundamentals.

One of the best illustrations of this is the continuing argument over the precise content of a United Nations Code of Conduct for Transnational – or, as they are often inaccurately described, 'Multinational' – Corporations.

It was in 1976 that OECD governments – anxious to get in first, before the United Nations did so – jumped in quickly with a set of 'guidelines' for 'multinational' corporations. They need not have been in such a hurry. Over five years later the intergovernmental working group on a Code of Conduct for Transnational Corporations had still not been able to agree on the preamble and were still arguing over the wording of almost half of the draft code's 71 provisions. The document contained a proliferation of bracketed alternative texts so subtly different that the real disputed issue was often unclear to the casual reader. And the relative irrelevance of the precise wording of the code makes this protracted negotiation even harder to understand. As the 1980 report of that group observed: 'Although consultation was recognised as necessary for the implementation of the code, particularly in cases where transnational corporations are subject to conflicting national requirements, it was generally agreed that it is for governments to decide whether and how they would consult on the issues related to the code.'[5] Just of course as it is for them to decide how far it need be observed.

There has been the same reluctance to admit the failure of multilateral negotiations in an area of rather greater political significance to both North and South – the Multi-fibre Agreement (MFA). This, it will be recalled, is the agreement first negotiated in 1974 to extend and take the place of the rightly named Long Term Cotton Textile Agreement of 1962. The MFA promised the developing countries interested in expanding their export markets for all kinds of textile products that the market shares allotted to them by quota restrictions in developed countries would be increased by 6 per cent each year. They had wanted 15 per cent a year but had more than compromised in return for the assurance that this agreement would replace and take precedence over arbitrary unilateral quota decisions and bilateral bargaining.

When it came to renewing the four-year MFA in 1977 it was only the last-minute intervention of the United States which prevented total disagreement from leading to the complete failure of the multilateral negotiation. In the recession, the industrialised countries were reluctant to keep to the 6 per cent rule any longer because of the accelerating loss of textile jobs to their own workers. Hit by rising oil prices and payment deficits, the developing countries found 6 per cent not nearly enough to help them pay their way. The US then intervened with a conciliatory protocol which, in effect, allowed bilateral agreements to be negotiated 'under the MFA' on any terms agreed by the parties (i.e. increasing at less than 6 per cent per year). The MFA principle was further diluted by making the 6 per cent apply overall, to all textile imports, not to 6 per cent in each specific category. The result was that by letting in more imports in non-sensitive sectors – T-shirts, for example – the rich countries could put a bigger squeeze on LDC imports in sensitive sectors like jeans or synthetic-fibre sweaters or dresses.

Exactly the same charade was played all over again in December 1981 except that this time the US hardened its attitude in the final week. Everyone had arranged to wrap it up and to go home for Christmas, but by the 18 December deadline, after months of preparation and fruitless negotiation, there was still a total impasse. So over the weekend before Christmas a frantic effort was made to patch up some sort of agreement. This finally emerged on 23 December. The *Financial Times* rightly observed that it satisfied no one.[6] It left the European Community free to renegotiate tougher bilateral agreements than ever when these ran out at the end of 1982. The promise of better market shares was whittled down to an effective annual rate of between 0.1 and 1 per cent.

Finally – although I could give other instances of the same trend – I shall point to one still more recent example of this somewhat puzzling reluctance to abandon the green baize table. At the end of January 1982, President Reagan revealed the conclusions of his administration's review of the work of UNCLOS – that marathon of all multilateral marathons which had started with an agreement as long ago as 1950 to convene a great new conference to revise the law of the sea in all its many aspects. That conference met in 1958 and after repeated efforts finally arrived at an agreed negotiating text some 20 years later.

The curious thing is not that President Reagan should be critical of it,[7] but that he should nevertheless go through the motions of making an offer to reopen the deadlocked negotiations. True, he then demanded that the Seabed Authority abandon all pretension to supranational powers, even including the independent authority to license operating companies searching for manganese and cobalt nodules. It must also renounce its right to reserve some part of the business to itself in deference to the ideas expressed in the UN resolution on the Common Heritage of Mankind in 1970. All these are considered incompatible with the national interests of the United States. But these national interests, one would think, could just as easily be achieved by simple non-participation. Why go to the trouble of reopening the multilateral discussion?

There are, I believe, three reasons which might account in varying permutations and combinations for such examples of paradoxical behaviour.

The first and undoubtedly most important is self-interest. In the MFA although the LDCs appear to have got the worst of the deal, some governments actually stand to gain considerable power – sometimes even substantial gain – from the right to allocate scarce and much-prized quotas. In Hong Kong they command a market price – ten to twenty dollars a dozen items in one case – and are legally bought and sold. By going along with any kind of MFA, LDCs also guard their exporters against the greater uncertainty that would result if there were no bilateral agreements and they were at the mercy of new rivals for market shares or of totally arbitrary changes in import quotas. MFA negotiations also give the Group of 77 ministers and delegates one policy area of substance and significance on which they can demonstrate – as they have done – their solidarity as a bargaining group.

Over UNCLOS, United States Ambassador Malone, in a statement at the Royal Institute of International Affairs in London, made it abundantly clear that the United States still hoped in February 1982 that by dangling the carrot of reopened negotiations before Britain and other developed countries it might be able to get them to move away from the semi-conciliatory position they had taken towards Third World demands and be persuaded to move closer to that of the United States, thus decreasing the isolation of the Reagan administration.

The second reason – not to be underrated – is fear, the fear of what would happen if the rickety and precarious arrangements that can only laughingly be described as an international economic *order* were to collapse. It is like fearing to sneeze in case a house of cards collapses. It is also like stepping aside rather than walking under a ladder – just in case. I believe this to be a very powerful motive and – again paradoxically – to be one to which the United States as the dominant capitalist country – I do not go along with all the whining cant we hear about the

decline of American power – is particularly susceptible. So long as no
major national interest is jeopardised, better go along with the charade
than break it up. In another context, Conor Cruise O'Brien once
characterised the United Nations as ritual drama, like the saying of mass
or the precautionary incantation of passages from the Torah or the
Koran. Keeping the discussion of UN codes going year after year is a bit
the same. And in some cases, like the MFA, it is more than that. For if
there were no MFA – or so some delegates believe – it is very possible
that the whole complex network of most-favoured-nation tariff reductions built up under the GATT over the last 30 years would cease to be
legally binding and would come undone, like a sweater slowly unravell-
ing when one stitch is dropped.

The third and last reason may be unmentionable in polite society but
ought not to be too easily discounted. It is what Cox and Jacobson once
referred to as 'private-regarding motives'.[9] After all, the UN is still a
growth industry with attractive fringe benefits for those employed in it;
long hours sometimes but also a lot of free travel and much enjoyable
business entertaining. More than that, the alternative to carrying on
with the debate is to devalue a lot of past professional experience and
many useful political contacts. And it is only fair to add that some
delegates to these wearisome marathons also genuinely believe that in
the long run their efforts are in the national and the global interest.
However slow the progress, one must not give up or give way to despair.

For some combination of these three reasons, the multilateral
discussions lumber on. But as can be seen from each of the discussions I
have mentioned and from many others, they all allow a great deal of
freedom to states at the same time to bargain bilaterally, both with each
other and with political groups or economic enterprises that happen to
be important to them. Indeed, the pace of bilateral bargaining often
seems to have accelerated of late. Look at the bilateral agreements on
nuclear materials after-care, now much more detailed and precise than
the multilateral agreements on non-proliferation. Even the Code of
Conduct report on multinationals I quoted earlier went on to admit this:
'It was noted that in practice most consultations would take place at the
bilateral level.'

And to these and other aspects of increasing economic uncertainty
one must add a far greater degree of *political uncertainty* where the
policies of the major countries – in what I have called the affluent
alliance – are concerned.[10] I will not speak of the United States and the
uncertainties of the Reagan administration. Closer to home, the
European Community's policies are almost as unpredictable if not so

influential. What has emerged as a clear trend in recent years I believe is the role of the European Community as a blocking agent in much multilateral negotiation. This first became apparent in the mid-1960s in the negotiations that led to the institution of Special Drawing Rights by the IMF. It was also evident in the MTN trade negotiations and again last year in the MFA renegotiation: no progress could be made until the European Community had resolved the differences which divided the liberal Germans, Dutch and Danes on one side from the more protectionist French, British, Italians and Greeks on the other. It does not seem to me that this is an element of uncertainty that is soon going to disappear.

PROSPECTS AND REFORM PROPOSALS

In view of these trends which I have rather briefly indicated, what prospects are there for diplomacy in the UN? Can it be speeded up and made more productive? And what do we conclude from all this about the study of diplomacy in general? Those are the last two questions I will try to answer.

There have been three sorts of moves to improve on the present situation in recent years. David Rockefeller's Trilateral Commission in the mid-1970s started with the idea that special expert taskforces drawn from America, Europe and Japan might discover areas of common ground from which new initiatives could be launched. In the event, despite an inordinate number of jetsetting meetings of these experts, it became largely discredited as an exercise overly dominated by the Americans and those who, if they did not think exactly as Americans did, at least did not differ too fundamentally from them.

Less publicised has been a proposal coming from the American Council on Foreign Relations and appearing in recent writings by Miriam Camps.[11] These have suggested the replacement of both the GATT and UNCTAD by a new Production and Trade Organisation (PTO) which would concede to the Third World the principle of unequal, preferential treatment but would nevertheless seek gradually to recruit and bind LDCs into a liberal world economy. Full members (i.e. the OECD countries) would agree not to go back on the consolidated tariff reductions of past GATT rounds. They would also agree to work towards a target programme aimed at total free trade, renouncing the use of all tariff and quota restrictions except when authorised by the proposed Trade Policy Review Board, or sanctioned by the IMF for balance of payments reasons. Such measures of liberalisation would also be made preferentially available to associated LDCs, but the better-off NICs (newly industrialised countries) would have to earn these benefits with some liberalisation of their own trade policies.

Why has this well-worked-out plan caused so little stir in diplomatic circles? First, because it would greatly circumscribe the present freedom of the United States to run with the liberal hare and hunt with the protectionist hounds. Second, because the LDCs also want it both ways: they want to invoke liberal principles in order to gain freer access to the rich countries' textile and other markets, but they also want to invoke Prebisch principles justifying selective protection in sectors where they cannot yet compete. Nor, frankly, are many of them sure that they can accept Mrs Camps's avowed objective: 'the need to find ways to incorporate the LDCs more fully into a global trading system'. That is not necessarily consistent with the declared objective of the Group of 77 – the achievement of greater collective self-reliance between developing countries. In short, Mrs Camps's basic problem is that her thinking is logical only within the bounds of the liberal paradigm and the value judgements which it presumes.

A rather different proposal was put forward some three or four years ago by a distinguished Indian diplomat, Rangarajan, in a book called *Commodity Conflict*.[12] His target was the caucus methods adopted in North–South bargaining over the UN integrated programme for commodities – yet another multilateral marathon that began with a resolution of the 1974 Special Session and finally resulted, six years later, in an agreement now open for signature. This procedure – and indeed that of the sterile Conference on International Economic Cooperation (CIEC) that went on in Paris in the mid-1970s – maximised the bargaining gap between the First and Third Worlds by aggregating the objections of the former and the demands of the latter before they ever got to the bargaining table. Rangarajan proposed instead an Agreement on Commodity Trade (ACT) which, like a GATT tariff-cutting round, would only be available to those states that accepted the whole package. This would encourage acceptance of the principle that a concession granted to one must be granted to all. The remarkable fact that such an eminently sensible idea was never taken up or discussed indicates two things. First, that the rich industrialised countries were never seriously convinced of the importance of stabilisation of commodity markets for primary producers – even though each of them was constantly intervening with markets for that very purpose on behalf of their own primary producers. Not wishing the end, they were therefore not interested in fashioning better means.

The second reason why the ACT idea fell on deaf ears lay on the other side, with the developing countries. These countries were bound – imprisoned, one might almost say – both by their belief in collective bargaining through the Group of 77 and by their curious symbiotic relationship with the UNCTAD Secretariat. This has been well described by Robert Mortimer who has explained how the latter has come to act as something more than guide, philosopher and friend to the developing countries' negotiators. 'UNCTAD personnel', he wrote, 'have for practical purposes fulfilled the function of a secretariat for the Group of 77 . . . it was natural for the developing countries to rely upon its administrative staff to prepare background papers, documentation and eventually proposals for their use.'[13] Therefore, to ask UNCTAD to concur in its own demotion and even demise, to be absorbed into a neutral, GATT-type broker dedicated not to a crusading campaign but to a sordid haggle, was to ask for a role change which this particular bureaucracy was unlikely to find acceptable.

In the Group of 77, too, the belief in the value of collective solidarity and the confrontational approach died hard. It was indeed not until 1983, at the Delhi meeting of non-aligned countries, that the first sign of disillusion with the pursuit of a New International Economic Order was to be seen. Such comments as the following began to be heard: 'The UNCTAD group system begins to appear as increasingly counter-productive and one which obscures analysis and negotiation of the real problems facing the low-income countries.'[14] Or again, 'The present system is designed to make confrontation almost continuous and to extend it to issues that are not merely unimportant but that do not even require international, and certainly not global, solutions.'[15]

And what of Brandt? The Commission's ideas are, of course, essentially social democratic; the commissioners were global Keynesians rather than free-market liberals. Their recommendations are therefore based on two assumptions: that there is a perceived community of interest between North and South, and that this can best be served by multilateral agreements on practically everything you can mention – energy, development, food, arms control, aid, multinationals, and so on. Now in the first place, though the community of interest may be real I do not think it is fully perceived on all these subjects. Rothstein recently concluded,

I believe that the quest for global rules is bound to be futile; the clash of interests and values is too profound, the intellectual uncertainties are too great, the probability of shocks is too high, and the available institutions are not capable of the quick and flexible reactions that are necessary in a very unsettled world.[16]

CONCLUSIONS

The record of multilateral negotiations in the last decade seems to me to bear out this pessimism. The closer one looks at the detailed reality of international economic diplomacy in the United Nations, the worse the prospects seem of implementing the Brandt Report. I think this may explain why many who have some familiarity with international organisations have involuntarily yawned over it. Well-intentioned and idealistic as it was, there yet seemed something redolent of the 1950s, a trifle *vieux jeu*, about its ideas. They did not really accord well with recent developments in the world economy nor with the recent record of international economic negotiations.

Yet the persistence both of the Brandt-type ideas and of various forms of the *dialogue des sourds* in international meetings is striking. And besides the superstitious, finger-crossing reason already suggested, it may be that both can also be accounted for by the predominance at such meetings of two out of the three major paradigms I have referred to – the liberal paradigm and the structuralist/dependency one. For each in a different way looks to international organisation as the best means of making good the shortcomings of the international political economy. In the liberal paradigm, the desirable open economy is threatened if there are no general rules for trade to restrain the nationalist tendencies of states, and if there is no source of order and discipline to inspire the necessary confidence in the monetary system. International 'regimes' are necessary at the best of times and more particularly when (as many Americans are convinced) the loss of American hegemony has robbed the United States of the power to provide these elements of order.

Meanwhile, in the structuralist/dependency paradigm, the counter-vailing power of international organisation is necessary in order to rectify the inherently unequal and asymmetrical consequences of involvement in a market economy. Thus, each mode of thinking about the system, in a different way, makes exaggerated demands on bodies like the United Nations, the World Bank and the IMF and on the machinery of negotiation over trade and industrial policies which cannot help at this point in the twentieth century but be disappointed.

The reasons for the disappointment are generally well understood. The inflation of membership in all these bodies, plus the increasingly obvious self-seeking of the affluent old-industrialised states, has robbed established international regimes of such support as they once commanded. The weakness is exacerbated, as noted earlier, by the blocking power acquired and often exercised (whether deliberately or through internal indecision) by the European Community and, as happened in the 1930s, by the lower priority given by governments to international matters as compared with domestic ones in the midst of a world depression.

But the pessimism is easily overdone. The probability that nothing much of importance is going on at the United Nations does not mean that everything has come to a fullstop. There are still cakes and ale – at least for some – but elsewhere.

Specifically, it is worth looking at some of the rates of economic growth in an assortment of developing countries in the latter half of the 1970s – just that period when multilateral economic diplomacy was grinding to a virtual halt. Between 1970 and 1976 the average annual increase in real GDP was over 10 per cent in Brazil and South Korea, nearly 9 per cent in Tunisia, and 6 per cent in Columbia and Thailand. Exports of manufactures from 59 developing countries grew on average at an annual rate of 19 per cent between 1970 and 1979 and from 5 states (Sri Lanka, Cyprus, Thailand, Indonesia and Peru) at an average annual rate of between 45 and 53 per cent. These are only some of the relevant statistics.[17] The truth is that despite the protectionism (much of it old, only some new) of the older industrialised countries, exporters in the Third World have been able to make astonishing inroads into their markets. And despite the world depression and the drastic decline of commodity prices in the early 1980s, growth rates were phenomenal for many countries in the 1970s and are still unusually good in Asia and the Pacific. The anarchy of the international economy has offered undreamt-of opportunities for economic development along with the risks – of commodity price collapse, of oil price rises, of mounting interest rates and debt service charges and of demands for 'voluntary' export restrictions as the penalty for being too efficient and too competitive on costs.

In that anarchy, there is little doubt that the developing countries have had two powerful allies whom few of their politicians care publicly to acknowledge: the international bankers who lent money so freely in the aftermath of the first oil price rise (and found it difficult to stop doing so even when the risks came along with the profits); and the castigated 'multinationals' who maintained *their* profitability by shifting production abroad and offering their know-how for managing large-scale production units as well as low taxes, the technology and market access, in return for low taxes and cheap labour. The result in many Third World Countries was very rapid economic and social change in the 1970s and then, when markets, prices and the money situation turned bad in the 1980s, the impact of world depression was often more political than economic: governments became more repressive and authoritarian and less tolerant of opposition. For this, international organisations did not pretend to have an answer. But in hard times, states also look naturally for special relations and bargains of mutual interest with close associates. Bilateral diplomacy, between states and between governments and foreign banks or corporations, takes the stage vacated by multilateral diplomacy. Regional policies – in Latin America for the United States, in Eastern Europe for West Germany, in Korea and Malaysia for Japan – seem closer to national interests than rhetorical confrontation at the UN.

NOTES AND REFERENCES

1. 'Keeping Alive a Withering Dream', *South* (October 1981).
2. R. Cooper, *The Economics of Interdependence* (New York: McGraw-Hill, 1968).
3. R. Mortimer, *The Third World Coalition in International Politics* (New York: Praeger, 1980).
4. *International Trade* (1980/81) p. 11.
5. Report of the Intergovernmental Working Group on a Code of Conduct for Transnational Corporations, UN Doc. 80/14296. For the previous comment, see *Transnational Corporations in World Development: Third Survey* (New York: UN/CTC, 1983) p. 112.
6. *Financial Times*, 29 December 1981.
7. Reagan's total opposition to some of the provisions of the text, especially the provisions for an International Seabed Authority, had been made abundantly clear even before he was a candidate for the White House.
8. C. C. O'Brien, *United Nations: Sacred Drama* (New York: Simon & Schuster, 1968), with illustrations by Feliks Topolski.
9. R. W. Cox and H. K. Jacobson, *The Anatomy of Influence: Decision-making in International Organization* (New Haven: Yale University Press, 1973).
10. S. Strange, *International Monetary Relations*, vol. 2 of A. Shonfield (ed), *International Economic Relations of the Western World, 1959–71* (London: OUP for R11R, 1976).
11. M. Camps and C. Gwin, *Collective Management: the Reform of International Economic Organization* (New York: McGraw-Hill, 1981); and M. Camps and W. Diebold, Jr, *The New Multilateralism: can the World*

Trading System be Saved? (New York: Council on Foreign Relations, 1983).
12. L. Rangarajan, *Commodity Conflict* (London: Croom Helm, 1978).
13. R. Mortimer, *Third World Coalition,* pp. 75–6.
14. D. Colclough, 'Lessons for the Development Debate', *International Affairs* (Summer 1982).
15. Ian Little, *Economic Development: Theory, Policy and International Relations* (London: Basic Books, 1983) p. 384.
16. R. Rothstein, *Global Bargaining: UNCTAD and the Quest for a New International Economic Order* (Princeton University Press, 1979). See also T. Weiss and A. Jennings, *More for the Least: Prospects for Poorest Countries* (Lexington, Mass.: D. C. Heath, 1983).
17. *Finance and Development* (June 1983) pp. 7–8.

9 The Paris Conference on Least Developed Countries, 1981

THOMAS G. WEISS
and A. JENNINGS

In contrast to the general malaise in multilateral economic diplomacy, growing consensus has emerged that much more significant efforts must be made on behalf of the poorest members of the international economy.[1] The UN system has expanded its activities to ameliorate the especially precarious situation and development prospects of the 36 least developed countries (LDCs) which in 1980 had a population of 283 million, or 13 per cent of the population of all developing countries.[2] These efforts took a decisive turn in Paris from 1 to 14 September 1981 when the UN Conference on the Least Developed Countries adopted the Substantial New Programme of Action (SNPA).[3] Domestic policy reform and international support measures are intended to eliminate their extreme poverty and transform their economies over the next ten years. Did the Paris Conference accentuate or counter the present paralysis in multilateral development diplomacy? The present chapter examines the preparations for this conference as well as its decision-making procedures with a view to making an evaluation of its value as an instrument of multilateral diplomacy.

THE CONFERENCE PREPARATORY PROCESS

As one critic of UNCTAD admits: 'The international recognition of the category would not have been possible without the tenacious commitment of UNCTAD to a category of countries that were generally not very active in multilateral affairs.[4] Indeed, without the vision and determination of one man, Jack I. Stone (Director of the Least

Developed Country Programme in UNCTAD), the Paris Conference
would probably never have occurred; the LDC category would probably have become inoperative in much the same way as the list of
countries 'most seriously affected' (MSAs) by the payments crisis
following the first oil shock of 1973–4.[5] At the third and fourth sessions
of UNCTAD, LDCs became a major agenda item and in 1977 a special
programme for them was created in UNCTAD, the first such unit within
the UN system which naturally determined UNCTAD's central role in
the Paris Conference.

To conclude that a decade had been wasted in the attempt to help the
poorest through multilateral diplomacy would be excessively cynical.
This period could more usefully be seen as a learning process during
which policy was formulated, and political will built up. A comparison
of resolutions on LDCs at successive UNCTAD sessions – 62 (III),-
98 (IV) with 122 (V) – provides a clear indication of the cumulative
appreciation of their problems, starting with a narrow preoccupation
with foreign trade and gradually extending to all aspects of economic
and social development.

The momentum was maintained between regular UNCTAD sessions
by the Intergovernmental Group on Least Developed Countries, which
met in 1975 and 1978, and a special meeting of multilateral and bilateral
financial and technical assistance institutions with representatives of
LDCs in 1977.[6] Opportunities were provided for governments, in
particular those of LDCs, to take stock and to propose the various
studies and actions that eventually influenced the character of
UNCTAD resolutions, and ultimately the Paris Conference itself.

In Resolution 34/203, the General Assembly agreed to convene the
UN Conference on the Least Developed Countries and designated
UNCTAD as the secretariat for the Conference. The General Assembly
called on each LDC to prepare its own case for additional resources. The
Intergovernmental Group was transformed into the Preparatory
Committee. Twenty-seven LDCs and a broad spectrum of multilateral
and bilateral aid partners were represented at the first two-week meeting
held in Geneva in February 1980 where few decisions were taken. The
international community was urged to assist the LDCs in drawing up
specific plans and programmes and identifying major priority projects,
which would 'enable each least developed country to increase its
national income substantially – even doubling it in appropriate cases –
by 1990'. Developing countries estimated that a minimum of $100
million, roughly $3.5 million per country, would be needed to assist each
LDC to prepare an adequate case for more aid. This estimate was

repeated at the second session in October 1980 but in the event only $50 000 per country was provided by the General Assembly and the United Nations Development Programme (UNDP).

The decision to hold the conference itself in September 1981 was against the wishes of the representatives from developed market-economy countries of Group B. The UNCTAD secretariat favoured a later date, February 1982, as providing more time to improve preparations, including documentation. Although not explicitly stated, the Group of 77 felt that any marginal differences in the quality of country reports which might arise from a shorter preparatory period would not really influence the views of donors. Moreover they were suspicious of delaying tactics, so much a part of multilateral development diplomacy. They wanted the additional aid yesterday.

The UNCTAD secretariat attempted to generate some discussion in the Preparatory Committee on substantive issues, for example on aid volume and quality as well as on the possible type of conference follow-up. Delegates of all groups argued that such discussion would be useful following the review meetings between individual LDCs and their aid partners, to be held by midsummer of 1981. Thus it was only at the third and final session of the Preparatory Committee, held in Geneva from 29 June to 10 July 1981, that key elements of the draft action programme were discussed seriously, leaving very little time for internal and intergovernmental debate before the conference in September 1981. Moreover, the open-ended contact group degenerated into a series of monologues rather than a constructive dialogue on alternative texts.[7] The Group of 77 took most of the two weeks to agree upon a text which they were careful to point out was not 'official', but nevertheless was not subject to discussion or modification. Group B proposed a variety of modifications in structure and content to the last-minute suggestion by the secretariat in its so-called 'non-paper';[8] but it too underlined that its suggestions were not governmental positions, merely some unofficial comments that had to be reconsidered in national capitals.

The impact on multilateral diplomacy of initiatives by international secretariats is not always fully understood. The issue of the non-paper illustrates this fact as well as the extent to which a haphazardly constructed statement can take on a life of its own. This brief document assumed an importance that was far greater for the Paris negotiations than the Secretary-General's own report to the Conference, although the latter had been carefully drafted and cleared while the former represented the views of a few staff members who had been asked to assemble it at the last minute.

International secretariats frequently provide raw materials for resolutions of the Group of 77 which, after internal consultations, eventually emerge as the draft position of these countries and form the basis for negotiations. However, because of the sensitivity of the nonleast developed among the developing countries within the Group of 77, UNCTAD needed to maintain its perceived neutrality as a broker for the entire group and had thus resisted pressures to produce a preliminary draft before the final session of the Preparatory Committee. In spite of indications to the contrary, it became obvious that no Group of 77 draft was under preparation. A secretariat draft was hurriedly finalised after almost no internal discussion and none at all with the Group of 77. As Group B was also in favour of some basis for discussions, the 'non-paper' made its appearance in photocopied form for the beginning of the third session of the Preparatory Committee.

The opening meeting witnessed an unusual reversal of roles. The representative of Group B congratulated the secretariat for its efforts to accelerate negotiations and agreed to take the non-paper as the basis for discussions, while surprisingly the representative of the Group of 77 simply noted its existence. As no preliminary consultations had occurred among the developing countries and as Group B had agreed to the basic outline, the Group of 77 was ironically forced to reject the secretariat's draft and go back to the drawing-board to produce its own.

The final version of the Group of 77 conference room paper eventually followed the overall structure of the secretariat's non-paper – which they had criticised as illogical and inadequate. Following the drafting process of the Group of 77 is never easy, but the meetings during the third session of the Preparatory Committee were particularly difficult, even for the initiated. A plenary working group – the 'Group of 15' – which actually was more like 45 or 50 countries for most sessions, was meeting along with all three regional groups (African, Asian and Latin American), as were their coordinators and other groups, including unofficially the least developed countries themselves.

Hence, the Preparatory Committee ended its deliberation with two 'non-texts' based on the secretariat's 'non-paper'. This confusion would be increased by texts emanating from subsequent regional meetings in Africa and Asia. The Senior Officials Meeting, planned for the eve of the conference, would thus be faced with a multiplicity of texts.

However, the Preparatory Committee easily reached a consensus on the agenda, organisation of work and rules of procedure during its final session. With minor exceptions, the rules of procedures and organisation of work essentially followed the models of other recent UN conferences. The only substantive decision, namely the allocation of work to the two sessional committees, came down to agreement on an action programme incorporating the domestic policies of least developed countries and international support measures, especially the volume and quality of external assistance, together with an institutional framework for follow-up to the Conference.[9]

In comparison with other UN conferences, the most salient feature of the Paris Conference was its concentration on individual countries. As one long-time observer has noted: 'There was a noteworthy innovation in the preparation for the Conference, compared with other UN ventures on a global scale. The preparations were both global in the sense of the traditional secretariat studies and reports; and country specific, consisting of country review meetings . . .'[10]

Instead of the secretariat's positing general analyses and recommendations to cover the socioeconomic situation of 31 countries and then asking each of them and their development partners to act accordingly, each LDC formulated its own policy objectives, priorities and assistance requirements; and then the sum of these requirements became generalised in the Substantial New Programme of Action adopted on 14 September 1981.

The secretariat certainly pushed its own conceptions of solutions to the problems of LDCs and took some important initiatives. In his *note verbale* of 14 May 1980, the Secretary-General of the conference requested each LDC to include the following three elements in its country presentation: an assessment of development potentials, bottlenecks and assistance requirements for the 1980s; an inventory of the status of projects and programmes requiring finance during this period; and a review of the quality of aid. Thirty LDCs produced country analyses which varied from 150 to 200 pages in length.[11]

The most critical element in each presentation was the estimate of total assistance required. Since no guidelines were provided, there were not surprisingly a host of different interpretations. Some governments listed projects and programmes from existing medium-term plans which were not yet funded. Others undertook special planning exercises to identify new projects and programmes. In many cases the aid requested was based only on projects already identified rather than any more ambitious list.

Although only two of the 30 country presentations were prepared entirely by governments without external assistance, the country presentations were governmental, and not consultant, submissions. This distinction is essential in evaluating the quality and impact of these presentations. Governments themselves were called upon to defend their content at the four clusters of review meetings held in Vienna, Addis Ababa, the Hague and Geneva from March to June 1981. Interviews with the Western donors – the main participants in these meetings as they provide over three-quarters of the aid to LDCs – indicated a surprising satisfaction with many of the presentations. While many observers did not believe that they were always realistic in light of their ability effectively to use resources, they none the less judged that they were an important first step. Donors and recipients both prefer dealing with the specifics of a particular country and its problems rather than with the vague generalities necessarily entailed in submissions covering 30 countries.

In general, the LDCs responded positively to the opportunity afforded by the review meetings. Invitations were issued to a wider range of development partners than would normally have been the case. Some countries crossed ideological frontiers; for example, Malawi invited the socialist countries to attend its review meeting. Other countries took the opportunity to renew formerly crucial relationships; for example, Ethiopia invited Western donors who had been largely absent following the revolution that overthrew Haile Selassie.

The reports of the individual meetings[12] were forwarded to Committee Two in Paris. While the content of individual reports was similar – in fact, there were what amounted to standardised intro-ductory and concluding paragraphs – mention was always made of donors' judgements of individual presentations. In addition to provid-ing the basis for subsequent follow-up meetings intended to secure concrete pledges, linking country reports to the global conference in Paris had one important potential advantage over UNDP or IBRD World Bank organised meetings of donors and recipients, which were relatively isolated and not linked to on-going international negotiations. While it is too early to determine whether the Paris Conference will ultimately be successful in terms of mobilising additional finance or shortening lead times for aid disbursements, the need to link national discussions with international monitoring was an important innovation in multilateral development diplomacy which attempted to ensure that commitments made at the global level would in fact be carried out in specific countries.

The final important step in preparations was a two-day consultation of senior officials held immediately preceding the conference (27–8 August). According to the now-established practice of the UN, such consultations are scheduled in order to settle all outstanding housekeeping matters.[13] The senior officials basically rubber-stamped most of the recommendations of the Preparatory Committee, leaving developing countries time to sort out their own internal political problems behind closed doors.

The major difficulty during the Senior Officials' Meeting concerned the election of officers. To an outside observer, the traditional bickering over officers appears trivial and as yet another indication of the truly byzantine quality of international discussions. Yet the composition of the general committee of any conference is critical for multilateral diplomacy. Its members have crucial roles to play in public and also participate in the closed discussions at the end of a conference during which bargains are struck.

The Group of 77 proposed that an African and an Asian LDC chair Committee One and Committee Two respectively. Group B expressed astonishment, since they had already publicly nominated the Swedish ambassador for Committee Two, who had, everyone agreed, done a superb job as chairman of the Preparatory Committee and who was in the chair of the Senior Officials' Meeting. A compromise was finally reached with the appointment of two Western vice-chairmen of the sessional committees to act as a team with the chairmen. The partial dissolution of Group B resulted in its inability to insist on the chairmanship. Already at the third session of the Preparatory Committee, the group had publicly expressed dissatisfaction with the rigidity of multilateral development diplomacy within UNCTAD's group system. At the Senior Officials' Meeting, this dissatisfaction intensified as the more pro-development members of Group B refused to be constrained by the minimalist, least-common-denominator stance of their group that had led increasingly to sterile confrontation rather than more meaningful negotiations.

THE UN LEAST DEVELOPED COUNTRY CONFERENCE, SEPTEMBER 1981

The location of the conference in Paris ultimately influenced the results, not only because of the press coverage that naturally ensued from holding the meeting in a major capital long associated with the development dialogue, but also because of the role played by the French government. Conferences occurring in New York or Geneva do not attract similar attention because they tend to be seen as yet another in a continuing series of talk-fests. In contrast, a special gathering in another capital tends to attract more attention locally and internationally. In particular, reporting by non-UN journalists tends to get better coverage because of the different date-line.

During the first half of 1980 the secretariat had attempted to find a major donor to sponsor the conference. After unsuccessful contacts with both Japan and the Federal Republic of Germany, the secretariat was somewhat surprised by the offer from the French foreign minister while the second session of the Preparatory Committee was deliberating in Geneva. The offer by President Giscard d'Estaing should be placed in the general context of France's relations with its former colonies. It is not far-fetched to suggest that behind the offer to host a global conference for the poor in historic Paris (almost half of the LDCs are French-speaking) were motives that sought to improve his image and credibility as a development statesman. While interviews suggest that the succeeding Mitterrand administration would not have made a similar offer,[14] it certainly did not wish to have a fiasco on its hands so soon after its arrival in power; and it worked hard to make the conference which it had inherited succeed.

The plenary provided the forum for general debate, was opened on 2 September and concluded on 10 September 1981. It was a ceremonial opportunity for heads of delegations to make general policy statements – not infrequently to a large empty hall – that could be reported with enthusiasm in national newspapers but which generally did not advance the work of the conference. Over 130 governments attended the plenary sessions in Paris which were addressed by four heads of state, heads of delegations from 106 countries, as well as the executive heads or other senior representatives from most of the specialised agencies and other United Nations bodies.

The 'friends of the *rapporteur*' were responsible for a non-controversial report on plenary proceedings in ten pages in which each group of countries was responsible for drafting its own text. A problem initially had arisen in that the *rapporteur-general* refused to consider his role as ceremonial and rejected the earlier decision that no summary of proceedings was necessary. He mobilised members of Group D to reverse temporarily this decision. The secretariat was appalled; it had made no provisions for writing or processing proceedings. After considerable shuffling and several all-night drafting sessions, every group voiced dissatisfaction with the secretariat's drafts. Subsequently, an ingenious diplomatic solution was found. As texts were meant to reflect each group's interventions in the debate in a favourable light, why not ask each to draft its own summary? Following such a procedure and having established limits, it was unnecessary for any time whatsoever to be spent agreeing on the prerogatives of other groups, which not infrequently was new material rather than what had actually been stated.

The final plenary was a masterful exercise in rubber-stamping. The president of the conference had insisted that the general debate end on 10 September, as originally planned, because he established his own negotiating team in the form of a 'contact group'. Forming such a group is the prerogative of a president, and Cot simply applied his usual businesslike manner and used the General Committee of elected officers as a base. He added certain key participants from governments (the spokesmen for the various groups, the vice-chairman from Sweden, Saudi Arabia and various French officials) and from international organisations. Instead of waiting until the last minute, the contact group was able to spend four days in marathon sessions and arrive at compromise texts. The final plenary was thus only a ceremonial agreement to the entirety of the pre-negotiated text. Although certain statements of interpretation[15] were made, no official reservations were made, the first time in the recent history of UN multilateral diplomacy.

While the plenary provided interesting commentary for journalists, actual negotiations took place in sessional committees and the contact group. It is to the heart of multilateral development diplomacy in Paris, the complex process of negotiating the Substantial New Programme of Action for the Least Developed Countries, that the analysis now turns.

Immediately following the opening of the conference, Committee One met in a room where delegations had been seated in alphabetical order. Delegates from developing countries requested to be seated in groups to facilitate intragroup discussion; but OECD countries resisted. The chairman converted Committee One into an informal working party, so that delegates could gather into the familiar alignments of Groups B, D and 77. The Group of 77 also questioned the status of Group B since they had been informed that for this conference no such group existed. The largely symbolic resistance of Group B was a public indication of cracks in their alliance that would influence the final shape of the action programme.

To facilitate redrafting on the basis of the synoptic paper drafted by the chairman of the Preparatory Committee,[16] Committee One was split into two. A significant reversal of roles was accepted: the vice-chairman from a donor country (Canada) undertook the drafting of desirable national measures for LDCs and the chairman from a least developed country (Cape Verde) undertook the drafting of desirable international support measures. Drafting subgroups were created when especially difficult measures were under scrutiny. The normally small delegations from least developed countries had serious problems of representation in so many parallel sessions; another common problem was that individual delegates were often negotiating on technical issues about which they had little or no expertise.

From the point of view of tactics, the least developed countries had laid their negotiating position on the table at the start of the conference. Indeed the crucial issue, additional aid from donors, had clearly been presented at the final session of the Preparatory Committee. Group B's first response had simply been to change the title of the section. Group D also was silent. At the start of the Paris Conference, donors still refused to be forthcoming about additional resources. Developed market-economy donors were divided as to the size and timing of additional commitments. For most of the European Community and the Scandinavians, accepting a 0.15 per cent of GNP target for aid posed no problem; other countries, for example Japan and the US, could not accept such a target since it would have entailed unacceptable increases in aid flows. Further, many donors had traditionally taken principled stands against specific targets or time-frames. With the developed market economies in disarray, not surprisingly no initiative came from Group D.

OECD countries were in continuous session, with separate and often parallel meetings for the member states of the European Community and the Scandinavians as well as for the North Americans and Japan. The UK delegation had a peculiar difficulty in that it was opposed to tying itself to any form of target, but as president of the European Commission at the time, Britain was speaking on behalf of the EEC and pressured to adopt a more liberal stance, particularly by the French.[17]

Three days before the end of the conference, the drafting group on 'international support measures – financial assistance requirements and policies' submitted a text to the chairman of Committee One which was littered with square brackets, indicating an inability to reach agreement. To break the stalemate in Committee One, Cot shifted the action to his contact group on 12 September. Because time for editing, translation, reproduction and distribution was necessary before the closing ceremony, the pressure on representatives of market economies to agree among themselves on an offer was intense; and they agreed to a compromise late on Saturday afternoon, only two days before the end of the conference. Very little time remained for real negotiation. Regional meetings were held among the Group of 77 during which disquiet was expressed, particularly by the Africans. Following non-stop sessions in the president's contact group, agreement was finally reached when the Group of 77 essentially accepted the *fait accompli* proposed by Group B.

Paragraph 63 of the SNPA notes that 'most donors' will devote 0.15 per cent of their GNP as aid to LDCs 'in the coming years', and that 'others' will double their aid to the countries 'in the same period'. The omission of 'the' before 'others' was deliberate and allowed an escape for a third category of donors who might do neither. A ragbag of loose and ambiguous phrases of good intentions filled out the remainder of this crucial paragraph.

The least developed countries had made significant concessions to have an action programme which all parties could support without reservations. An optimistic interpretation was that the donors were to be congratulated for rallying together at the eleventh hour. A more cynical interpretation was that they had once again made the most of multilateral development diplomacy. They had negotiated a crucial loophole to avoid further commitments. Group B had also retained its solidarity. In particular the European Community, under the very active and effective presidency of the UK, had succeeded in holding together, despite the widely different stances of the UK, Germany and France towards the aid volume target issue.

Negotiations in Committee One concerning the other international support measures were more straightforward. On the quality of external assistance, or 'aid modalities', a close measure of agreement among groups existed even at the start of the conference. This agreement was due to the research previously carried out by OECD, as well as to studies by the conference secretariat that had focused attention on major issues discussed earlier during the country reviews.[18] On commercial policy, discussion was tempered by the realisation that such measures would have almost no significance, other than rhetorical, for LDCs.

If the least developed countries looked upon multilateral diplomacy in Paris as an opportunity to pressure donors on the volume and quality of aid, the donors saw this conference as a forum in which they could finally extract from recipient governments the admission that a number of national policy reforms were essential. This *quid pro quo* was at the heart of the bargaining process.

Group B had worked over the summer to define those changes in domestic policy that the LDCs should adopt. Before the end of the first week of the conference, an outline was submitted by the European Community; and a few days later the vice-chairman of Committee One presented a completed draft for consideration by the committee. The efficiency of donors in drafting measures to be taken by least developed countries stood in sharp contrast to their pace in drafting measures to be taken themselves.

During negotiations, donors pressured the Group of 77 to include national measures omitted entirely from earlier drafts, and also to add greater weight to policies which had barely been mentioned. An example of the former was energy policy and an example of the latter, which had the support of both OECD and socialist countries, was the emphasis on the need for a planning framework. On such key issues as food self-sufficiency, structural adjustment and human resources and social development there was general consensus.

The work of Committee Two appeared to be less difficult, namely the steps necessary to implement and monitor the decisions of the conference. The consideration of country presentations and the review meetings was simply a means to introduce the discussion on follow-up details. That some sort of follow-up would occur was a foregone conclusion, but long-standing and controversial issues were obvious again in Paris – the exact nature of future country reviews and global monitoring as well as their financial implications.

The donor's lack of appreciation of review meetings contrasted starkly with the satisfaction of almost all least developed countries. According to the LDC delegates, these reviews had been conducive to a fruitful exchange of information with actual and potential development partners, as well as constituting the basis for agreement about the nature of assistance needs. They also approved the unique emphasis of these meetings on individual countries, albeit within the global context.

The striking differences in perspective between donors and recipients reflected disagreement over the desirability of UNCTAD's continued involvement. No one disputed the ability of UNCTAD to organise such meetings – in fact all parties paid tribute to the impressive series of meetings organised within an impossibly hectic calendar – or its role as the logical leader in the exercise of global monitoring. However, traditional donors and other UN organisations sought to prevent UNCTAD playing a major role at the country level. Its well-known biases on such issues as debt or special measures for LDCs would ensure country discussions in which donors would be on the defensive. UNCTAD was also obviously intruding upon organisational territory that had previously been staked out through IBRD consultative groups and UNDP round tables.

UNCTAD senior officials concentrated on Committee Two negotiations, in which the secretariat was unable to retreat from its original proposals for leadership in national follow-up, even when developed donor countries, the major United Nations organisations (IBRD and UNDP) and eventually even the majority of LDCs did not support an expanded role for UNCTAD at the country level. The deliberations and negotiations of this committee would have proceeded more quickly had the conference secretariat been able to read the handwriting on the walls. The UN system could also have avoided unnecessary negative publicity about empire building.

Brackets around controversial sections were rapidly removed by the contact group. The final text stressed the importance of strengthening and broadening existing mechanisms of the IBRD, the UNDP or the OECD and basically eliminated UNCTAD from involvement at the national level except in gathering information. For global monitoring, there was general agreement that UNCTAD should play the focal role. The LDC representatives initially argued for regular meetings of the Inter-Governmental Group as a monitoring committee; but the donors, horrified at a calendar of annual meetings, eventually achieved a compromise of reviews at regular UNCTAD sessions in 1983 and 1987 as well as a mid-term review in 1985 with the possibility of reconvening the United Nations Conference on LDCs at the end of the decade.

THE PARIS CONFERENCE AND MULTILATERAL DEVELOPMENT DIPLOMACY

Does the outcome of the Paris Conference suggest that such a form of multilateral diplomacy is an effective instrument in helping the poorest countries to begin to escape from poverty? As for all international gatherings, the proof of the Paris pudding will lie in the eating – the actual implementation of its programme of action. None the less, some lessons for multilateral development diplomacy can already be derived. Least developed countries, by their nature, are least well placed to benefit either from a 'warrior' or alternatively from a 'shopkeeper' view of diplomacy. The least developed countries have neither 'the ability of force to produce intimidation' nor 'the ability of the credit idea to produce confidence'. If, however, diplomacy is viewed as 'common sense and charity applied to international relations', then the Paris Conference witnessed both.[19]

First and foremost, the international support measures reflected a willingness by the international community to introduce an LDC clause in aid and trade policies that positively discriminated in favour of these countries. Whatever the rate of implementation, the fact that unanimous and even enthusiastic agreement was reached on a comprehensive set of policy measures for a group of poor countries must be looked upon as a solid achievement, particularly in light of the unpropitious international climate of the early 1980s.

Another very positive development of the Paris Conference was that it clearly specified the shared responsibility of the LDCs and the international community. Previous discussions within the UN avoided directly considering the responsibility of developing countries for their own plight. A convenient villain was normally found in the behaviour of developed countries. Respect for the 'independence, sovereignty, and territorial integrity of every country' (Paragraph 13 of the International Development Strategy) had become synonymous with the uncritical acceptance of the *status quo* in developing countries. The fact that over half of the SNPA is devoted to needed domestic reform reflected a maturing and represented a welcome outgrowth of 'common sense' from multilateral development diplomacy.

The Paris Conference also focused the attention of the international community on the plight of some 280 million of the globe's most desperately poor people. Such a propaganda value of the conference, particularly for those democratically elected governments whose budget decisions are subject to pressures from electorates, should not be easily dismissed because the popular awareness of poverty in the Third World is negligible.

Agreement on a follow-up mechanism to monitor implementation at the national and global levels over the next decade must also be regarded as a major achievement. Multilateral diplomacy led to an agreement on a country-specific action programme combined with a global attack on least development in the follow-up. Since the Paris Conference, World Bank consultative groups have been sponsored for four LDCs and UNDP round tables have taken place for ten others. An intensive schedule of such meetings is planned which should provide an opportunity for coordination of assistance among donors, and between donors and a recipient, as well as monitoring performance in the 1980s at the national level. Regional level meetings have been organised by ECA and ESCAP. At the global level, UNCTAD is preparing in-depth analyses of the progress, and of policy issues affecting the implementation of the SNPA, drawing upon the results of review meetings as well as other sectoral studies. The system of focal points in each UN agency used in preparations for the Paris Conference has been strengthened, and further interagency meetings held.[20]

In contrast to this guarded optimism concerning multilateral diplomacy in Paris, two critical observations should be made. First, according to estimates made by UNCTAD, the financial assistance required by the LDCs to achieve the growth rate of about 7 per cent envisaged in the SNPA would be $14 billion in 1985. However, estimates on the basis of commitments made by various donors in Paris suggest assistance to the LDCs in 1985 will be only $8 billion, a gap of some $6 billion (i.e. the size of the actual annual flows). In the year 1981, ODA receipts by the LDCs declined both in current and real terms, and further declines in aid receipts were reported in 1982. Thus, the global recession has meant that even the earlier estimates on increased resources for least developed countries were too optimistic and must be adjusted downwards. In short, the practical pay-off for goodwill from the multilateral development diplomacy at Paris is uncertain and the prospects of LDCs remain extremely bleak.

Second, the validity of the central focus of the conference should also be questioned. The emphasis on external aid was so significant that one could, with some justification, label the approach to LDCs as 'neo-colonialist'. Critical consideration was not given during the Paris Conference to conceptual problems about the nature of least development. The SNPA was based simply on a repetition of the traditional model of development which rested on the type of assistance provided to developing countries from the beginning of the postwar period through the late 1960s.[21]

In explaining the mixed results of the conference reference should be made not only to the specificity of the issue under discussion, but also the particular bureaucratic context within which negotiations took place. In this respect, Goran Ohlin has argued that 'Multinational global diplomacy would in any case stand to gain from paring its agenda down to essentials which would restore its capacity for the double task of political dialogue and technical negotiation.'[22] While the Paris Conference was an excellent example of agenda reduction, one explanation for its mixed results was its partial breaking of what one observer has called the 'golden rule' of successful conference diplomacy – good preparations.[23]

A distinction must be made between logistical and substantive preparations, on the one hand, and political preparations, on the other. There was general agreement that the conference secretariat must be complimented for a superb contribution as regards the former. Indeed, the effective preparation time for the conference itself had been only ten months, following the decision made on timing by the Preparatory

Committee during which time four clusters of review meetings had also been organised. Logistical preparations were as sound as for many other conferences when normally three years lead time had been available, and costs proportionately lower.

Unfortunately the same cannot be stated for preliminary political spadework. While the extremely tight calendar was perhaps partially responsible, the conference secretariat could have exerted more leadership. In contrast with activist secretariats for other UN conferences, UNCTAD was more inclined to allow things to take their own course. There was too little effort to secure advance agreement on a package of priority items that the LDCs would have considered substantial and meaningful, but which the important donor countries would also have found negotiable. During sessions of the Preparatory Committee, no real effort was made to lobby donor countries on the crucial issue of the volume and quality of aid. In contrast with other senior officials who shuttle among important national capitals in the important last weeks before a conference opens, UNCTAD passiveness on the political front appears striking. UNCTAD was unwilling to offend other non-LDC members of the Group of 77 by becoming committed to the cause of only one part of its membership.

The plethora of documentation produced for the conference probably confused more than enlightened the negotiations as well. Whatever the value to organisation and governments in the long run of research and analysis, the vast majority of the actual documents produced for UN conferences are not read or used. This generalisation was particularly true in Paris, where the checklist of documents itself took up eight pages. Waste is suggested by the task of a delegate who could not be expected to carry, let alone read, the 30 country presentations or even the 32 submissions from UN organisations. A main policy statement from a conference secretariat is, however, imperative and useful, whether or not its recommendations are actually followed; it outlines the parameters of debate and sets the tone for it. The main substantive document for the Paris Conference was criticised by many as being too 'UNCTADish' and technocratic, but it did provide facts and justifications for many of the central elements of the SNPA.

The importance of adequate political preparations is further highlighted because the actions by diplomats involved in the Paris negotiations suggested that technical expertise and substantive arguments are of relatively little consequence in what was ultimately a political gathering. The process in Committee Two illustrated most clearly the dominance of politics and the exclusion of substance. Interventions during the public and restricted sessions were mere statements of preferences without a substantive discussion of the various merits of alternatives. All available time was spent drafting compromises without discussing the substance behind the language. Committee One never discussed even the simplest calculations concerning donor commitments and the needs of LDCs if the proposed aid targets were implemented.

Another important variable in explaining the mixed results of multilateral diplomacy in Paris was the respective leadership roles of the conference secretariat and of the host government. While in annual sessions of the General Assembly or governing bodies of specialised UN agencies the room for manoeuvre of international secretariats is severely circumscribed, the same is not true for global conferences. With their combination of specific focus and high visibility during a concentrated period of time, global conferences provide an unusual opportunity for international civil servants to influence national government policies.

In almost all previous conferences, ultimate responsibility remained with the General Assembly or ECOSOC and a highly visible outside political figure was named by the UN Secretary-General to head an autonomous secretariat. The secretariat was normally attached to a department of the UN or one of its specialised agencies in order to make maximum use of available technical and logistical expertise; but the secretariat and its leadership were independent.

The selection of Gamani Corea, and the almost exclusive use of the UNCTAD secretariat to prepare the Paris Conference, was an exception to this general rule. Better results would have probably ensued had this not been the case. As already stated, the preliminary political consultations and preparations among all interested parties to negotiations would have been better and the main background document for the conference more original and useful, and less bureaucratic in-fighting among UN organisations would have occurred.

The pre-conference period is ordinarily the time that a secretariat and its head exert maximum influence. The on-going responsibilities and organisational ideology of UNCTAD and its Secretary-General provided a partial explanation for the secretariat's low-key profile. Corea was preoccupied by a number of issues of importance for his organisation and North–South negotiations more generally, and he personally spent little time on preparations before the actual opening of the conference. Maintaining the solidarity of all developing countries was primordial. The complete omission of LDCs from the *Trade and Development Report, 1981* – the organisation's most prominent annual publication released just before the conference – reflects the minor role of LDCs in UNCTAD's evaluation of major world economic developments.[24]

During global conferences, both international and national officials can influence negotiations. In previous conferences executive heads have sometimes played crucial roles, for example Maurice Strong at the Conference on the Human Environment and Sayed Marei at the World Food Conference. International officials usually cede their places to national decision-makers once an intergovernmental conference opens. The Paris Conference was unusual in that in the exercise of leadership not only the conference secretariat but also all other national delegations were almost totally eclipsed by France.[25] In particular the President of the Conference, Jean-Pierre Cot, made it clear from the opening session that he was an activist. He abandoned his honorary seat at the centre of the podium, giving the opportunity for limelight to his 19 vice-presidents and thereby liberating himself for his own highly personalised style of multilateral development diplomacy. Four days before the end of the conference, Cot formed his presidential contact group which reached agreement quite expeditiously on square-bracketed sections of the SNPA, which the main committees and their subcommittees had been labouring upon to no avail.

Effective United Nations decisions on economic and social affairs must be negotiated. The tenor of the multilateral diplomacy surrounding the negotiation of the SNPA differed from the earliest years of the UN's existence; decisions may have been effective because they were imposed as a result of the lack of universal membership. Paris diplomacy also differed from more recent decisions that have been less than effective as a result of sterile confrontations between the numerically superior South attempting unsuccessfully to impose its views on the powerful but numerically inferior North.

The qualified success of the conference may be explained in terms of three conditions that characterised the bargaining. First, a significant fund of political goodwill about the LDCs already existed. Humanitarian concerns and parliamentary directives had made this issue an unassailable priority; and shifts in policy had already occurred within bilateral and multilateral programmes related to finance and trade.

Second, flexible coalitions characterised the multilateral development diplomacy in Paris, a significant departure from recent UN practice. Since the first session of UNCTAD in 1964 in Geneva, a group system has been adopted, refined and generalised to almost all intergovernmental meetings within the UN system.[26] While the group system was originally effective in organising discussions and led to the launching of various debates of concern to the Third World, its rigidity is rapidly becoming counterproductive.

Differences in views within groups in Paris may have been as great as differences among them. The existence of divergent views – or ambivalence – of subgroups within the Group of 77 towards the LDC category had been noted. Unease with the group system surfaced in Paris because poorer nations no longer uniformly believed that oil was the only weapon for improving their lot. The cumulative damage from successive price increases forced LDCs to reevaluate their traditionally supportive and sympathetic view of OPEC, and indirectly the shibboleth of Group of 77 solidarity.

In Group B the more pro-development partners (in particular the Scandinavians and Dutch, joined by the French and Canadians) were no longer willing to be associated with the lowest common denominator that necessarily resulted from compromising with the most conservative members of Group B (the United States, the United Kingdom, Japan and the Federal Republic of Germany). The recent frustration with multilateral development diplomacy reflects not only the insensitivity of developed nations to the need for change, but also the inflexibility of the lowest-common-denominator approach of the group system. The erosion of uniformity in forums such as the Paris Conference may therefore be seen as a positive development.

Third, the Paris Conference witnessed a willingness of the principal parties to compromise. Mahbub ul Haq has argued that in retrospect the call for a New International Economic Order should not have been a 'demand' of the developing countries – the stance taken by negotiators – since they were too poor to have anything to offer, as well as because they were only asking for rights that should not be subject to bargaining. More emphasis should rather have been placed on the global needs of the world economy, and the interests of the North.[27] The Paris Conference permitted the international acknowledgement of the need for developing countries to make policy changes in order to assist their own development. In return for a reasonable consideration of this Northern concern, developed countries agreed to significant inter-national support measures for the poorest members of the South.

Attempts to measure the precise impact of the Paris Conference are presently premature and should more properly await the mid-1980s. In the meantime, one can safely state that multilateral diplomacy has contributed to the increasing attention paid to the problems of the 36 countries presently at the bottom of the United Nations development ladder. The creation of a special category has proved a useful policy tool, singling out countries that have hardly begun the long and arduous struggle that can eventually lead to some measure of economic independence and a minimum domestic capacity to meet essential local requirements.

NOTES AND REFERENCES

1. For a more extensive discussion of the problems and prospects of these countries, as well as the process of this conference, the reader is referred to *More for the Least? Prospects for Poorest Countries in the Eighties* (Lexington, Mass.: D. C. Heath, 1983). Some of the material in the present article was also utilised in T. G. Weiss, 'The UNCLDC: The Relevance of Conference Diplomacy in Paris for International Negotiations', *International Affairs*, vol. 59, no. 4 (1983). Material reproduced by permission of the publishers, D.C. Heath and Butterworth.
2. These countries are Afghanistan, Bangladesh, Benin, Bhutan, Botswana, Burundi, Cape Verde, Central African Republic, Chad, Comoros, Democratic Yemen, Djibouti, Equatorial Guinea, Ethiopia, Gambia, Guinea, Guinea-Bissau, Haiti, Lao People's Democratic Republic, Lesotho, Malawi, Maldives, Mali, Nepal, Niger, Rwanda, Samoa, Sao Tome and Principe, Sierra Leone, Somalia, Sudan, Togo, Uganda, United Republic of Tanzania, Upper Volta, Yemen. Five of these – Djibouti, Equatorial Guinea, Sao Tome and Principe, Sierra Leone and Togo – were added at the 37th session of the General Assembly, which took place after the Paris Conference. Consequently, this chapter discusses the list as it existed in 1981, although the five recently added countries will benefit from the SNPA. In generalisations about the present economic situation and prospects, however, data on them have been included.
3. *The Least Developed Countries and Action in their Favour by the International Community*, 'The Substantial New Programme of Action for the 1980s for the Least Developed Countries', A/CONF.104/22/REV.2, pp. 1–22.
4. Andre Champmarin, 'Les PMA dans les negociations internationales: la tentation du neo-colonialisme multilateral', in G. Mignot with Pierre Jacquet and Jacques Loup (eds), *Les Pays les plus pauvres: quelle co-operation pour quel developpment?* (Paris: Institut français des relations internationales, 1981) p. 196.
5. A certain irony marked the leadership of the Paris Conference. Stone reached mandatory retirement age at the end of 1980 and was unable to see through completion of the exercise he had taken such pains to shape, although he was a consultant responsible for initially drafting the report of the Secretary General of the conference.
6. See TD/B/577, TD/B/719 and TD/B/681.
7. The Group of 77 text is found in A/CONF.104/CRP/5 and that of Group B in A/CONF.104/CRP/4 which both appear in the synoptic table annexed to

the report of the Preparatory Committee on its third session (A/CONF.104/L.1). As is normally the case in international negotiations in the UN, the real participants were the developing countries and the Western bloc. The socialist countries of Eastern Europe which comprise Group D made only a few suggestions to the preamble (A/CONF.104/CRP/2–3), and China made none at all.

8. UNCTAD/LDC/misc. 2.

9. This allocation followed the secretariat's suggestions in A/CONF.104/PC/14 (Annex A/CONF.104/Add.1, and A/CONF.104/PC/L.4).

10. A. F. Ewing, 'UN Conference on the Least Developed Countries', *Journal of World Trade Law*, vol. 16, no. 2 (March–April 1982) 171.

11. These documents are found in the series LDC/CP/1 to 31, summaries of which are found in A/CONF.104/SP/1 to 31. Chad, which was still in the midst of civil strife, was the only country not to put forward its case, although a number in each series was reserved for it.

12. These are found in A/CONF.104/3, 4, 5 and 6 for the countries present respectively in Vienna, Addis Ababa, the Hague and Geneva.

13. See 'Guidelines on the Preparation, Organization and Servicing Arrangements of Special Conferences of the United Nations and Their Preparatory Meetings', annexed to General Assembly Resolution 35/10, 3 November 1981.

14. See the speech given at AAPSO–AFASPA colloquium by Jean-Pierre Cot, then Minister for Cooperation and Development, and President of the Paris Conference, 6 July 1981, mimeograph which describes the Paris Conference as 'un heritage que M. Giscard d'Estaing nous a laisse, et je dois dire que c'est un heritage qui n'est pas commode'.

15. A/CONF.104/22, pp. 37–45.

16. A/CONF.104/L1, the synoptic paper set out the various groups proposed draft for each section of the SNPA.

17. M. Mitterrand visited Mrs Thatcher during the conference's deliberations, and one of the issues raised was measures to assist LDCs. Most delegates in Paris believed that he was exerting maximum pressure on the British Prime Minister to ensure a successful outcome of the conference.

18. L. Gordan, Aid Modalities in Bangladesh, LDC/RM.1/1, A. Jennings, Aid Modalities in Tanzania, LDC/RM.2/1, and R. Roberts, Aid Modalities in Sudan, LDC/RM.2/2.

19. H. Nicolson, *Diplomacy*, 3rd edn (Oxford University Press, 1963) p. 25.

20. For a discussion of these meetings, see TD/276, pp. 44–8 and Annex I.

21. There is a considerable literature on the limits of aid including: J. Galtung, P. O'Brien and R. Preiswerk, *Self-Reliance: A Strategy for Development* (London: Villiers Publications, 1980); P. Bauer and B. Yamey, 'The Political Economy of Foreign Aid', *Lloyds Bank Review* (October 1981) pp. 1–15; John Healey and Charles Clift, 'The Development Rationale for Aid – Re-examined', *ODI Review*, no. 2 (1980) 14–18.

22. G. Ohlin, 'Negotiating International Order', in M. Gersovitz *et al.* (eds), *The Theory and Experience of Economic Development* (London: Allen & Unwin, 1982) pp. 215–18.

23. Nicolson, *Diplomacy*, p. 87.

24. TD/B/983.

25. In terms of the effectiveness of individual delegations, some delegates argued that the European Community also played a dominant role. The French, however, were not without influence in defining the EEC's positions.
26. A discussion of these developments, as well as the overall context of UNCTAD, where group politics have been perfected, can be found in R. L. Rothstein, *Global Bargaining: UNCTAD and the Quest for a New International Economic Order* (Princeton University Press, 1979). For a discussion of the internal and external politics surrounding UNCTAD's foundation and its group system as an alternative to the domination by the North in other international organisations, see Branislov Gosivic, *UNCTAD: Compromise and Conflict* (Leiden: A. W. Sijthoff, 1972); Diego Cordovez, *UNCTAD and Development Diplomacy: From Confrontation to Strategy* (London: Journal of World Trade Law, 1970); and Kamal Hagras, *United Nations Conference on Trade and Development: A Case Study in UN Diplomacy* (New York: Praeger, 1965).
27. M. ul Haq, 'Negotiating the Future', *Foreign Affairs*, vol. 59, no. 2 (1980/81) 398–417.

10 The Third UN Law of the Sea Conference

R. P. BARSTON

The UN Convention on the Law of the Sea was opened for signature at the final session of the conference in Jamaica on 10 December 1982.[1] The enormous task of codifying and revising existing maritime law established by the Geneva conventions has spanned a period of over eight years. During this time the UN Conference on the Law of the Sea (UNCLOS) met in session for a total of over 90 weeks and held extensive intersessional consultations, producing ultimately a text containing 320 articles, with nine technical annexes and four resolutions. For many states, especially the core delegations, the conference provided a unique meeting ground, which facilitated the discussion and, to an important degree, the resolution of deep-seated problems. This process was undoubtedly aided by the 'insulation' of the conference from the wider effects of major international conflicts. In all, the Convention and Final Act was signed by 117 states, plus the Cook Islands and the United Nations Council for Namibia. Amongst the signatories were the Soviet Union and Eastern European bloc, five members of the EEC (France, Denmark, Greece, Ireland and the Netherlands) and the bulk of countries in Africa, Asia and the Middle East. In addition, 23 states which did not sign the Convention signed the Final Act.[2]

This chapter will examine two broad themes. The first explored is the political process and main features of the regimes which were negotiated at the conference. The second part focuses on the evolution of state practice from the final phases of the conference.

MULTILATERAL CONFERENCE DIPLOMACY

The Framework of the Conference

The mandate for revising the law of the sea was established by General Assembly Resolution 3067 (XXVIII) of 16 November 1973. Prior to this the Assembly had considered, on the initiative of Malta, a broad range of questions concerning the peaceful uses of the seabed and ocean-floor from 1967 until 1969. In the following year, on 17 December 1970, the General Assembly adopted Resolution 2749 (XXV) containing the Declaration of Principles Governing the Seabed beyond the limits of National Jurisdiction, and in Resolution 2750 c (XXV) of the same date decided to convene a conference on the law of the sea in 1973. Preparatory discussions were held within the framework of the enlarged Ad Hoc Committee to Study the Peaceful Uses of the Seabed at UN headquarters in New York and at the office of the United Nations in Geneva between 1971 and 1973. The first procedural session of the Law of the Sea Conference was held in New York between 3 and 14 December 1973.

From the outset, membership of the conference was based on the principle of achieving universality. Accordingly invitations were extended to all states members of the United Nations or specialised agencies, parties to the statute of the International Court of Justice, and observer status was given to interested intergovernmental organisations, as well as states not fully independent at that time, and national liberation movements recognised by the OAU and League of Arab States. At the final session in Jamaica, 6 to 10 December 1982, the Credentials Committee accepted the credentials of 144 delegations participating at the session. In all 168 states were invited to attend, although 24 did not submit credentials or appoint representatives.[3]

The work of the conference was conducted through the plenary, three main committees, the drafting committee, two *ad hoc* Groups of Legal Experts (from the eighth session), with the presidency providing an important focal point in the decision-making process and overall coordination and harmonisation of texts. The conference elected Ambassador Hamilton Shirley Amerasinghe (Sri Lanka) as president. Ambassador Amerasinghe remained president until his death on 4 December 1980, when he was succeeded by Ambassador Tommy T. B. Koh (Singapore), who took over on 13 March 1981.

The complex of issues before UNCLOS was grouped, as indicated above, around three main committees: the deep seabed and related matters (First Committee), the Exclusive Economic Zone (EEZ) and a wide range of other issues (Second Committee) and preservation of the marine environment, pollution control and marine scientific research in the Third Committee. At the sixth session (New York, 23 May to 15 July 1977), the conference approved the formation of a group, known as 'the collegium', consisting of the conference president, chairman of the three main committees, chairman of the drafting committee and *rapporteur-general*, to prepare an Informal Composite Negotiating Text (ICNT), pulling together the work of the various committees.

Apart from the negotiations in these committees, the business of the conference has been conducted through less formal groups, bloc or group consultations during the sessions of the conference and, of course, intensive intersessional negotiations. During the earlier stages of the conference, the three committees tended to operate in a somewhat self-contained manner and indeed produced separate documents. It was not in fact until the publication of the ICNT in 1977 that overlap between the work of the three committees was reduced and texts were reordered and combined in a single document forming the basis for a draft treaty. The chairmen of each of the main committees, Paul Engo (Cameroon, First Committee), Andrés Aguilar (Venezuela, Second Committee) and Alexander Yankov (Bulgaria, Third Committee), along with the president of the conference (Shirley Amersinghe, Sri Lanka), were collectively responsible for any revision of the negotiating text. An interesting and remarkable feature of the conference has been the absence of formal voting on substantive proposals throughout the majority of the history of the conference. Under the so-called 'gentleman's agreement',[4] which forms part of the 1974 rules of procedure, states participating in the conference accepted that differences should be resolved on the basis of consensus and that formal voting should be avoided until negotiations had been completed.

On several occasions, especially during the middle and later phases of the conference, the formal machinery was supplemented by innovative, *ad hoc* negotiating 'structures'. These were essentially conceived of as devices for crystallising issues, and reviving the momentum of negotiation. At the seventh session of the conference, for example, in April, an attempt was made to break the impasse by defining the remaining hard core issues. Seven negotiating groups were as a result established on the following subjects:[5]

(i) the system of exploration, exploitation and (deep seabed) resource policy;
(ii) financial arrangements relating to the International Seabed Authority;
(iii) the institutional machinery of the Authority;
(iv) access to the resources of the economic zone for landlocked, 'geographically disadvantaged' and certain developing coastal states;

(v) settlement of disputes arising from the exercise of sovereign rights by coastal states in the exclusive economic zone;

(vi) the definition of the outer limits of the continental shelf and revenue-sharing of profits from offshore operations between the outer limit of the EEZ and the continental margin;

(vii) delimitation of maritime boundaries between adjacent and opposite states and dispute settlement.

At the eighth session of the conference in 1978 work was halted in the three new negotiating groups set up to deal with seabed questions and a Working Group of 21 instead was established.[6] This move, coming at a time when many delegations considered that outstanding issues should be rapidly resolved, was a further important procedural innovation. Unlike previous formal groups, membership was restricted and drawn from ten developed industrialised states, including the United States, United Kingdom, France, Federal Republic of Germany, Canada, Australia and the Soviet Union, and ten developing countries represented *inter alia* by Brazil, Peru, Mexico and the People's Republic of China. The size of the group did, however, tend to increase after the initial phase through the presence of alternates and observers.

In terms of the overall progress of the conference, it is worth adding that by the resumed ninth session (28 July–29 August 1980) the ICNT had, under the direction of the collegium, been put through three revisions in the various formal and informal groups both during and between sessions – an immense and exhausting task. The revised text, which by this stage had come to resemble the form and substance of the final document voted on in April 1982, was entitled 'Draft Convention on the Law of the Sea (Informal Text)'.

Multilateral Negotiations

The Law of the Sea Conference is distinguished above all by the highly politicised nature of its negotiations. In contrast to procedure in the First and Second Law of the Sea Conferences, negotiating texts in the Third were prepared and discussed through the three main committees and other forums, rather than being initially drawn up by a representative legal drafting committee prior to general debate. The language used in the ICNT is as a result often ambiguous and loosely drafted to reflect political negotiation and differing interpretations. Obligations are frequently qualified to make allowances for a state's level of development. Thus the requirement to establish international rules and practices to prevent the marine environment being polluted by land-based sources such as factory effluent and industrial discharge is qualified by allowing for 'the economic capacity of developing states and their need for development' (Article 207). During the conference, the issue of 'double standards' frequently arose as in this case and similar issues (cf. Article 194.1).

A further distinctive feature of UNCLOS is that negotiations, bargains and conflicts have involved many types of crosscutting alignments. In this way, negotiations have been characterised by changing and shifting groupings drawn together by limited or specialist interests, such as the regime for straits or the outer limit of the continental margin. In other cases, 'strategic' groups were formed to agree and promote negotiated 'packages', for example on the general regime for the EEZ. In some cases negotiation and contact groups were limited in their composition and basis of membership, such as the five major powers group, the Soviet and Eastern European group and the Arab group. Others spanned both Western and Eastern Europe, such as the Group of 17, which included the Soviet Union, several socialist states, the United States, Japan, Norway, Finland and the United Kingdom; this was formed to discuss particularly Third Committee questions. The so-called Evensen group,[7] for example, chaired by a Norwegian minister Jens Evensen, was set up before the Geneva Session in 1975 to bring together representatives of the main interest groups, especially major maritime powers and key members of the Group of 77, at the level of heads of delegation and legal experts. During 1975–6 the Evensen group concentrated on Second Committee questions, whilst at the sixth session it dealt with the International Seabed Authority. Jens Evensen continued his important role by subsequently chairing one of the two Groups of Legal Experts which were set up at the resumed eighth session to deal with technical aspects of the Final Clauses of the convention.

THE MAIN OUTLINES OF THE LAW OF THE SEA REGIME

Within the Second Committee of the conference the major issues of debate centred on the regime for the territorial sea, passage through straits used for international navigation, the EEZ regime and the outer limit of the continental shelf. The convention extends the breadth of the territorial sea from three to twelve nautical miles (Article 3). A contentious issue during the territorial sea debate was the regime for innocent passage. The major maritime powers, such as the United States and Soviet Union, together with those states with large shipping interests, were concerned to minimise as much as possible restrictions on passage in the territorial sea. The resultant regime, however, modifies the 1958 Geneva Convention, in line with the widespread concern of many developing countries over violations of this territorial sea, by broadening substantially the categories (Article 19) of activity which render passage not innocent to include, for example, propaganda, interference with communications and military activity. With regard to straits, provision is made for a new concept of transit passage, for which no prior authorisation is required (Articles 37–45).

Beyond the territorial sea, the convention provides for what is effectively a resource 'zone', out to 200 nautical miles, measured from the base line of the territorial sea. The regime for the zone (Article 56), in an effort to strike a compromise between those states which sought greater coastal state powers (e.g. Brazil, India, Ecuador, Peru) and the 'freedom of the high seas' group, relies on a distinction between sovereign rights and jurisdiction (Article 56) in the zone. In the EEZ, the coastal state has sovereign rights over the exploration, exploitation and management of resources and lesser jurisdiction, e.g. marine scientific research (consent may not normally be withheld for pure scientific research in the EEZ),[8] protection of the marine environment[9] and offshore installations. The jurisdiction of the coastal state over controlling pollution from vessels[10] is extended to include the power to board and inspect vessels, detention and the institution of proceedings (Article 220) and a new concept of port state devised to facilitate inspection and forwarding information on pollution offenders (Article 218).

As for the continental shelf regime, the traditional Geneva regime of the outer limit being the limit of exploitability or a depth criterion (200 metres) is revised by new outer limit criteria. Efforts to restrict or place limitations on the outer limit predictably came from the wide shelf states (e.g. United Kingdom, Australia, New Zealand, India). The revised regime, based on Irish and Soviet proposals, puts the outer limit as a distance criterion based on the geological characteristics of the continental slope. The Soviet proposal (Article 76.5) sets the limit at 100 nautical miles from the 2500 metre isobath or no more than 350 nautical miles.

The regime for the deep seabed (the 'international area') ultimately proved the most difficult issue for UNCLOS. The main lines of the regime[11] – the Authority (made up of an Assembly, the 36-member council and Secretariat) and its operating arm, the Enterprise – were established by the close of the sixth session of the conference. Under the convention, it is envisaged that the Enterprise would conduct independent deep seabed mining operations and set up joint-venture or production-sharing contracts with mining contractors. Other principles and regulatory powers in the Part xi provisions include the power of the Authority to control international polymetallic production limits, facilitate the transfer of technology at commercial rates from mining contractors licensed to operate in the area to the Enterprise and developing countries, and participation in international commodity agreements. The failure of the United States, in particular, to modify the seabed regime, led to two major reviews of US policy towards UNCLOS.[12] Although President Reagan announced on 29 January 1982 that the United States would rejoin the conference, the conditions set made it likely that the United States would not sign the convention. As a result of its failure to achieve the amendments sought, the United States pressed for a vote, and the conference closed on 30 April 1982, with the draft convention being carried by 130 votes to 4 (United States, Turkey, Venezuela, Israel) with 17 abstentions.

THE DEVELOPMENT OF STATE PRACTICE

So far this chapter has discussed the institutional framework and the political process within which a multilateral convention is negotiated. The remaining part of the chapter examines a question which is seldom if ever dealt with: the fate of a multilateral UN convention once it is signed. In other words, in the period after the convention or agreement is opened for signature, until eventual entry into force through the necessary ratifications or accessions (in the case of UNCLOS the required figure is 60, with entry into force the following year), how or to what extent does a multilateral instrument influence or shape state policies?

A feature common to many multilateral instruments requiring ratification including those negotiated under the auspices of the United Nations or through its specialised agencies, is the long period between signature and entry into force. Conventions signed with much ceremony eventually find their way to foreign ministry archives to be filed and often forgotten, as new interests and preoccupations seize the attention of decision-makers. The international diplomatic world moves on, though this is not to say that after signature the principles, ideas and certain elements of the substance of a convention or agreement have no effect. The Geneva Conventions took six to eight years before entry into force but nevertheless had an important influence on state practice in the interim.

In the case of UNCLOS, we might conclude that in the lengthy period of negotiation, a number of the ideas and concepts discussed and negotiated within UNCLOS have been incorporated into customary international law, particularly the 12 mile territorial sea and the concept of a coastal state having a resource zone beyond the territorial sea. By 1977, some 17 states had declared Fisheries Zones (FZs) and 23 Economic Zones (EZs); the following year these rose to 25 and 45 respectively, and, by 1982, 30 states claimed FZs and 59 EZs.[14] Nevertheless the scope for differences of zonal construction, and regulation within zones, remains, as we shall discuss below, considerable.

Some indication of state approaches to the convention, and their future practice pending entry into force, was provided in the closing statements made during 6–9 December 1982 at the final Jamaica session. A large number of delegations took the opportunity to present interpretive statements and comments on the various provisions, despite Article 310 of the convention which, in keeping with Article 18 of the Vienna Convention on the Law of Treaties, ruled out statements which purport to modify the legal effect of the provisions of the convention. Apart from those dealing with the seabed regime,[15] three general areas of reservation could be seen in the interpretive statements which were made. In the first place, those states which had unsuccessfully sought to have a provision for prior notification or authorisation for the passage of warships in the regime for the territorial sea (e.g. the Democratic Republic of Korea, Romania, Sudan, Yemen, UAE[16]) repeated their position. In Yemen's view, for example, the passage of warships through the territorial waters of a small developing country was a violation of its sovereignty. Malta, whilst accepting the compromise on passage, nevertheless reserved the right to submit a declaration. Similar concerns too were expressed, for example by Spain, with respect to the provision on transit passage of straits used for international navigation.

The question of delimitation was a second area which predictably revealed several different approaches. A number of states expressed dissatisfaction with the failure of the convention to provide clear rules, rather than the open-ended formula adopted in Articles 74 and 83, which provide that delimitation of the continental shelf and EEZ should be effected between opposite or adjacent states 'on the basis of international law'. The Bahamas, for example, restated its preference that the median line should be the mandatory factor in determining where maritime boundaries should lie. Venezuela reaffirmed its objections to the provisions.[17] Four Mediterranean states (Israel, Greece, Turkey, Cyprus) presented differing views on the application of the convention's provisions to enclosed and semi-enclosed seas.[18]

Thirdly a number of the landlocked states and so-called geographically disadvantaged states in general expressed dissatisfaction with the provisions of the convention with regard to transit rights, and access to the EEZ, of neighbouring states (e.g. the German Democratic Republic, Hungary, Mongolia, Nepal). The German Democratic Republic, for example, commented on the adverse impact on its deep-sea fishing industry of the introduction of Exclusive Economic Zone, whilst several landlocked states viewed the rights provided in the convention as very limited. In contrast, several coastal states with landlocked neighbours viewed transit rights and access to resources not as inherent rights but matters for bilateral or regional negotiation – a point stressed by Angola, Mauritania and Pakistan.

It is worth adding that many of those states which did not sign either the convention or Final Act, such as Albania, or signed only the Final Act, are located in areas which are politically or strategically sensitive. This, of course, is also true for some states which signed the convention, although the positions of most of the Final Act group are substantially at variance with the intentions of the convention. The group includes Venezuela, which has delimitation and other maritime disputes; Libya, Israel and Korea, in areas of international tension; and others such as Spain and Oman whose geostrategic location played an important part in the line they unsuccessfully sought to achieve. In addition there are those states whose existing maritime regimes are incompatible with the convention, such as Peru (200 miles territorial sea) and Ecuador, which considered its archipelagic claim to the Galapagos Islands compromised by the archipelagic state provisions of the convention. In a written statement to the conference, Argentina indicated that it was unable to sign the convention or the Final Act because of Conference Resolution III, on the rights and interests of territories which have not gained independence. The Argentine statement referred to the Malvinas, South Sandwich and South Georgia islands as an integral part of Argentine territory, and refused to recognise the right or title of any other state relating to resources protected by the resolution.[19]

The above approaches to the extent of the territorial sea and states' rights within it and zonal regulation suggest several broad categories of practice. These include conventional territorial sea (12 nm); territorial seas in excess of 12 nm but less than 200 nm (e.g. Albania, Oman); 200 nm territorial sea (e.g. Latin American patrimonial Sea Group); archipelagic; archipelagic island claims (e.g. Ecuador); restrictive regimes for straits used for international navigation (e.g. Spain, Iran); selective/comprehensive zoned regulation; and limited international regulation of deep seabed resource activity beyond the limits of national jurisdiction (e.g. United States, United Kingdom, the Federal Republic of Germany).

Maritime Capability and Regulation

The question of how state practice will develop can be examined in a number of ways. Two important determinants are the willingness to implement appropriate national legislation and, correspondingly, possession of adequate capability to enforce a wide range of potential jurisdictions in the maritime zone. Taken together these factors will influence the extent to which the approach taken is selective or comprehensive. As we have argued earlier, a large part of the work of UNCLOS was devoted to changing the balance of rights and control over resources to coastal states, through the EEZ and continental shelf provisions, and limiting or revising traditional high seas freedoms. However, whilst this technically may have been achieved through the convention, extended jurisdictions pose several difficulties for many states. At an administrative level, extended maritime areas face states with the difficult problem of interministerial coordination, since relatively few have single fully pledged departments of marine affairs or the personnel to staff them. Related to this is the budgetary question of allocating, or increasing, resources to offshore maritime functions such as marine police, coastguard, installation security and marine research. The problem of enforcing vast sea spaces (including fisheries, pollution control, passage of vessels) can be illustrated through the case of Indonesia.[20] Under the archipelagic concept Indonesia, which comprises over 13 000 islands, has converted over 2.2 million sq km into internal waters. Again, Kiribati in the Pacific has a population of some 56 000 and potential control of a sea area of 3 million square kilometres, of which the 200-mile fisheries zone of the former Gilberts Group covers an area of 1 061 300 sq km.[21] Kiribati has virtually no capabilities for fisheries control – its principal source of offshore interest. The extended maritime area of the Philippines, South West of Palawan, incorporated by presidential decree on 11 June 1978, provides an illustration of the difficulties of regulating and controlling large areas of contested sea space. The extended box area south of Palawan, known as Kalayan, approximately follows the boundaries of the area called 'Freedom land', claimed by a Philippine merchant adventurer, Thomas Cloma, in 1956. The area includes within it a number of island features which border or are part of the disputed Spratly Group, including Aboyna Cay, others which are claimed or already occupied by Vietnam, the People's Republic of China, Taiwan and the Philippines itself. The contested claims as a result make future development of this area hazardous or improbable.

EEZ Boundaries

A related aspect of the capability to enforce offshore jurisdictions is the problem of the delimitation of overlapping EEZs. As with those states whose existing maritime regimes are substantially incompatible with the law of the sea convention, similarly, those which have long-standing boundary, territorial or significant EEZ delimitation problems are unlikely in the short term to adhere to the convention, preferring to rely on interpretations of existing international law (e.g. Geneva Convention on the Continental Shelf), leave unresolved the question of the outer limits or general 'shape' of the EEZ, or reach *ad hoc* agreements where possible (e.g. Malaysia–Indonesia archipelagic agreement, March 1982). On delimitation of EEZs, a number of areas of difficulty arise on which the convention itself gives little or no guidance. In many cases the base line used by states to measure the territorial sea and the EEZ itself (200 nm) frequently departs considerably from the coast, with the effect that substantial sea areas are included on the landward side of the base line as in the Malacca Straits. So-called 'closing' base lines have also been drawn across bays and gulfs with similar effect. One of the longest straight base lines in this respect is that drawn by Burma across the Gulf of Martaban, which is some 224 nm. The Gulf of Sirte, claimed by Libya, encloses a similar sea area, south of Misurata to Benghazi. In fact not all base lines of this type conform to the convention. In such cases much depends on the meaning and weight attached to the concept of 'historic' bay. Historic bays as such are not subject to breadth limitations under the convention. Several such claims are the subject of considerable dispute.

Further difficulties arise from the tendency of states to use remote islands both to construct the base line and the outer edges of the EEZ, e.g. Rockall (Atlantic Ocean, United Kingdom), Narcondam Island (Adaman Sea, India), Ile Bac-long-vi (Gulf of Tonkin, Vietnam). In cases such as these the general effect is substantially to alter the configuration of the zone, complicating delimitation negotiations between opposite states with overlapping claims. A related question in contested areas also is the relative weight to be attached to uninhabited islands and reefs as against remote inhabited or occupied islands. Whether remote, uninhibited features can be discounted or claimed across is subject to differing practice. In the case of Brunei, for example, a number of best or worst case solutions to the configuration of the EEZ can be derived, depending on which islands or reefs are discounted south of the Spratly Group. The outer limits of a Brunei EEZ, as well as that of Malaysia, remain contested in view of the claims of Vietnam and four other states to the whole or part of the group.[22] The overall effect, as this example from the complex overlapping EEZ and continental shelf claims in the South China Sea indicates, is to preclude or seriously hinder the delimitation and regulation of the EEZs of a number of the parties. In addition, as in these and other similar cases, naval operations to contest and acquire island features have become noticeably more marked following the final phases of the law of the sea conference.

With regard to EEZ regulation a number of broad types of state practice can be seen. A large number of economic zone declarations follow the language of the convention, although in regulatory terms consequential national legislation is frequently selective, depending on the interests of the states focusing on fisheries for example, and/or hydrocarbon resources. Relatively few of the zonal regulations include provisions on a contiguous zone beyond the territorial sea. This would seem to suggest that whilst such a zone was felt important under the narrower territorial sea regime of the Geneva Convention, the extension of the territorial sea to 12 nm makes a contiguous zone out to 24 nm, covering customs, health and related regulations, either unnecessary, or the regime of the area is for practical purposes considered indistinguishable from the EEZ. In some regions, particularly those with highly developed institutional connections, some degree of harmonisation of regulations has been possible, such as in the EEC, though integrated fisheries policies on access and catch limitation remain highly contentious. Elsewhere the pattern is one of *ad hoc* national regulation, with some bilateral collaboration.

In general, the framing and development of national legislation is influenced to an important extent by the degree of local or regional conflict. The extension and selective regulation of resource zones out to 200 nm (and beyond) has, especially in the greatly contested areas, meant either loss of access to EEZs, or continuous arrest of 'straying' fishing fleets. For example, Thailand, a major fishing nation, with the world's sixth largest fleet, exporting 2.2 million tons worth US$434.7 million in 1982, has increasingly had to rely for 50 per cent of its total catch on fishing grounds in or around the territorial seas of neighbouring South and Southeast Asian countries.[23] The 200 nm EEZ declarations by neighbouring countries have meant loss of access to at least some 300 000 square kilometres of fishing waters and caused Thailand considerable concern. Thai efforts to establish joint ventures with Burma and Vietnam have made no progress, although an agreement was reached with Bangladesh in August 1982. Whilst Thailand signed the UNCLOS convention, it remains ambiguous towards it and was the last state within the region to declare an EEZ. Thailand's position is further complicated because of continental shelf claims in the Gulf of Thailand, particularly by Vietnam and Kampuchea.

High Seas

A major issue of importance for the development of customary practice and accepted rules in maritime law is the question of the status of the high seas. The issue of rights and obligations beyond the territorial sea will remain highly contentious, especially over seabed mining and other resource activity. This is also the case with regard to assertions of traditional high seas rights and freedoms, such as over-flight and navigation. In addition to the broad categories of territorial sea and zonal approaches discussed earlier, there is, with respect to the use of the high seas, what might be termed the modified 'high seas' school, which includes the United States and other major maritime powers. The Soviet Union, at least as far as navigation is concerned, might be considered a *de facto* member of this group.

The United States 200-mile EEZ declaration of 10 March 1983[24] is of interest in at least three respects as an indication of the modified high seas doctrine. In the first place the United States accepted, in its proclamation, the maritime claims of other states which are consistent with international law, as reflected in the convention, providing United States rights and freedoms are respected by the coastal state. Secondly, however, the breadth of the United States territorial sea has not been changed but remains at 3 nautical miles, rather than at the UNCLOS 12-mile limit, forming the base line for the EEZ. Territorial sea claims greater than 3 nm miles and up to 12 nm, will only be recognised if the United States is granted full rights under international law in the territorial sea of other states. A third departure in the EEZ proclamation is the exclusion of jurisdiction over marine scientific research from the list of jurisdictions within the United States EEZ in the 'interest of encouraging marine scientific research and avoiding any unnecessary burdens'. The American position recognises, however, the right of other coastal states to exercise jurisdiction over marine scientific research within 200 nautical miles provided that jurisdiction is exercised 'reasonably, in a manner consistent with international law'. Together, the above three elements in the EEZ proclamation constitute a restatement of the legal philosophy and assumptions of the 'high seas' school, which has underpinned its positions and policies from the outset of the Law of the Sea Conference: the preference for unimpeded commercial and military navigation, research and over-flight.

International Seabed Mining

Considerable jurisdictional uncertainty surrounds the mining of poly-metallic minerals from the seabed. Whilst it will be some time before significant commercial production is achieved, the issue was considered important enough for the United States to withold its signature to the convention, and seek interim solutions with other industrialised states. In terms of mineral exploration, the most likely location remains the nickel and copper finds in the northeast Pacific Clarion–Clipperton area, tested, along with other areas, by major Western consortia since the mid-1970s. Potential deposits of cobalt, manganese and other metals exist in other parts of the Pacific and Indian Oceans. Other potentially important areas include the Red Sea metalliferous sedimentary deposits, located east of Port Sudan.

In anticipation of an unsatisfactory seabed mining regime, the United States administration put through the Senate on 28 June 1980 the Deep Seabed Mineral Resources Act,[25] to protect existing US deep seabed mining and facilitate if necessary a separate international seabed mining treaty with other interested parties. The United States was subsequently joined by several other West European states, including the Federal

Republic of Germany, France and the United Kingdom, which passed similar, though not identical, legislation. The Soviet Union and Japan delayed legislation as long as possible, although both eventually passed national licensing laws on 17 April and 9 July 1982 respectively.[26]

As far as the institutional aspects of the seabed regime are concerned, the convention takes into account the likelihood of political difficulties in implementing the Part XI provisions on the International Seabed Authority, by permitting the 36-member Seabed Council to be set up on entry into force (Article 308.3) in a manner consistent with the appropriate provisions (Article 161), even if that article cannot be strictly applied. Furthermore, the convention is unusual in the extent to which it allows the Preparatory Commission to assume various functions before the convention comes into force, such as approving 'pioneer' investors and liaison on overlapping claims with states who authorise mining.[27] The early proceedings of the Commission were in part devoted to the dispute arising from the attempts of India and the Soviet Union to register as 'pioneer' investors before any agreed general rules for resolving overlapping claims had been reached by the Commission.[28]

As for states outside the convention, non-ratification by the US in conjunction with some of the important West European high technology states would undoubtedly seriously weaken the International Seabed Authority both technically and financially. It is possible that the major industrialised states not participating in the convention might develop some form of loose cooperation amongst themselves short of a formal seabed treaty. The national legislation referred to earlier allows for collaboration between so-called deep seabed mining states in order to avoid duplication of effort and competing claims, and facilitate licensing. As part of this development the United States, United Kingdom, Federal Republic of Germany and France concluded an interim agreement on 2 September 1982.[29] The agreement deals, inter alia, with procedures for resolving overlapping claims, exchange of information and procedures for examining licence applications. However, it is possible that at least some of the major industrialised states will prefer to participate, and, working through the Enterprise, enable the 'parallel' system envisaged in the convention to come into operation – two sites being designated by an operator one of which be set aside for the Enterprise. Further financial investment by states outside the convention will inevitably make it much more difficult to break off existing operations and transfer them to the ISA on entry into force of the convention.

International Institutions

The convention devolves considerable responsibility on international organisation and diplomatic conference to develop and harmonise rules and standards. In the main, the contribution such institutions make is in specialised sectors of maritime policy such as shipping, pollution control and marine research, rather than in acting as agents for persuading states to adopt a comprehensive approach to the law of the sea.

Organisations such as the ILO, IMCO, UNEP and FAO have in fact already influenced the content of the convention and begun to implement a number of the ideas in it. In shipping, for example, several of the ideas contained in the 1973 IMCO International Convention for the Prevention of Pollution from Ships and the accompanying 1978 (MARPOL) Protocols, such as special areas vulnerable to pollution, find their way into the UNCLOS convention. Following ratification by Italy in October 1982, the MARPOL convention, which is now ratified by 15 countries with over 50 per cent of international shipping tonnage, entered into force on 2 October 1983. Ship routing schemes are now being increasingly adopted, as in the Malacca and Dover Straits, and the provisions of the UNCLOS convention on routing have been tightened, as mentioned earlier, following the *Amoco Cadiz* tanker disaster in 1978. The concept of port state jurisdiction for controlling shipping standards and preventing pollution has been further developed following the signing on 26 January 1982 of the Paris memorandum. Under the Paris scheme, 14 European states have agreed to inspect up to 25 per cent of the vessels arriving in their ports according to seven international conventions and the 1976 merchant shipping (minimum standards) convention (ILO Convention 147).[30]

Military Uses of the Sea

A final set of general issues relating to state practice concerns offshore security and access to internal waters, EEZs, international straits and airspace. The question of access through straits has been underlined by the Iran–Iraq War, which has highlighted the general danger to merchant shipping, and the vulnerability of the Straits of Hormuz in particular to closure or disruption since passage is restricted to the relatively narrow channel following the Omani coastline. Again, in the Far East, the decision by Japan to take a more active role in the defence of sea lanes has been influenced by the increasing Soviet build up in

Sakhalin and the sea of Okhotsk, as well as the shooting down of the KAL airliner on 1 September 1983. In a revision of defence policy, the defence perimeter now extends out to 1600 km, including two major sea lines of communication – the southeasterly route using Tokyo– Yokohama as the starting point for the 1600 km coverage, and the southwesterly route from Osaka/Kobe, extending to the Mariana Islands and Guam.

The law of the sea convention has very little to say on the military uses of the sea.[31] This to a large extent is a reflection of the origins of UNCLOS and the large amount of attention subsequently given to questions connected with the ownership and control of living and non-living resources. The Iran–Iraq War illustrates a further gap in the convention in terms of the problem for third parties of maritime access, war zone charter risks and the threat and damage caused by high levels of pollution from war-affected refineries. In general, it is clear that the convention will have to be supplemented by new and comprehensive international rules and guidelines on third party shipping, neutral zones, the conditions for *ad hoc* ceasefires, access to war zones for pollution control and humanitarian assistance, in respect to military conflicts which have a maritime dimension.

CONCLUDING OBSERVATIONS

The United Nations Law of the Sea Conference has made an important contribution to the codification, revision and development of existing maritime law. During its work, the conference drew on a number of innovative negotiating methods and tried wherever possible to operate on the basis of consensus. A crucial feature in this process was the perceived need to maintain the momentum of the negotiations both during and between sessions, until as many options had been explored as possible. The effect was to create a *developing* consensus on the main lines of the issues at stake. Where this consensus was imperfect, the effect was to produce articles which were of an open-ended nature, as for example on the delimitation provisions or the methods for dispute settlement. The convention, therefore, is a political instrument in the sense that it reflects the level of state agreement or conflict on any issue or group of issues. Put differently, an indication of the extent of the consensus was the gradual incorporation of a number of the ideas discussed during the course of the conference into customary law.

The seabed issue showed ultimately that the consensus could no longer be maintained. The repercussions of the absence of major powers from the convention has yet to be fully felt. It remains to be seen whether the effect is confined to deep seabed mining alone or extends more generally into other areas of maritime law, producing a legal 'dualism' between states party to the convention and those not. The problem of divergent approaches to offshore jurisdictions is most clearly illustrated in incidents of the Gulf of Sirte type, when rights of passage through an area are tested. In general, however, the convention provides an essential framework both for the moderation of state interests and the future development of public maritime law.

NOTES AND REFERENCES

1. A/CONF. 62/122, 7 October 1982, and (Final Act) A/CONF. 62/121 October 1982.
2. The 23 states signing only the Final Act were: Belgium, Benin, Botswana, Ecuador, Equatorial Guinea, Federal Republic of Germany, Holy See, Israel, Italy, Japan, Jordan, Libya, Luxembourg, Oman, Peru, Republic of Korea, Samoa, Spain, Switzerland, United Kingdom, United States, Venezuela and Zaire. The Final Act was also signed by the ANC, EEC, Netherlands Antilles, PLO, Pan African Congress of Azania, SWAPO, the Trust Territory of the Pacific Islands and the West Indies Associated States. Of the 168 states invited to attend the conference 24 did not submit credentials or communicated the appointment of representatives. The 24 states not participating in the final part of the eleventh session included Afghanistan, Albania, Argentina, Bolivia, Democratic Kampuchea, Saudi Arabia, South Africa and Syria, see UN Press Release, SEA/MB/12 9 and 10 December 1982.
3. Report of the Credentials Committee, A/CONF. 62/123, 9 December 1982.
4. Appendix to 1974 Rules of Procedure, 27 June 1974. The agreement was reached on 16 November 1973.
5. A/CONF. 62/62, 13 April 1978.
6. Report of the Working Group of 21, A/CONF. 62/C1/L.26, 21 August 1979.
7. See R. P. Barston and P. Birnie (eds), *The Maritime Dimension* (London: Allen & Unwin, 1980) p. 156.
8. The qualified consent regime, a compromise between the 'freedom' for research and full consent positions, was based on the draft articles submitted by Colombia, El Salvador, Mexico and Nigeria in May 1975. See A/CONF. C3/L.92, 6 May 1975.
9. For a detailed discussion of international efforts to regulate pollution of the marine environment, see R. P. Barston and P. Birnie, *The Maritime Dimension*, ch. 5.
10. Largely as a result of the *Amoco Cadiz* tanker accident off the Northwest coast of France at Ushant in March 1978, the text of the draft conven-

tion (Article 211) was amended at the eighth session the following year to require states to establish routing schemes designed to minimise accidents. For details of the *Amoco Cadiz* incident, see *Interim Report of the Formal Investigation of the Marine Board*, Republic of Liberia, February 1979. The grounding of the *Hydo* off Brittany on 14 October 1982 (Cypriot/Panamanian register) also revived the controversy over flags of convenience.

11. For the background to these changes, see A/CONF. 62/WP 10/Add. 1, 22 July 1977, pp. 68–9.

12. The United States did not participate in the tenth session of UNCLOS in 1981 pending the second major review of United States policy. For a discussion of United States objections to the deep seabed mining provisions, see R. P. Barston, 'The Law of the Sea', *Journal of World Trade Law*, vol. 17, no. 3 (May/June 1983) 207–10.

13. SEA/498/3 December 1982. Those abstaining on the vote on the adoption of the convention were Belgium, Bulgaria, Byelorussia, Czechoslovakia, German Democratic Republic, Federal Republic of Germany, Hungary, Italy, Luxembourg, Mongolia, Netherlands, Poland, Spain, Thailand, Ukraine, USSR and United Kingdom. Liberia later announced that it wished to be recorded as abstaining. Albania, Ecuador and the Holy See announced that they were not participating in the vote, see, SEA 498, 3 December 1982.

14. FAO, *Limits of Territorial Seas, Fishing Zones and EEZs*, September 1982.

15. See Department of State *Bulletin*, May 1982.

16. SEA/MB/13, 10 December 1982.

17. SEA/498, 3 December 1982.

18. SEA/498, 3 December 1982.

19. A/CONF./62/WS 35.

20. For details of shipping incidents and problems of regulating shipping in the Indonesian archipelago see *Asiaweek*, 1 (April 1983).

21. Fisheries are the main export of the group. The major licensing agreement with Japan of June 1978 was the subject of protracted renegotiations during 1982. For the text of the International Agreements (Government of Japan) Order 1978, see Kiribati *Gazette*, 29 May 1981.

22. See J. V. R. Prescott, 'Maritime Jurisdiction in Southeast Asia: A Commentary and Map', *Research Report* (Honolulu, Hawaii: East-West Environment and Policy Institute, 1981).

23. *Business Times* (Malaysia), 28 September 1983, and SEA/498.

24. Presidential Proclamation, 10 March 1983.

25. Public Law 96–283, 28 June 1980 (HR 2759).

26. See G. Marston 'United Kingdom: Legislation on Deep Sea Mining', *Journal of World Trade Law*, vol. 16 (January 1982) 86; Decree No. 81, 555, *Journal Officiel*, no. 115 (16 May 1981); R. P. Barston, 'The Law of the Sea', *Journal of World Trade Law*, vol. 17 (May/June 1983) pp. 217–18 on Soviet and Japanese legislation.

27. See LOS/PCN/1, 14 March 1983 on the agenda of the Preparatory Commission.

28. For the text of the Indian *Note Verbale* see LOS/PCN/21, 13 May 1983, and LOS/PCN/19, 4 May 1983 for the Soviet letter. India and the Soviet Union

held bilateral talks on 29–30 April 1983 concerning the coordinates of their respective claims in the central Indian Ocean and Pacific. For the views of countries opposing these procedures and claims, see *inter alia* France, LOS/PCN/12, 29 April; Japan, LOS/PCN/11, 28 April 1983; Italy, LOS/PCN/10, 28 April 1983; Indonesia, LOS/PCN/20, 12 May 1983, and United Kingdom, LOS/PCN/13, 29 April 1983.

29. *Agreement concerning Interim Arrangements relating to Polymetallic Nodules of the Deep Sea Bed*, Treaty Series No. 46 (1982) Cmnd. 8685.

30. Since the signing of the Paris Memorandum, over 5000 ships have been inspected, including 1300 in France. The French authorities found 190 defective and detained them in port.

31. For a detailed discussion of the development of zones in military conflict see R. P. Barston and P. Birnie, 'The Falkland Islands/Islas Malvinas Conflict: A Question of Zones', *Marine Policy* (January 1983) 14–24.

Part III
Bilateral Diplomacy

11 'Old Diplomacy' in New York

G. R. BERRIDGE

It is a commonplace of commentary on the United Nations that much time is spent in the corridors of UN headquarters on consolidating or sabotaging alliances constructed for the purpose of propaganda exchanges in the Security Council and the General Assembly.[1] Whether or not offstage activities also usefully include the private promotion of agreements with more pacific purposes in view, as well as the fulfilling of certain of the subsidiary functions of what is usually referred to as 'bilateral' or 'old' diplomacy, is a matter of more contention. Those who adopt a negative position on the latter issue, who, in other words, are sceptical of the proposition that the UN is a significant centre for the ordinary conduct of general business between states, include supporters of the United Nations as well as its enemies. Thus, while it is not surprising to find the authors of *A Dangerous Place* contending that 'Nations interested in reaching agreements almost always ignore or avoid the United Nations',[2] it is perhaps more remarkable that Shirley Hazzard should arrive at the same conclusion.[3] Neither is it comforting to the hypothesis that the UN is an important centre of 'old diplomacy' that those who have insisted on this most frequently should have been those with a vested interest in salvaging something from the United Nations in the light of its manifest failures in other regards, namely the highest officials in the Secretariat, and in particular just about every Secretary-General since Trygve Lie.

It is not difficult to understand why the idea in question has been greeted with such widespread scepticism. Normally the great powers and the middle powers, at any rate, have representation in each other's capitals and also, in most instances, at the headquarters of regional standing conferences such as that of the EEC in Brussels. In addition, they are able to support rapid and extensive travel for key politicians and home-based civil servants, and in any case have sophisticated systems of direct communication which can fulfil some of the functions of diplomacy. When to all this is added the fact that certain great cities on all continents have traditions of providing hospitality to diplomacy both old and new, it is not surprising that the most important bilateral negotiations of recent years, for example on arms control and Vietnam, should not principally have taken place in New York but in Washington, Moscow, Helsinki, Geneva and Paris.

If the great powers and the middle powers, at least, appear to be embarrassed with opportunities for diplomatic contact rather than short of them, and therefore not in need of the United Nations in New York for this reason, the permanent missions which almost all states maintain there do not seem the most appropriate instruments of old diplomacy in any case. For these missions, given the public setting of formal agenda business at the UN, are necessarily charged with vital *propaganda* functions. If these functions are fulfilled with zest – and, of course, they often are – the permanent missions have little time and certainly do not create the right sort of atmosphere for real bilateral diplomacy. On the contrary, as is so often said, they may actually exacerbate the differences between member states. Nevertheless, there remain grounds for believing that the possibilities for private contact provided by the presence of so many permanent missions in New York mean that the United Nations has diplomatic compensations as well as diplomatic drawbacks. At the least, the convergent scepticism of the realists and the disillusioned idealists needs to be qualified.

As John Barratt stresses at the beginning of the following chapter, diplomacy involves, *inter alia*, communication and information-gathering as well as negotiation, and that the United Nations is an important 'listening post' for all member states there can be little doubt. According to Richard Pedersen, who at the time of writing was Chief of the Political Section of the US Mission to the United Nations, the UN 'is a unique centre for obtaining quick and reasonably authoritative answers on all kinds of questions, even on short notice when delegates may be without instruction from their governments . . . The acquisition and exchange of information', Pedersen continues, 'involves a large percentage of the time of UN delegations.'[4] Supporting this, Alger and Best, in a pioneering and unfortunately unrepeated study based on interview data collected from permanent missions in 1960, tentatively concluded that diplomats found it easier to exchange 'off the record' information at the UN and also that the United Nations was in general a more important source of information than national capitals.[5] While none of this evidence can be considered impartial, it would be extremely surprising indeed if the United Nations in New York were *not* to be one of the world's more important diplomatic listening posts even if not the most important of all.

If it seems likely that the United Nations is of some value for communication and information-gathering even to the great powers and the middle powers, it is sometimes said to be of special value to the dialogue between such powers when their relations descend into pronounced hostility, and also to be of special value to the diplomacy of small states in all circumstances.

SMALL STATES

The United Nations is commonly said to be of special value to the diplomacy of small, poor states, and especially micro-states, because representation in the midst of so many other permanent missions in New York saves such states the expense (in personnel as well as resources) of maintaining a full network of diplomats across the globe. As Kay puts it: 'The head of a typical mission from a new state may find himself also serving as his country's Ambassador to the United States and *de facto* representative to 80 or more other states.'[6]

The claim that the United Nations assists the diplomacy of small states has some substance and is widely accepted.[7] It is important, however, that this point should not be exaggerated. After all, small states other than micro-states do not in practice tend to regard their UN missions as acceptable substitutes for representation in the capitals of the bigger powers, or in the capitals of states which are of lesser weight but remain important for such reasons as aid or ideology, or indeed in the capitals of their neighbours. This is for the very good reason that it is particularly with these states that negotiation, *inter alia*, will be necessary and that, as Sir Geoffrey Jackson says, 'Successful negotiation is best assured by the experienced diplomat's easy-seeming but hard-earned familiarity with a country, its people and their ways.'[8] Cosmopolitan though New York undoubtedly is, such familiarity can hardly be acquired at the United Nations. Thus Sierra Leone, for example, in 1975, maintained embassies or high commissions in China, France, West Germany, the Soviet Union, the USA, the United Kingdom, Cuba, Egypt, Ethiopia, Gambia, Guinea, Liberia, Mali and Nigeria, while Guatemala, in addition to maintaining embassies in seventeen of the most important states of central and south America, was also represented at embassy level in Benelux, China (Taiwan),

France, West Germany, Haiti, Israel, Italy, Spain, Switzerland, the USA and the Vatican.[9]

Neither, of course, do great and middle powers have a monopoly on representation in international organisations other than the UN itself. Thus in 1975, Peru, as well as maintaining representation in 61 countries, had missions to the Latin American Free Trade Area, the EEC, the FAO, the OAS and others, in addition to the UN in New York.[10]

If most small states thus tend to retain high-level direct representation in the places where policy most intimate with their interests is actually made, this is not the case with micro-states. Indeed, in 1975 the 16 micro-states (population under 300 000) listed by Plischke, with the exceptions of Iceland and the Vatican, averaged less than one mission abroad each.[11] On the face of it, therefore, states such as Grenada and Equatorial Guinea might be expected to find more diplomatic value in the United Nations than the majority of small states.

The fact remains, however, that the United Nations is not the only recourse for contact with the states which fall outside the direct embrace of ambassadorial representation for *any* of the small states. On the contrary, there is a variety of means whereby every kind of small state might expand the range of its diplomacy beyond this limit. Plischke lists these as unilateral representation, multiple accreditation, third-country representation, joint representation and representation at a major diplomatic centre such as London, Vienna or New Delhi.[12]

Unilateral representation, or the unreciprocated representation of one state in the capital of another, is in fact quite a common device whereby small states can conduct a limited diplomacy on the cheap. Plischke records Cyprus as accrediting envoys to only 11 countries but receiving them from 46, and Sierra Leone as sending missions to 13 countries but receiving 50 in return.[13] A special case of unilateral representation, also commonly employed, is the special envoy.

Multiple accreditation, or the accreditation of an ambassador in one country to others in the vicinity, is also a common practice among small states, although not quite to the extent that one might have expected.[14] Formally endorsed by the Havana Convention of 1928 and the Vienna Convention on Diplomatic Relations, 1961,[15] multiple accreditation has obvious advantages for small states. Thus in 1975 the Sudan maintained embassies in 26 countries but, through multiple accreditation, had formal ambassadorial representation in 32 more. With a firm grasp on political realities which certain other countries might do well to emulate, the Sudanese Ambassador to the Soviet Union was also accredited to Czechoslovakia, Bulgaria, Hungary, Poland and Romania.[16]

Third-country representation consists in the protection of one state's interests in the country of a second by the embassy of a third. This requires either great trust or unqualified domination and is thus – except in the event of hostilities – rare. Nevertheless, it is a device employed by some micro-states.[17]

Joint representation, where two governments accredit a single envoy to represent them both in a third country, is even rarer than third-country representation itself.[18] However, the final device – the cultivation of contacts within the diplomatic corps of a major diplomatic centre – is assuredly more important, even if, because in the main it is conducted informally, its precise extent is unknown and unknowable. (The United Nations in New York itself falls into this category, of course.) 'London', as the Report on the Commonwealth Seminar on the Diplomatic Service, held in Singapore in 1970, said, 'is of particular value for this purpose within the Commonwealth, since all Commonwealth countries maintain significant missions there, and most foreign countries are also represented.'[19]

In light of the evidence on the direct representation of small states other than micro-states in national capitals, and in light of the variety of other diplomatic mechanisms available to all small states, the case for the value to their diplomacy of the UN in New York seems weak indeed. This impression is intensified when it is further considered that the more commonly employed alternatives to full representation actually have advantages which are not shared by permanent representation in New York. Thus unilateral representation, while providing no more first-hand insight into the affairs of foreign countries than a UN mission, at least costs nothing. Multiple accreditation, for its part, allows an ambassador access to the countries in the vicinity of his main posting, while the atmosphere around the diplomatic corps in, say, Warsaw, Vienna or Bangkok might be expected to be more conducive to successful diplomacy than that enveloping the permanent missions in New York. It needs to be added, too, that some micro-states actually do not have permanent representation in New York.[20]

But this is to present only half of the picture. On the other hand, unilateral representation does not permit the dramatic symbolic assertion of the state, a vital diplomatic service provided magnificently by UN representation; multiple accreditation can only provide superficial knowledge of the countries neighbouring the ambassador's principal posting and may be counterproductive if the device is considered by those countries to be tantamount to relegating them to second-class status,[21] while, by contrast, the latter is impossible at the UN, where, in any case, the equality of states is a religion; and the use for bilateral diplomacy of London, for example, rather than New York, while certainly making possible contact with American diplomats will not provide first-hand experience of conditions and attitudes in the United States itself, a vital consideration for most small states. In addition to all this, the General Assembly in New York is the principal battleground in the war of propaganda between the poor states and the rich states and, in view of the 'parliamentary' character of that war, is the place where alliances are best *negotiated*. (A rich irony of diplomacy used to this end in New York is that the governments of small, poor states in particular find it necessary to allow considerable discretion to their permanent missions on some issues of policy as well as on tactics;[22] such ambassadorial discretion is, of course, associated normally with the 'old diplomacy'.)

To sum up so far, permanent representation in New York cannot adequately replace representation in the capitals of the countries, or at the seats of the other international organisations, most important to individual small states, and in practice it does not. Nevertheless, it helps them in their dealings with states which lie outside this inner core, especially in the forming of propaganda alliances; it provides for dramatic symbolic assertion of the state; and it can double as representation to one of the world's two great powers, the United States. In short, the United Nations in New York is useful but – in normal circumstances – not indispensable to the bilateral diplomacy of small states.

HOSTILE STATES

Lack of resources is not, however, the only reason why small states may sometimes find the UN a useful point of diplomatic contact; neither does the utility of New York for the great and middle powers always reside in its listening-post function alone. There is another category of states or, rather, of interstate relations, for which the United Nations is possibly of greater diplomatic value and, because of its nature, certainly of great importance to all of us. This is the category of states (subsuming some small states) which are either so hostile to each other that they have never opened embassies in each other's capitals, or have closed their embassies, or – as during the worst years of the Cold War between the

United States and the Soviet Union – have embassies which are under such a state of siege as to be of extremely limited diplomatic use. Such relationships are, by definition, the most dangerous in international politics, especially if they involve the great powers. If the permanent missions of such states at the UN can assist in the establishment of serious diplomatic contact, therefore, they are clearly of considerable importance. Bailey and Bloomfield, amongst others, have both made this point,[23] and it is evidently what Kurt Waldheim had in mind when he noted in the course of an address in September 1979 that 'There are many forms and channels of communication well short of full diplomatic recognition . . . The United Nations itself serves both as a channel *and as a place* for communication in many difficult situations' (emphasis added).[24]

Contacts outside the UN

Of course, as Dr Waldheim himself conceded, the United Nations is only one among a number of ways in which hostile states may preserve, or reestablish, *direct* diplomatic contact. They may also employ some of the alternatives to full representation already discussed in this chapter under the heading of 'Small states'. One such alternative, which is increasingly popular with states in conflict, is a variation on third-country representation, namely, representation through an 'interests section' in the embassy of a third state.

It has long been common for states to entrust their interests in a hostile state to the embassy of a third state. A device which is employed by some small states as an economy measure has, in other words, often been used for political reasons as well. In the latter respect the embassies of Switzerland and Sweden have been popular choices.[25] However, largely because the severance of diplomatic relations these days is normally a limited political gesture rather than a prelude to war, and also because of its obvious advantages to all concerned, it is now common to find a state's interests in a hostile state being protected by a small group of its *own* diplomats within the embassy of a third state.[26] Furthermore, the practice having caught on, it has been employed recently by states at war.

According to Eileen Denza, the practice of employing interests sections staffed by nationals of states in conflict was started by the United Kingdom when seven African states broke off relations as a protest at the weakness of the British response to Rhodesian UDI in

1965. With the agreement of the African states themselves, 'British Interests Sections' sprang up in the embassies of third states.[27] More interesting still, even during the Falklands War between Britain and Argentina in early 1982, prior to which diplomatic relations were severed, a British Interests Section was established in the Swiss Embassy in Buenos Aires. In the event, it was shunned by the Argentine government and by most of the diplomatic corps in Argentina as well (including Britain's partners in the European Community).[28] The point is, however, that it was there throughout the fighting and was a channel for personal contact – albeit at a low level – should one have been needed. Amongst other states, Israel finds this new method valuable.[29]

Direct contact between hostile states may also be made within the diplomatic corps resident in a third state with which each has diplomatic relations. Thus the United States and mainland China had embassies in Warsaw and took advantage of the fact to have regular discussions during much of the period of their intense hostility following the Communist revolution.[30] The American Ambassador also attempted at least one 'chance' encounter with his Chinese counterpart at a Yugoslav fashion show held at the Warsaw Palace of Culture, though unfortunately the Chinese Ambassador fled in panic. Of the 134 meetings held prior to January 1970, all but one, according to Henry Kissinger, were completely sterile. Nevertheless, the connection played a vital role when both powers decided to explore, with great caution, the possibilities of a *rapprochement*.[31]

Finally, direct contact between hostile states may be made by the simple expedient of the special mission, which may be public or secret depending upon the odium which it might be expected to attract or the alarm which it might be expected to excite. Secret ones, of course, tend to be better known. Henry Kissinger's secret visits to China during the fragile early stages of the *rapprochement* are a case in point. So, too, are the secret trips which were made into black Africa by John Vorster, South Africa's Prime Minister, and his Foreign Minister, Dr Hilgard Muller, in the course of 1974.[32] A secret visit to Israel by a high-level Liberian mission in early August 1983 was important in the sequence of events which led to the reestablishment of relations between Liberia and Israel shortly afterwards.[33]

There are thus at least three methods other than use of the UN permanent missions themselves whereby hostile states may make direct diplomatic contact. And, in addition to these, there are of course various *indirect* methods other than recourse to the UN Secretary-General. Third-party diplomacy may involve the assistance of the embassy of a third state which is located in one of the hostile states, the same device employed by some small states as an economy measure; or it may entail help at the highest governmental level in a third state. In the latter category the use made of Yahya Khan's regime in Pakistan by China and America in the early 1970s comes to mind. But non-governmental organisations and private individuals may be employed as well. Amongst the latter, journalists and businessmen are particular favourites; during the Cuban missile crisis the Soviet Union used both to convey messages to Washington.[34]

Although there is a variety of methods by which hostile states might make contact, most of them have serious limitations. In the case of national 'interests sections' the limitations are imposed by the junior status of the diplomats, the smallness of their number and the extreme hostility – in some cases – of their immediate environment. Special missions may seriously damage a state's prestige if they are made with public knowledge and fail to produce results, and may in any event invite sabotage of the policy initiatives which are behind them. If they are made in secret there are formidable obstacles to be overcome in order to ensure that they remain secret. The contact provided by special missions is, in any case, by definition spasmodic. Where intermediaries are employed instead there is more chance of misunderstanding, no confidentiality, and invariably a price to be paid; this may be of considerable significance if the intermediary is a state. President Nixon's 'tilt to Pakistan' in 1971 was in part a *quid pro quo* for Yahya Khan's good offices in the early stages of America's *rapprochement* with China.[35] In fact, the only method by which hostile states might make contact which seems to be without serious limitations of this kind is the contact made by their diplomats within the diplomatic corps of a third state with which they both have diplomatic relations. In these situations ample opportunity for discreet contact is added to existing proximity. But the advantages for hostile state diplomacy of the diplomatic corps in a national capital – with the important exception of the difference in atmosphere, already noted – are precisely those of New York. The UN centre on the East River is simply the biggest diplomatic corps of them all.

Contacts within the UN

The fact that the UN in New York is the largest of all diplomatic corps is, however, no reason in itself why hostile states should sometimes prefer it to a national capital should they desire a meeting place, or employ it to supplement contacts in national capitals. What, if any, are the advantages of contact in New York? Since very little emerges about the contacts which actually do take place, this question is not easy to answer with any confidence. Nevertheless, the following would seem to be among the more important reasons why the UN is sometimes employed.

First of all there is the claim of the UN diplomats interrogated by Alger and Best in 1960 that they were more likely to have formal and informal contacts with representatives of 'unfriendly states' than were diplomats posted to national capitals.[36] This is principally because of the great many meetings which they all have to attend. While it may not be of any significance in itself, this greater *familiarity* may be an asset in some situations.

Secondly, the choice of the United Nations might help to underline the seriousness of an approach from one hostile state to another if this is desired. The reason for this is that the heads of permanent missions are frequently individuals of some political weight in their own countries and, even if they are not, they will have some international prominence by virtue of their position at the United Nations.

Thirdly, it is a reasonable supposition that the United States might choose the UN to make contact with its many enemies in view of the proximity of New York to Washington. Communications presumably provide fewer problems here than do those with embassies abroad, while key government figures can easily be whisked north should the necessity arise.

Fourthly, government leaders may themselves be at the United Nations when a crisis involving their states is seen to require discussion. This is usually the case – in both respects – at the beginning of each new session of the General Assembly in autumn. In this sense the United Nations has the same importance for diplomacy as the funeral of a great statesman, an event normally attended by many world leaders anxious not only to pay their last respects but also to have a confidential exchange of views. The only differences are that at the United Nations it is usually the funeral of a state which is the occasion of their consultations and the embalmed remains of the deceased are never actually interred.[37] In any event, because of the value of these contacts at least one commentator felt that the Soviet Union had made a serious error in not allowing Mr Gromyko to attend the opening of the 1983 session of the General Assembly (the funeral of Lebanon), following the declarations of the governors of the states of New York and New Jersey that, in the light of the shooting down of the KAL flight, they could not guarantee his safety at their states' commercial airports.[38]

Fifthly, a dialogue started between the permanent missions of two or more hostile states at the United Nations can always fall back on the assistance of the Secretary-General himself, while if he takes the initiative by offering to act as an intermediary it would not make much sense for the parties to respond by suggesting that he deal with their ambassadors in, say, Harare.

Finally, the issues which divide states are often on the UN's *formal* agenda in any case and while this is usually a reason for *not* attempting a serious negotiation in New York the reverse is sometimes true. In particular, New York is a good place to negotiate when it is important to be seen to be negotiating, even if the prospects for success are remote.

Whatever the reason, or reasons, the fact is that the United Nations is sometimes chosen as a point of diplomatic contact by hostile states; this also occurs sometimes within the context of formal UN involvement in a dispute. Riggs investigated such 'cases of record' over the period from 1946 until 1970 and found that 'Of the hundreds of questions discussed by the Assembly or the Security Council . . . only six represented a serious attempt by the United States to use the United Nations to achieve a negotiated settlement of an East–West question.'[39] In addition, in only three of these was the UN negotiation helpful in producing agreement. It would, however, be quite absurd to decide the issue of the UN's importance in this respect on the basis of numbers alone. When the *nature* of the East–West questions which the UN helped to settle is also taken into account the value of New York appears in a different light. The three issues in question were arms control, the peaceful uses of outer space and the Cuban missile crisis, in the last of which Riggs reports that 'Both parties used their UN ambassadors to channel informal suggestions and semiofficial messages that reinforced and supplemented more direct communication.'[40] If the UN had helped in the Cuban missile crisis alone it would have justified its existence as a diplomatic meeting ground. Besides, Riggs's research is confined to cases of record in only one set of hostile state relations, namely, Soviet–American.

In addition to the negotiations which have occurred between hostile states at the UN within the context of the Organisation's agenda and which are, therefore, known, some diplomatic contact goes on outside this context; it follows that this is private although, in the event, not necessarily secret.

Until recently the most famous of these cases was the series of conversations in the early months of 1949 between Philip Jessup, America's deputy representative to the UN, and Yakov Malik, the Soviet representative, which contributed to the lifting of the Soviet blockade on Berlin. These conversations, it should be noted, did not begin by accident: Jessup was directed by the State Department to try to open this 'private channel'.[41] In August 1979, however, it was revealed that in the previous month America's UN Ambassador, Andrew Young, had met privately in New York with the Head of the PLO's Observer Delegation to the UN. This caused a sensation because in 1975 the United States had formally committed itself to a policy of no contact with the PLO until this organisation changed its own policy on the recognition of the state of Israel. Shortly afterwards, Ambassador Young resigned.[42]

Two points of interest emerge from the Andrew Young affair. The first is that while New York may be suitable neutral ground for many hostile states, it is probably *not* the best place for the USA and the PLO to make 'secret' contact. This is partly because of the intense passion generated by the Arab–Israeli dispute in the General Assembly, and partly because New York has an extremely large number of Jewish residents.[43] The second and probably related point is that another American diplomat had *three* encounters with the PLO during the same period at a different meeting place – Vienna.[44]

A decade earlier the Americans had similarly failed to keep the Israelis in the dark about an approach to the Arabs at the UN. With diplomatic relations between Washington and Cairo ruptured by the Six Day War, the US Secretary of State, Dean Rusk, had taken advantage of the Egyptian foreign minister's appearance at the opening of the 1968 session of the General Assembly (the funeral of Czechoslovakia) to commend to him personally a document containing America's latest proposals for a settlement in the Middle East – 'Rusk's seven points'. Unfortunately, news of the American approach quickly reached the ears of the Israeli Ambassador to Washington. Mr Rabin, whose contempt for the style of the American approach was rivalled only by his dislike of its substance, 'protested vigorously' to the State Department, and nothing more was heard of 'Rusk's seven points'.[45]

More effective than this was the use to which the UN was put by the Americans and the Chinese in the period between Communist China's admission to the UN in late 1971 and the semi-official exchange of diplomats in 1973. In his memoirs Henry Kissinger records that he had agreed with Peking that 'the new Chinese mission to the UN be authorized to deal with its American counterparts in an emergency . . . This link', Kissinger continues, 'was soon to be needed during the India–Pakistan war. In fact, I met secretly in New York about a dozen times over the next year and a half with Huang Hua, who was quickly moved from Ottawa to become China's UN Ambassador. These meetings', says Kissinger, summing up, 'together with my annual trips to China, became the principle channel of communications until the creation of the Liaison Offices in Washington and Peking in mid-1973.'[46] Kissinger, it is worth recalling in this context, is not a man with a reputation for inflating the importance of the United Nations.

Another notable contact of recent years was that which took place at the General Assembly in September 1981 (the continuing funeral of Afghanistan) between the Israeli and Soviet foreign ministers. The Soviet Union had broken off diplomatic relations with Israel at the time of the Six Day War, and the 90-minute discussion which took place between Shamir and Gromyko in 1981 was reported to have been the first direct diplomatic contact between the two countries since 1976.[47]

The few examples of informal contact between hostile states at the United Nations which I have mentioned are some of the important ones which have come to light. In themselves they do not, of course, present a strong case for the value of the United Nations in these circumstances. On the other hand, if the UN is to be of value in this respect then it is important that these contacts *remain* secret for at least as long as the disputes which make them urgent continue. In view of this, and in view of the reasons which argue for the value of the UN as a neutral meeting ground for some hostile states, it seems reasonable to conclude that the examples which I have recorded are indeed only a few among the many that have probably occurred.

CONCLUSION

Those who have written off the United Nations as *merely* 'a dangerous place' have committed the characteristic error of polemic: they have thrown out the baby with the bathwater or, in this case, expelled the diplomat with the hot air. The United Nations has diplomatic advantages as well as drawbacks, especially for hostile states and for states which are friendly but poor; these ought to be properly recognised. Whether the good which the UN does to diplomacy outweighs the harm is, of course, a separate question and one to which I do not know the answer; neither do Yeselson and Gaglione. It is tempting to suggest that this problem would be solved by the abolition of both the Security

Council and the General Assembly but there are reasons for lamenting this prospect and, in any case, the permanent missions would be unlikely to remain in their absence. In New York, propaganda seems to be the price of diplomacy.

NOTES AND REFERENCES

1. I would like to thank Jack Spence and Maurice Keens-Soper for their helpful comments on this chapter.
2. A. Yeselson and A. Gaglione, *A Dangerous Place: The United Nations as a Weapon in World Politics* (New York: Grossman, 1974) p. 6.
3. Shirley Hazzard served in the UN Secretariat for many years and was devoted to the founding principles of the United Nations. After she left she wrote a bitter and brilliant attack on the quality of Secretariat leadership: *Defeat of an Ideal: A Study of the Self-Destruction of the United Nations* (London: Macmillan, 1973). For her views on the present theme, see pp. 115–16, 145–6 and ch. 6.
4. R. F. Pedersen, 'National Representation in the United Nations', *International Organization* (Spring, 1961) 256–66.
5. It is important to note Alger's admission that there was a particularly high non-response rate to the question on the importance of the UN as a source of information compared to national capitals, and also that a general weakness of the study was its reliance on answers from those with a vested interest in boosting the importance of the UN. As he concedes, a proper investigation would need, at the least, comparable information from diplomats accredited to national capitals, C. F. Alger, 'Personal Contact in Intergovernmental Organizations', in H. C. Kelman (ed), *International Behaviour: A Social-Psychological Analysis* (New York: Holt, Rinehart & Winston, 1965) pp. 531–2.
6. D. A. Kay, *The New Nations in the United Nations, 1960–1967* (New York: Columbia University Press, 1970) p. 21. It is true, of course, that not *all* 'new states' in the 1960s were 'small states'.
7. See, for example, S. D. Bailey, *The General Assembly of the United Nations*, rev. edn (London: Pall Mall, 1964) p. 15; T. Hovet, Jr, 'United Nations Diplomacy', *Journal of International Affairs*, 17 (1963) 29–41, and A. Watson, *Diplomacy: The Dialogue Between States* (London: Eyre Methuen, 1982) pp. 173–4.
8. Sir Geoffrey Jackson, *Concorde Diplomacy: The Ambassador's Role in the World Today* (London: Hamish Hamilton, 1981) p. 151.
9. J. Paxton (ed), *The Statesman's Yearbook, 1975–1976* (London: Macmillan, 1975). The year 1975 is the last for which *The Statesman's Yearbook* records this sort of information.
10. Ibid.
11. E. Plischke, *Microstates in World Affairs* (Washington, D.C.: AEI, 1977) p. 46.
12. Ibid., p. 46ff.

13. Ibid., p. 49.
14. Plischke recorded 32 states employing this device at the time when he was writing, of which only about a third could reasonably be classed as poor states, pp. 54–5 and Appendix A.
15. E. Denza, *Diplomatic Law: Commentary on the Vienna Convention on Diplomatic Relations* (New York: Oceana, 1976) p. 28.
16. Paxton, *Statesman's Yearbook*.
17. Plischke, *Microstates*, pp. 52–3.
18. Ibid., pp. 53–4.
19. The Commonwealth Secretariat, *Diplomatic Service: Formation and Operation* (London: Longman, 1971) p. 72.
20. Belize, Comoros, Solomon Islands and Vanuatu, endnote 2, ch. 7 above.
21. The Commonwealth Secretariat, *Diplomatic Service*, p. 74.
22. E. Luard, *The United Nations: How it Works and What it Does* (London: Macmillan, 1979) endnotes 6 and 7, pp. 173–4, and Kay, *New Nations in the UN*, pp. 20–1.
23. Bailey, *General Assembly of the UN*, p. 15 and L. P. Bloomfield, *The United Nations and U.S. Foreign Policy*, rev. edn (Boston: Little, Brown, 1967) pp. 130–1.
24. Kurt Waldheim, *Building the Future Order* (New York: The Free Press, 1980) p. 240.
25. Denza, *Diplomatic Law*, pp. 278–81.
26. Watson, *Diplomacy*, pp. 128–9.
27. Denza, *Diplomatic Law*, p. 280.
28. According to David Watt, reporting on a recent visit to Argentina in *The Times*, 4 November 1983.
29. It was reported that in August 1983 there were, in West Africa, Israeli Interests Sections in embassies in Ghana (also handling Togo) and Ivory Coast (also handling Gabon), *The Times*, 15 August 1983.
30. This is Eileen Denza's example, *Diplomatic Law*, p. 281.
31. H. A. Kissinger, *The White House Years* (London: Weidenfeld & Nicolson and Michael Joseph, 1979), especially p. 165, pp. 188–90 and pp. 684–5. The one meeting which was not 'sterile', according to Kissinger, was that of 10 September 1955, when 'an agreement was reached on repatriation of some nationals', p. 165.
32. See C. Legum, *Southern Africa: The Secret Diplomacy of Detente, South Africa at the Cross Roads* (London: Rex Collings, 1975) p. 6.
33. *The Times*, 15 August 1983.
34. T. C. Sorensen, *Kennedy* (London: Pan Books, 1966) p. 787 and A. M. Schlesinger, Jr, *A Thousand Days: John F. Kennedy in the White House* (London: Deutsch, 1965) p. 702. For other cases, see M. R. Berman and J. E. Johnson (eds), *Unofficial Diplomats* (New York: Columbia University Press, 1977).
35. Kissinger, *White House Years*, p. 895.
36. In Alger, 'Personal Contact in Intergovernmental Organizations', pp. 529–30.
37. I am indebted to Maurice Keens-Soper for the second of these observations.
38. Zoriana Pysariwsky, UN Correspondent of *The Times*, writing on 5 October 1983.

39. R. E. Riggs, *US/UN: Foreign Policy and International Organization* (New York: Meredith, 1971) p. 125.
40. Ibid., p. 140.
41. C. E. Bohlen, *Witness to History, 1929–1969* (London: Weidenfeld & Nicolson, 1973) p. 284. Bohlen's full account of this case is clearly authoritative.
42. *Daily Telegraph*, 14–17 August 1979.
43. It is interesting to recall here that during the discussions at the end of the Second World War on the site for the UN the Arabs had actually opposed the choice of New York on these grounds, P. Gore-Booth, *With Great Truth and Respect* (London: Constable, 1974).
44. *Daily Telegraph*, 17 August 1979.
45. Y. Rabin, *The Rabin Memoirs* (London: Weidenfeld & Nicolson, 1979) p. 109.
46. Kissinger, *White House Years*, p. 786.
47. *Financial Times*, 26 September 1981.

12 South African Diplomacy at the UN

JOHN BARRATT

Accepting as a starting-point Sir Ernest Satow's brief definition of diplomacy as 'the conduct of business between states by peaceful means',[1] one can immediately recognise two essential aspects of the concept. First, and of basic importance, diplomacy is a peaceful practice in the sense that the use of force or other coercive measures, such as economic sanctions, is excluded. Although the *threat* of coercion is legitimately used as a diplomatic tool in negotiations over a dispute, putting the threat into effect would mean that diplomatic means had failed. Second, the phrase 'conduct of business' indicates the wide scope of diplomatic functions. They do not include only negotiations, as implied in Sir Harold Nicolson's more restricted definition,[2] but also symbolic representation (stressed by Morgenthau),[3] the exchange of information in the broadest sense, simple consultations to clarify respective policies, and generally the maintenance of normal interstate relations, so that the multitude of contacts between states in the modern world – in trade, finance, technology, information, politics, culture, etc. – can proceed unhindered as far as possible. Negotiations to settle differences, or to reach some other agreement between states, are an essential part of diplomacy, but not the only part. Regular, day-to-day, diplomatic activity is more concerned with the various means of keeping open the channels of communication between states and affirming the latters' identity.

A special point has been made here of the broad nature of diplomacy because, when the focus is on the United Nations, there is a tendency to think simply in terms of negotiations. The image of the UN is one of conferences and meetings, at which it is assumed that the representatives of states gather to negotiate agreements on a variety of subjects and to try to negotiate the settlement of disputes within a limited time-span. The other, continuous functions of diplomacy are often overlooked in the UN context and it is the purpose of this chapter to present the view that, in South Africa's case at any rate, these other functions, usually associated with bilateral diplomacy, are not only exercised at the UN to an important extent but are of greater diplomatic significance than what often passes for diplomacy at the Organisation's public multilateral gatherings. That South Africa should want to exploit the potential of the UN in this particular way is immediately plausible since, although it has reasonably wide diplomatic and consular representation in Western countries and also, to a lesser degree, in Latin America, it is excluded from whole groups in Africa, Asia and Eastern Europe as a result of its reputation for racialist domestic policies, and is also now excluded from participation in most of the *formal* proceedings of the UN itself.

THE FAILURE OF CONFERENCE NEGOTIATION

The contrast between South Africa's status at the birth of the United Nations four decades ago and its position in the Organisation today is remarkable. At the San Francisco Conference Prime Minister J. C. Smuts was considered one of the foremost world statesmen present. He had personally prepared the first draft of the Preamble of the UN Charter, and he was elected Chairman of Commission II of the Conference. He represented a country which had played a very creditable role for its size as one of the allies in the Second World War and which was one of the 51 founding members of the new organisation. South Africa thus seemed destined in 1945 to play an active role in the development of the UN and in the work of its various organs. Today, however, that unfulfilled destiny is but a dim memory. For the past decade in fact South African representatives have been excluded from the UN General Assembly, its subsidiary bodies, most related international agencies (but not the IMF) and all UN-sponsored conferences. Although South Africa remains a member and its flag flies with all the others in front of UN headquarters, it could hardly be more isolated in this international organisation, with a total membership now of 158 countries.

South Africa's problems began in the earliest days of the UN over two issues: the future of the former mandated Territory of Southwest Africa, and race policies within South Africa itself. After four decades neither issue has been resolved; instead South Africa's relations with the UN have become progressively worse. All UN organs, including the International Court, have been involved.

At first attempts were made, using the multilateral machinery of the UN to resolve these disputes *within* the Organisation by negotiations between member states, including South Africa. This was in accordance with the Charter aim in Article 1 to bring about, *inter alia*, 'the settlement of international disputes' and the 'harmonising [of] the actions of nations' to that end. But since the mid 1960s any prospect of a resolution of the disputes through multilateral diplomacy within the General Assembly and the Security Council, or through evenhanded legal proceedings in the International Court, has largely disappeared.

It is true that the negotiations of the past six years over Namibia (as Southwest Africa is now termed in the UN) between South Africa and the group of five Western states have been conducted under a broad mandate of the Security Council. But the Western group is by no means representative of the full UN membership, and the negotiations have clearly taken place *outside* the UN context, albeit with the hope of obtaining Security Council approval of the eventual agreement – if there is any agreement (which at the time of writing seems unlikely). In fact, the negotiations in this form were initiated by the United States and the other Western states precisely because there was no hope of a resolution of the Namibian issue *within* the UN. The Western group is thus in a sense trying to perform a 'third party' diplomatic role between South Africa and the UN majority. Certainly, the majority in the General Assembly does not think that the negotiations being conducted by the Western Five are likely to produce the kind of independence for Namibia which it – the majority – wants. Resolutions of the General Assembly have in fact served (perhaps intentionally) to undermine the current negotiations of the Western group. Only by using their constitutional powers in the Security Council have the major Western states managed to keep the door slightly open for a possible compromise agreement.

The only occasion in over 20 years (since an abortive mission by the UN Committee on Southwest Africa in 1962) when diplomatic methods more clearly of UN origin began at least to come to grips with an issue involving South Africa was when the Secretary-General personally intervened in negotiating attempts. In 1972–3 Dr Kurt Waldheim held talks directly and through a personal representative with the South African government over Namibia, until they were terminated by a decision of the Security Council, because no concrete results were being achieved. A similar negotiating effort over the apartheid issue had been made by Dag Hammarskjöld in the aftermath of the Sharpeville crisis at the beginning of the 1960s, and it was reported that several South African diplomats said after his death in a plane crash in September 1961 that no talks created such doubt about the policies of apartheid in Prime Minister Verwoerd's mind as those with Hammarskjöld in January 1961.[4] In 1983 the new Secretary-General, Dr Pérez de Cuéllar, became marginally involved in attempts to break the deadlock in the Western Five's negotiations over Namibia, and he held discussions in Cape Town with Prime Minister P. W. Botha in August of that year. However, in the event, these rare forays have done little more than underscore the weakness of multilateral diplomacy with the UN, since it was, after all, the failure of conference negotiation which made Secretariat intervention necessary in the first place.

There is now clearly a contest between the UN majority on the one hand and the South African government on the other, which is reflected particularly in the long list of condemnatory and punitive resolutions passed annually by the General Assembly and in South Africa's defiant disregard of them. Neither in the Assembly's resolutions, nor in South Africa's reaction to them, are there any suggestions of negotiations as a means of resolving the contest. Many of the resolutions now simply advocate sanctions under Chapter VII of the Charter to *force* South Africa to comply, although the Assembly itself is, of course, powerless to impose mandatory sanctions and, given the opposition of the major Western powers, the Security Council has only once agreed to do so, when it imposed an arms embargo in November 1977.[5]

In the case of South Africa, therefore, the United Nations has failed in its primary purpose, in terms of the Charter, of resolving these issues through diplomatic methods within the conference context, and it has long ago given up any real attempt to do so. Instead, debate and the passing of resolutions in the General Assembly and Security Council are now used simply as weapons by the majority for propaganda or 'moral pressure' against South Africa.

THE BROADER DIPLOMATIC VALUE OF THE UN TO SOUTH AFRICA

South African representatives were still playing a relatively normal role in the UN until 1960, participating fully in the meetings of the General Assembly and its committees. They participated towards the end of the 1950s in negotiations for the setting up of the United Nations Economic

Commission for Africa, and in 1959 the South African foreign minister was even elected to a vice-presidency of the General Assembly as the agreed Commonwealth candidate. South Africa's membership of the Commonwealth group, even though the group was never a cohesive voting bloc in the UN, also gave South African representatives the opportunity for contacts and the exchange of information with representatives of a variety of other states. During the annual General Assembly sessions South Africa was also represented at the meetings of the group of 16 states which had contributed to the UN force in Korea, a group which included predominantly Western, but also some other, states.

The year 1960 was, however, a turning-point for South Africa, as it was for the United Nations as a whole. In that year alone 16 new states from Africa joined the Organisation, while in South Africa there were serious racial disturbances which became associated with the name of 'Sharpeville'. From that point on the pace at which South Africa was isolated was accelerated until eventually, in September 1974, the Republic was finally denied participation in the General Assembly itself, through the rejection of its delegation's credentials. For several years before this the South African delegation had been unable to play a meaningful role in the General Assembly: statements were seldom made in debates, because they were invariably met with a walk-out of more than half the other delegates, and there was no chance of South Africa ever being invited to co-sponsor a resolution. After leaving the Commonwealth in 1961, neither was South Africa any longer a member of any group in an organisation where group politics were of primary importance.

In the process of isolating South Africa, the final step of complete expulsion from the United Nations has often been advocated. This would probably have happened, too, if it had not been that the Charter requires that the Security Council makes the final decision on expelling a member, and the United States and other Western powers had clearly indicated that they would oppose such a step on the grounds that it would be contrary to the principle of universality.

In spite of its treatment at the hands of the UN majority, the government has been determined to maintain South Africa's membership of the UN and its permanent mission in New York. For certain brief periods, it is true, the mission has been downgraded, with no ambassador permanently resident, as a sign of disapproval of UN action. This occurred in the late 1950s, when the government said it was maintaining only 'nominal representation' in New York, and for about two years at the beginning of the 1980s the ambassador commuted between Pretoria and New York. But for most of the time the mission and its staff have been maintained at reasonable strength, and at present there is a senior career ambassador in the post as permanent representative. (A more consistent expression of disapproval has been the deduction by the government of a proportion of the annual contribution to the Organisation, since the mid-1970s. This deduction has been based on a calculation of the amount spent by the UN on 'anti-South African activities'. But the bulk of the contribution is paid regularly each year, in spite of the fact that South African representatives have no say in the discussion and adoption of the UN budget.)

It is also true that South African Prime Ministers have in the past made statements threatening withdrawal from the UN, if South Africa's rights as a member were denied and if South Africa was humiliated in the Organisation. For instance, when the South African delegation's credentials were being challenged in the General Assembly in the early 1970s, Prime Minister Vorster stated that, if South Africa's rights to participate in the General Assembly were actually denied, it would have no other option than to withdraw from the UN 'for the sake of our self-respect'.[6] Although in the following year the South African delegation's rights to participate in the General Assembly were in fact denied, no action was taken by the government. In 1975 the South African foreign minister was questioned on this matter in Parliament, and he agreed that the General Assembly was making it impossible for South Africa to exercise its rights of membership and that, as the government had always said, it would not allow South Africa to be humiliated and trampled on. It would not crawl in front of the UN, he said. But he also maintained that the government standpoint was very clear: 'We want to remain in this organisation, as long as this is possible, in practice, and our future relations with the UN will therefore depend on further developments, in practice.' He refused to say any more on the question.[7]

These comments are typical of government statements on the UN: while frequently criticising the Organisation in response to widespread dissatisfaction with the UN among the white electorate, the government does not make any actual commitment to withdraw from membership, always putting off a decision to the future. In fact, in the years since 1975, there has been little serious talk of withdrawal, and the government does not seem any longer to consider it as a major issue.

There is no doubt that there is a very strong anti-UN feeling among the white electorate of all parties. No political party in the South African Parliament ever defends the UN. White public attitudes vary between those who regard it as a very dangerous place, controlled by the Communist states which use the countries of the Third World for their purposes, and those who consider it largely as an expensive joke. So there are no significant domestic pressures to retain membership; in fact, quite the contrary.[8]

In the past, as the result of this public opinion, various pressures did build up in the governing National Party favouring withdrawal. The most serious occasion was apparently 20 years ago in the early 1960s, when the South African white electorate was in an inward-looking mood. In 1963 there were reportedly intense Cabinet discussions regarding UN membership, but eventually those who opposed withdrawal, on the grounds that it would further isolate South Africa, prevailed.[9] There was no categoric decision not to withdraw, but rather an agreement to put off a decision, which has been characteristic of the government's position ever since. However, that was probably the point at which South Africa came closest to terminating its membership, and the Prime Minister himself was in favour of doing so. That was not surprising, because it was a time when the threat of effective action by the UN against South Africa seemed stronger than at any time since. The agreement not to withdraw then was a demonstration of the belief, maintained ever since, that continued membership and representation at UN headquarters in New York has some value in countering the growing trend towards international isolation.

What advantages, then, does the South African government obtain from continued representation in New York, or into what practical language does 'countering the trend towards international isolation' translate? What, in other words, makes the humiliation of the Republic's representatives at the UN and foregoing the domestic applause which would greet a defiant withdrawal worthwhile? The problem in trying to provide the answer to this question is that the government is understandably reluctant to state publicly its real reasons for maintaining UN membership and its permanent mission. Given the popular view of the UN, it is not in the government's interests to encourage public debate on the question, particularly if it should be asked to justify the expenditure involved, both for the annual UN contribution and for the costs of the office and staff in New York. Justification of this expenditure, when the government does not *appear* to be receiving any benefits from membership and is not even allowed to state its case against the attacks on it, would require a public explanation of its reasons, the most important of which are by their nature not for public consumption. They would either not be understood by the electorate as good and sufficient reasons, or they might prove embarrassing diplomatically.

Aside from the fact that the Western powers have encouraged the South African government to retain UN membership in order to avoid a weakening of the principle of universality, probably the main reason for its retention is to do with the interest which the government has in symbolic representation at the UN. Whatever the faults and inadequacies of the United Nations, and in spite of its failure to provide a forum for meaningful multilateral negotiations on political disputes, the symbolic value of membership is regarded as enormous by all states.

It soon became the rule in the postwar period that a newly independent state applied for membership of the United Nations almost as its first act of independence. Membership thus became the seal of independence and a sign of international recognition and national legitimacy. This is not only a question of recognition and legitimacy of the *state* concerned, but also of its *government*, as the disputes over the representation of several states have shown, e.g. China and, in more recent times, Cambodia. If this is an important reason for most countries to maintain an effective permanent mission at UN headquarters, it is especially so for South Africa, since the argument for rejection of its delegation's credentials in the General Assembly was that the government did not truly represent the people of the country and was therefore not the legitimate authority to issue the credentials. Suggestions have been made in the past that the government's representatives should be replaced by others considered more truly representative (i.e. the African National Congress, which is now externally based and campaigning to overthrow the government), but no formal proposal has been submitted. There is thus the danger, which is no doubt in the South African government's mind, that if it were to withdraw from the UN or even simply close down its permanent mission in New York, it might be easier for the ANC to take its place and thus achieve a greater degree of recognition, legitimacy and support than it already has. It therefore has to be recognised that this is a basic reason of national interest for clinging to membership and for maintaining representation in New York at almost any cost.

Also, as a 'listening post', any permanent mission performs a regular diplomatic function. In South Africa's case, even though the ambassador and staff cannot attend formal meetings (with the important exception of those of the Security Council when Namibia, for example, is being debated), they remain at a good vantage point to make continuous reports to Pretoria on *all* significant developments at the

UN, but especially on any matters affecting South Africa. The ability to watch closely what is happening in connection with Namibia is, of course, particularly valuable. In addition, New York is an important centre of information on many other international issues, through contacts with a wide range of diplomatic representatives and as a result of the fairly frequent visits of foreign ministers and even heads of government to the UN. Moreover, a great variety of non-governmental organisations have offices in New York providing information which may often be of use. Of special interest to the South African government are, of course, the activities of organisations such as the ANC and the South West African People's Organisation (SWAPO), as well as other related 'liberation movements'.

Another diplomatic function performed by the permanent mission in New York is the provision and dissemination of information on South Africa and its government's policies. In the first place, the mission provides the channel for government communications to the Secretary-General (which it may still, as is the right of a member, request be circulated as UN documents to all other members); this is especially important at the moment with regard to the Namibian question. The mission also issues statements to the media, which often take the place of statements which would have been made at General Assembly meetings. There is considerable interest in South African views and policies (even if not generally *approved*), and those serving in the South African mission find that their press releases are widely read. Because of this special interest in South Africa, the mission is also able to use its access to the press corps of the UN to publicise information on government policies generally, and special attention is paid to South African statements. South African representatives have noted, too, that when press conferences are occasionally called by the mission for particular purposes, they are always very well attended, compared with similar events held by other missions.

In general, as far as the media are concerned, there are indications that less and less attention is being given to the formal proceedings in the General Assembly and its committees and more to what the 'players' say and do outside. In this sense, in the view of South African representatives, South Africa is still very much a 'player' in and around the UN. Apart from the media, other missions, including many from African countries, show intense interest in information from and about South Africa, probably because many of them have very little access to such information from anywhere else.

In performing this diplomatic function of providing information, the

South African mission is able to do it more effectively in New York than in a national capital, in view of the wider audience and the special interest in South African issues at the UN. This illustrates an advantage of maintaining the mission in New York. It could be said that this is simply a product of the barrage of criticism the government faces there, which it has to try to counter by its own propaganda. In that sense South Africa is a special case, in which the government and the mission have learned to exploit the attention paid to them.

These diplomatic functions, of acting as a 'listening post' and of disseminating information, are thus performed by the South African mission in spite of its formal isolation. What about more direct bilateral diplomacy with other countries, through their representatives at the UN? Two levels are involved: one is the on-going contact with other permanent missions, and the other is contact with more high-level government representatives at particular times, such as during General Assembly sessions.

On the first level, it is the view of those who have been involved in the South African mission, including the author, that the opportunity for contact with other missions provides a very useful channel of communication with governments with which South Africa has no direct diplomatic relations, including countries which are not willing to have formal relations for political reasons. The channels can be maintained or developed socially, and used very informally for the exchange of information or passing on of messages. They may also be used more formally on particular occasions and for special purposes when, for instance, a contact in New York is viewed as most convenient at that time. (Washington and London are used for such exchanges, too, as they are centres where there is wide diplomatic representation and where South Africa has representatives.)

The bilateral contacts in New York are useful, in the first place, for explaining and discussing South African issues before the UN, but also for purposes outside the UN context. However, the problem in assessing the significance of the latter is that by their nature these bilateral diplomatic contacts are kept secret. The secrecy is all the more important in New York because of the possible embarrassment for other governments, given South Africa's 'pariah' status in the UN. But of the fact that such contacts have taken and do take place with the representatives of countries outside the range of South Africa's open and formal relations, there is no doubt. These countries include, for instance, the Soviet Union, African states and Latin American states. In some cases the matters concerned are very practical ones, with little or no controversial political content, such as the provision of information or an enquiry about a particular incident or about a citizen of the other country. But these relatively minor matters are, after all, the usual stuff of diplomatic intercourse, formal or informal, anywhere.

In other cases, however, the contacts may have been concerned with more substantial matters, such as establishing new links with states in Africa and Latin America, as well as trying to promote a dialogue with such states on political differences. For instance, there has been speculation that contacts in New York were used as a channel of communication for arranging at least one high-level South African visit to West Africa, when the government was attempting to develop a policy of 'dialogue' with other countries of Africa.

At the higher level, the few weeks at the beginning of the annual General Assembly session, when many foreign ministers attend for the General Debate, is particularly important. It is well known that this provides a time for meetings between individual foreign ministers on many issues of common interest. Until the early 1970s, the South African foreign minister attended regularly. He took the opportunity, like other ministers, to meet his colleagues from many other countries. Dr Hilgard Muller, who was foreign minister from 1963 to 1977, is known to have found these opportunities for meetings and discussions particularly useful. There has been speculation that during the period of South Africa's so-called 'outward' foreign policy in the late 1960s, when the foreign minister paid special attention, for instance, to expanding South Africa's links with countries of Latin America, he used his visits to New York annually to meet with foreign ministers from those countries.

This level of contact is not as significant now, although the foreign minister still visits New York from time to time, mainly for negotiations on the Namibian issue. It should be noted in this regard that these negotiations are not conducted strictly within the UN, except occasionally with the Secretary-General, but rather with representatives of the Western Five in their 'third party' role. But these visits do give him the opportunity of discussion also with other representatives as a means of attempting to influence the policies of their governments in favour of South Africa.

There have been no suggestions that there have ever been any secret meetings between official South African representatives and representatives of SWAPO itself over the Namibian issue. Instead the Western

Five have negotiated separately with each side, sometimes including the African 'frontline' states, together with SWAPO. The nearest to direct negotiations were the 'proximity talks' arranged by the Western Five in February 1978, with both South African and SWAPO representatives in New York at the same time and with the Western foreign ministers acting as intermediaries between them. The former US Secretary of State, Cyrus Vance, has described these negotiations, which were aborted when the South African foreign minister withdrew.[10] It is clear that New York was the most convenient venue for these 'proximity talks', because all the parties were represented, even though the negotiations did not reach a successful conclusion. In other words, the venue had nothing to do with their failure.

The question, however, still remains as to whether the South African government is able to engage in meaningful bilateral negotiations in New York on issues directly concerning it, namely Namibia and South African internal political developments. As a centre for such negotiations, New York does have limitations, compared with, say, Washington or London, because of the highly charged atmosphere and the sensitivity of these issues in the UN context. Other African permanent representatives, for example, are bound to be reluctant to have discussions with South African officials, and even more reluctant to be seen publicly to be having such contacts. This would be interpreted as undermining the joint African policy of excluding South Africa from the United Nations. There is, of course, also sensitivity from the South African side, because of the hardline domestic political attitude towards these states and what is seen as their support for subversive movements in South Africa and Namibia. These problems apply less when there is 'third party' involvement by the Western Five, as there has been over the past six or seven years, or occasionally by the Secretary-General. Unfortunately, even in the cases of 'third party' diplomacy on South African issues, it is still impossible to refer to the successful conclusion of any negotiations.

Nevertheless, in spite of the limitations and the lack of success on these major issues, there is no doubt that representation on a permanent basis in New York is seen by the South African government to have practical advantages for the pursuance of its diplomatic activities. Experience over the years has shown that the contact that its representatives have had with the representatives of other countries in all geographical groupings have proved to be very useful. They are channels for bilateral diplomacy, which are available to be used when the need arises and when they are considered to be appropriate.

NOTES AND REFERENCES

1. Sir Ernest Satow, *A Guide to Diplomatic Practice*, 4th edn (New York: Longman's, 1957) p. 1.
2. Sir Harold Nicolson, *Diplomacy*, 3rd edn (New York: Oxford University Press, 1964) p. 4.
3. Hans, J. Morgenthau, *Politics Among Nations*, 5th edn (New York: Alfred A. Knopf, 1973) pp. 522–3.
4. Mark W. Zacher, *Dag Hammarskjöld's United Nations* (New York and London: Columbia University Press, 1970) p. 107; referring to an interview with Andrew W. Cordier of the UN Secretariat.
5. The Security Council's previous arms embargo resolutions in 1963 and 1964, although widely observed, were not mandatory in terms of the Charter.
6. *The Times* (London), 6 October 1973.
7. South Africa (Republic), *House of Assembly Debates*, no. 11, 25 April 1975, columns 4811 and 4812.
8. It can be assumed that voteless *black* South African opinion would be largely indifferent to a decision by the government to end UN membership. There are no indications that any significant segment of black political opinion any longer entertains expectations that the UN can bring any meaningful influence to bear on the government, through South African membership, to change its policies.
9. See B. M. Schoeman, *Van Malan tot Verwoerd* (Cape Town: Human and Rousseau, 1973) pp. 234–44.
10. Cyrus Vance, *Hard Choices: Critical Years in America's Foreign Policy* (New York: Simon & Schuster, 1983) pp. 302–3.

13 The United Nations and Israel

BERNARD REICH
and ROSEMARY HOLLAND

The relationship between the United Nations and Israel has undergone substantial change since the 1940s. Israel was a product of the United Nations, and yet a growing portion of the membership of that Organisation continues to question the very legitimacy of the state. Initially Israel ardently sought United Nations membership but by the 1980s few Israelis saw value in the Organisation. The evolution of the Organisation's relationship with Israel illustrates not only the changing nature of the United Nations but also the altered roles that it can play in Israeli foreign policy. It is our purpose here to consider the altered nature of the relationship and to provide some assessment of the factors underlying this change.

ORIGINS AND EVOLUTION

The United Nations played a major role in the creation of the modern state of Israel. When the British announced the decision, in the spring of 1947, to relinquish the Mandate, the United Nations established the Special Committee on Palestine (UNSCOP) in April 1947 to examine the issue and report its suggestions. Its majority proposed the partition of Palestine into independent Arab and Jewish states and a separate status for Jerusalem under United Nations auspices. The partition plan was adopted by the required two-thirds of the General Assembly on 29 November 1947.

The British withdrew from Palestine as scheduled in mid-May 1948, Israel declared its independence, and the Arab League launched its invasion of Palestine. The United Nations was unable to ensure implementation of its partition resolution or to prevent the first Arab–Israeli War. Ultimately the UN was instrumental in securing the armistice agreements between Israel and the four contiguous Arab states in the spring of 1949.

STAGES IN THE CHANGING RELATIONSHIP

In the initial two decades Israel saw the United Nations primarily in a benign or even positive light.[1] Israel was not the target of overwhelming special antagonism on the part of the Organisation or its membership. The United Nations continued to deal, albeit at a low level of interest and concern, with various aspects of the Arab–Israeli conflict (including making provisions for the refugees and establishing the UNEF in Sinai after the 1956 Suez War) but did not focus its attention on the problem to the same extent as in later years.

The June War of 1967 was a major watershed in the relationship. It marked the inauguration of a new period in which the United Nations helped to establish the diplomatic parameters for future efforts to resolve the Arab–Israeli conflict and increasingly it became a forum for anti-Israeli rhetoric, resolutions and actions.

The change in perspective began to develop during April and May 1967, as the events leading to the war were unfolding, and the United Nations was not seen, in Israel, as an effective barrier to conflict. This view was the result of various actions, although the decision, on 19 May, to withdraw UNEF from the Israel–Egypt frontier, at Egypt's request, and the manning of its positions by contingents of the Palestine Liberation Army and Egypt's armed forces, was seen as particularly crucial. Abba Eban has described Israel's mood and reaction in these terms:

> While Israel steadied itself for the assault . . . the United Nations Security Council, in ignominious silence, heard the Egyptian representative announce 'an overt state of war' with Israel. It did and said nothing. It thus kindled the greenest of green lights before the exultant aggressor. Israel would not soon forget the abdication of the United Nations from its duty to defend her Charter rights.[2]

Effectively the United Nations was precluded from acting and the conflict was not prevented. The United Nations was not seen as an effective organisation for the prevention of war in the Arab–Israeli sector, by Israel and others.[3]

Security Council Resolution 242 of 22 November 1967 was the major achievement in the immediate aftermath of the 1967 war and has since become the central resolution concerning the peace process. It is significant for Israel in that it calls for an end to hostilities and seeks to ensure, *inter alia*, Israel's peace and security. Its central theme, concurred in by Israel, is the trade of peace for territory. The subsidiary clauses also comported well with Israel's position. Although Israel had some minor concerns with Resolution 242, it was not, on the whole, problematic from the Israeli perspective, in that its overriding objective was the termination of hostilities and the establishment of peace between a secure and recognised Israel and its Arab neighbours. In addition, the general tenor of debate in the General Assembly and the Security Council during the summer and autumn of 1967 was not inimical to Israel's interests and was accompanied by votes favourable to Israel when the Soviet Union and the Arab states sought to place blame on it for the war and sought to obtain reparations for Arab losses, to no avail.[4]

The 1967 war had an additional effect on the UN–Israel relationship as a consequence of the changes resulting from the war. The increased numbers of Arab refugees and the issues resulting from Israel's military occupation of substantial territory, including the eastern sector of Jerusalem, with its attendant control of a considerable population, provided increased opportunities for questioning and condemning Israel's policies and actions. Existing UN bodies, and others newly created for the purpose, focused on various aspects of Israel's policy, thus presenting an expanded opportunity for the Arab states (and, later, the PLO) to raise questions about, and secure condemnations of, Israel. The failure of the Arab armies and their Soviet patrons to secure Israel's battlefield defeat during the 1967 war generated an increased interest in securing a political victory over Israel in the ensuing period by utilising UN forums to secure anti-Israeli resolutions.

General Assembly consideration of the problem of refugees also underwent an important shift of emphasis. The terminology emphasised the rights of the Palestinian people as opposed to the rights of refugees. In the Security Council, meanwhile, attention was focused on the wider Arab–Israeli conflict in the framework of Resolution 242, and the narrower question of Palestinian rights was not there addressed.

The role of the United Nations in the Arab–Israeli peace process and the consequent relationship with Israel took significantly varied forms between the 1967 and 1973 wars. In the earlier years there was a prominent public role for the Jarring Mission, despite its ultimate failure to achieve any significant breakthrough.[5] Immediately preceding the 1973 war the United Nations role was virtually non-existent. Ultimately the Arab states and Israel clashed in combat once again due to the failure of the several peace efforts, including the limited ones of the United Nations. The United Nations could not prevent war between Israel and the Arabs in 1973. With the outbreak of hostilities it was paralysed, until the super powers reached accord and were able to secure the resolutions necessary to halt the conflict.

The Security Council adopted Resolution 338 which, for the first time in the history of the Arab–Israeli conflict, required the parties to engage in negotiations to resolve it. Resolution 338 also called for implementation of Resolution 242, thus reconfirming its centrality in the peace process. Although the initial postwar peace efforts were primarily those of the United States, and particularly of Secretary of State Henry Kissinger, the United Nations was significant in providing the forces needed to ensure implementation of the disengagement agreements Kissinger helped to negotiate in January and May 1974. The new United Nations Emergency Force (UNEF) in Sinai and the United Nations Disengagement Observer Force (UNDOF) in the Golan Heights proved important to securing the agreements worked out between Israel, on the one hand, and Egypt and Syria on the other. The United Nations thus served an important role for Israel and its presence was welcomed in that it supported Israeli policy.

The 1973 war also modified the general environment in which the United Nations had to function. Unlike 1967, the 1973 war worked more to the advantage of the Arab states. They, particularly Egypt and Syria, were able to relieve the humiliation associated with the 1967 conflict and they became more confident of their positions. They also appeared to understand that, despite their improved performance, they were unable to dislodge Israel from the occupied territories and thus, increasingly, they sought to take advantage of the opportunities provided within the diplomatic–political framework of the international community. At the same time, the relative power of the Arab states within the international community, and the United Nations in particular, was enhanced with the considerable increase in oil prices, generating substantial petrodollar revenues, and with the creation of a presumed 'oil weapon'. There was also an erosion of Israel's carefully established relations with African and other Third World states which increased its isolation in the international community and affected the extent of support it could secure in the United Nations and other international bodies.

The period after the 1973 war witnessed an intensification in the efforts by the Arab states to focus international attention on Israel and to secure anti-Israel resolutions in the various organs of the United Nations and in related bodies of the UN system, as well as in other international organisations and forums. These efforts took numerous forms and were successful in achieving a large number of anti-Israel resolutions and some anti-Israel actions.

As a prelude to subsequent developments in the General Assembly, the Conference of Arab Heads of State and Government at Rabat, in October 1974, endorsed the right of the Palestinian people to self-determination and to return to its homeland, and recognised the Palestine Liberation Organisation as the sole legitimate representative of the Palestinian people. Given that the Palestine National Covenant viewed Israel as an illegal entity and the PLO sought the destruction of Israel, the position of Israel had been and remained that it could not recognise or negotiate with the organisation. Developments in the General Assembly challenged the Israeli position. In September 1974 the 'Palestine Question' appeared as a separate item on the Assembly's agenda for the first time since 1952. In the same year the PLO was accorded observer status in the General Assembly and in other UN–sponsored conferences. A year later it was invited to participate in all UN discussions of the Middle East 'on an equal footing with other parties'.

The process by which member states are nominated for inclusion in the various specialised councils and commissions of the UN has become tied to the bloc system, which increasingly permeates every facet of the Organisation's work. Since Israel belongs to no bloc or group of nations, it has become practically impossible for Israel to be nominated for membership in the major UN organs: the Security Council, the Economic and Social Council and the Trusteeship Council.

In the case of the Economic Commission of Western Asia, (ECWA), which was established in August 1973, Israel lies in the same geographic location as the member states of this body, and is obliged to contribute to its budget, but is excluded from participation in its proceedings. Not only is this questionable on legal grounds, since article 1, paragraph 3 of the Charter calls for international cooperation in economic, social, cultural and humanitarian matters 'without distinction as to race, sex, language, or religion', it is contrary to Israel's interests. On 9 May 1975, according to Resolution 12 (II), the ECWA accorded the PLO observer status and invited it to participate in and avail itself of the Commission's services. At its third session, in May 1976, the ECWA launched two projects in cooperation with the PLO.

This illustrates Israel's dilemma. Israel's right to participate in the various United Nations organisations is compromised either by procedural arrangements or deliberate efforts to exclude her and decisions are made in these bodies which affect Israel and which apparently favour the Arabs, or more specifically the PLO. Other examples of this situation abound.

In November 1975 the Arab-sponsored campaign to discredit Israel and question its legitimacy reached a new level with the adoption by the General Assembly of a resolution equating the Jewish national movement – Zionism – with racism. The object was to equate Zionism with whatever qualities were deemed to be the most reprehensible in the prevailing atmosphere and jargon of the world community. Racism, as manifested in the apartheid regime of South Africa, constituted a rallying cry for opposition among the African member states of the General Assembly.

To equate Zionism with racism was thus to bring it into disrepute with states not directly involved in the problems of the Middle East. This served the purposes of both the Arab states and the Soviet Union in the politics of the United Nations. The resolution equating Zionism with racism was the culmination of a process which was begun much earlier and which included 1972 and 1973 resolutions on terrorism and apartheid.

The process surfaced as a specific campaign at the World Conference of the International Women's Year held in Mexico City in late June and early July 1975. The 'Declaration on the Equality of Women' issued by the conference makes repeated reference to the part played by women in the struggle against neo-colonialism, foreign occupation, Zionism, racism, racial discrimination and apartheid. The following October the Third Committee of the General Assembly of the United Nations voted by a substantial majority that Zionism was a form of racism, and called upon the General Assembly to follow suit. Resolution 3379 (XXX) on the 'Elimination of all forms of racial discrimination', which determined that 'Zionism is a form of racism and racial discrimination', was approved by a large majority despite many abstentions. Subsequently, this resolution has been made the basis for a series of further condemnations in different agencies and at various meetings of the United Nations. The Programme of Action for the Second Half of the United Nations Decade for Women, held in Copenhagen in 1980, endorsed the 'Zionism is racism' resolution of 1975 and urged the United Nations to 'provide assistance in consultation and co-operation with the PLO, the representatives of the Palestinian people'.

The votes in favour of the resolution did not represent a united or equally committed opposition to Israel, *per se*. The majority, having no direct stake in the Arab–Israeli conflict, were either beguiled by slogans or influenced by specific material needs to support the resolution's sponsors.[6] The sponsorship was a combined effort of the Arab states and their associates, pursuing an anti-Israeli policy, and the Soviet bloc, pursuing its general effort against the West, its institutions and its friends. The motivation for the Arab sponsors was in keeping with their consistent position on Israel, that is to question Israel's right to exist. The objective in linking Zionism with racism was to delegitimise the state of Israel. The condemnation of Israel's ideological basis, for whatever reason, was seen as an important step towards expelling Israel from participation in various international bodies, such as UNESCO, and ultimately from the UN itself.

The effort to register a link between Zionism and racism did not end in 1975. By reiterating this association in statements and resolutions since 1975, the anti-Israeli forces in the United Nations have sought to keep alive the stigma. It has become rather commonplace for the UN to adopt unbalanced resolutions condemning Israel without compensatory language voicing concerns about Arab actions. In late 1979 the General Assembly adopted a resolution proclaiming 'The Inadmissability of the Policy of Hegemonism in International Relations'. Included in the wording of this resolution was a condemnation of 'racism including zionism'. The document was adopted by a vote of 111 to 4 (Australia, Canada, Israel and the United States), with 26 abstentions, mostly Western European countries. In addition to this explicit mention of the 'Zionism is racism' dictum, about a dozen resolutions between 1975 and 1980 referred back approvingly, if indirectly, to the 1975 formulation. Almost every UN conference or Third World gathering expressed the idea that Zionism is racism or Israel is racist.

Meanwhile, attempts were made to exclude Israel from participating in the General Assembly of the United Nations[7] and related international organisations. A motion brought before the International Atomic Energy Agency on the last day of its meeting in 1982 rejected the credentials presented by Israel, and Israel was thereby unable to participate. An attempt to exclude Israel from participating in the activities of the International Telecommunication Union failed primarily because the United States delegation made it clear that if such a measure succeeded, the United States would withdraw from the conference, withhold its contributions and evaluate its future membership. The motion was defeated.

Membership in the United Nations is the concern of the Security Council, where the United States would be expected to use its veto if ever Israel's membership were questioned there. It does, however, lie within the power of the General Assembly to move to reject the credentials of any one member when they are presented before the opening session. If rejected, the member in question would not be allowed to participate in the session. An attempt to question the validity of Israel's credentials was made unsuccessfully, in the General Assembly, at Iran's instigation, on 24 October 1982. The vote against considering the challenge was 75 to 9 with 31 abstentions. The only country to have its credentials rejected by the Assembly (in a move declared illegal by the UN Legal Counsel on 11 November 1970 [A/8160]) is South Africa. Not even South Africa was accused of the crimes attributed to Israel, however. The proposal to reject Israel's credentials was based on charges embodied in two Assembly resolutions, of 5 February 1982 and 28 April 1982, that Israel is a 'non-peace-loving state', and thus does not meet the membership requirement. The Iranian action sought to bring into question the legitimacy of Israel's membership in the Organisation, beyond simply excluding Israel from participation in the forthcoming session.

In the autumn of 1983 an attempt was made by Iran and Libya to unseat Israel's delegation to the General Assembly. The motion was not voted on directly. Rather, following the procedure devised in 1982, the Assembly voted 79 to 43, with 19 abstentions to take no action on the challenge to Israel. Israel's ambassador to the United Nations, Yehuda Z. Blum, noted: 'The assault in the United Nations by the forces of bigotry, irrationality, international gangsterism and international lawlessness has once again been turned back.'[8]

Cumulatively, the various tactics adopted by Israel's opponents in the UN represent a continuing effort to associate Israel with both racism and bellicosity, both of which are qualities reserved for special condemnation by the membership in general. By inference, the continuing effort has been to question repeatedly and publicly the legitimacy of the state of Israel.

CURRENT PERSPECTIVE

Israel's view of the United Nations has changed dramatically since the independence of the state. At the outset Israel saw the UN as a positive force important to its future and well-being and sought to associate itself with that Organisation through membership. Although some of the initially perceived benefits remain valuable and the Organisation might display occasional positive virtues, Israel now regards the Organisation as essentially inimical to its interests.

Israel sought membership in the United Nations for a number of reasons. Key among its perceptions was the belief that such membership would help to demonstrate the legitimacy of the state, as it would be tantamount to world recognition. Moshe Sharett, Israel's first foreign minister and later its Prime Minister, told the Knesset on 15 June 1949:

> By our admission to the United Nations, the highest seal has been placed on our international recognition, even though that recognition is not yet universal. This was more than a major political occurrence: it was a deeply moving human event. It brought Israel back into the community of nations. It conferred upon the Jewish people regathered in their ancient land equal rights with all free nations. It closed the dark chapter of persecution, degradation and discrimination. It seemed difficult to gauge the full import of that revolutionary change. Those who represented Israel on that unique occasion were very far from any sense of complacency . . . By the decision of the General Assembly the status of our delegation was completely transformed. From a group demanding help it became an official body whose support was solicited by others. Thus we entered the ring of international contest and mutual dependence. A new and complex responsibility devolved upon us.[9]

Several other considerations prompted the quest for membership. Admission would lead to almost automatic membership in related specialised agencies, with access to the services they provide as well as participation in their decision-making. Accordingly, by December 1949, Israel had been admitted to the ILO, the FAO, UNESCO, the International Civil Aviation Organisation, the World Health Organisation, the Universal Postal Union, the International Telecommunication Union, and had ratified the Convention of the World Meteorological Organisation. Later Israel joined the International Maritime Consultative Organisation, the IMF, the World Bank, and the International Atomic Energy Agency, among others.

By bringing Israel within the collective security arrangements contained in the Charter, membership would generally strengthen Israel's own security arrangements and prospects. Abba Eban argued: 'The time had come for the United Nations, if it wished Israel to bear the heavy burden of Charter obligations, to confer upon Israel the protection and status of the Charter.'[10] The belief that membership in the United Nations would facilitate and hasten the country's integration in the Middle East through the instrumentality of the Organisation was also part of the Israeli rationale. Abba Eban remarked that until the scars of conflict were healed and Israel became integrated with its immediate world, 'the UN might be the only forum in which it could sit as a colleague and partner of its neighbouring states in the transacting of international business and in the paths of social and economic co-operation'.[11] Israel's admission, being 'fully consistent with UN policy in Palestine', would 'contribute to the stabilization of the Middle East and to the cause of international peace'.[12] There was also a conviction that Israel's membership would accelerate the solution of outstanding political–social problems – including the major problems of Israel–Arab relations, Jerusalem and the Arab refugees.

Admission would be consistent with the country's own ideals, since the aims of Israel and those of the UN Charter coincided. Eban noted: 'Israel was bound to the UN and its Charter by many links of peculiar intimacy and strength. The doctrines of the Charter founded on the hopes of international brotherhood had been bequeathed to modern civilization by Israel's prophetic writings . . . '[13] This perspective continues to prevail. Thus, Israel sees a philosophical/ideological linkage to the United Nations even now. Ambassador Blum has described it in these terms:

the philosophy underlying the United Nations Charter is basically the philosophy of the Jewish prophets. It is universal peace, social justice, equality of man, the dignity of the human being – all concepts that were first proclaimed in Jerusalem some 3,000 years ago. And these are concepts the Jewish people have been standing for during these three millennia. I hope the philosophy of the UN will be *respected* by the UN – and, if so, that the UN does indeed have a future.[14]

Israel thus identified many reasons for joining, and remaining associated with, the UN system.

The alterations in Israel's viewpoint concerning the United Nations resulted from its status in, and treatment by, that body over an extended period. The United Nations has altered its approach to Israel as a result of various factors, including changes in the body itself and in the international environment in which it operates.

The United Nations has changed dramatically since the early years. It is no longer a small club of essentially like-minded European and American states subscribing to a similar conception of the world and of such concepts as justice and morality. The membership has grown more than threefold and the orientation of its majority is quite different from that of its founders some four decades ago. It is a body more oriented towards Third World concerns and practical issues than towards those matters which motivate the powers and some of the other Western-oriented states, such as Israel. The United States (and, to a lesser extent, the Soviet Union) can no longer mobilise an automatic majority in support of its positions and faces increasingly strident opposition to many of its views.

The Arab states have increased not only their membership in the various bodies of the UN system, they have increased their power through a growth in the significance of oil and associated products. Petrodollar power has enhanced the political importance of the Arab world. The UN now counts Arabic as one of its six major languages and Arab states are routinely represented in the significant elected bodies of the UN system. Their ability to mobilise votes on issues of direct concern to them can be very impressive. The cohesiveness of the Arab position on matters concerning Israel has been a result of strong ideological discipline on this issue. The Third World has similarly shown a remarkable consistency on this and similar matters. Deviation from the 'norm' position adopted within the Arab, Islamic or Third World caucuses on matters concerning Israel is increasingly rare. Many of the Third World states have little direct knowledge of, and no basis for understanding, the Israeli position and perspective in ways that are common within the Western world. At the same time the Third World can identify, and sympathise with, the Arab viewpoint of the Arab–Israeli conflict and Israel.

The Arab states apparently have learned to improve their use of international bodies for their own political and diplomatic purposes. They seem to believe there is a utility in amassing UN resolutions condemning Israel, and have learned to secure the votes needed to achieve them. The Arab states seem to be interested in securing, and publicising, substantial numbers of UN resolutions condemning Israel for various actions and inactions. This appears to be part of an effort to build a case that Israel is not a legitimate entity and defies the collective will of the international community as expressed by the United Nations and its various associated bodies and organisations. This could be used to provide a base for actions to be taken to unseat Israel in the United

Nations and related organisations.[15] They seem to understand the political leverage that derives from increased numbers, from the increased dependence of much of the modern world on oil, and from the power associated with wealth.

The result of much of the change in the United Nations is a situation whereby its actions often make little overt sense and tend to contradict many of the very goals it claims to seek. This is particularly evident in the case of Israel and the Arab–Israeli conflict. United States Ambassador Jeane Kirkpatrick has provided the following example:

> it is a good example of how common sense can be confounded, and confounded overwhelmingly. At issue was a resolution which called on the Security Council to take steps to establish an independent Palestinian state in the Israeli occupied territories, to create it by fiat and impose it on Israel. Now of course such an action would cut directly across the major Security Council resolutions on the Middle East, 242 and 338, and everyone knew that the Security Council was never going to do this. Equally, everyone knew that such a resolution was quite worthless in terms of advancing the settlement on any of the outstanding Middle East issues. In fact, the resolution was as good an example as one could find of UN action which exacerbates differences rather than settling them. Nevertheless, 113 states voted for the resolution and only two, Canada and Costa Rica, joined the United States and Israel in voting against it.[16]

Straightforward procedural developments have contributed to the change in the environment for Israel in the United Nations. The practice of bloc voting is perhaps the most pertinent. Many countries are pledged to support the policies of the blocs to which they belong. Such a system encourages 'deals' between blocs, and curious coalitions. Israel belongs to no bloc or voting group. From the perspective of Jeane Kirkpatrick: 'the waters at the U.N. are not only muddied but churned up by the participation of parties that have no direct interest in settling the Arab–Israeli conflict and, in many instances, are committed precisely to its perpetuation and intensification'.[17]

Facilitating the Arab effort to mount an anti-Israeli campaign is the image of Israel as a Western-imperialist element in the Middle East rather than an advanced member of the developing world. Israel is increasingly seen as a militaristic state serving the interests of Western colonialism rather than as a member of the developing Third World. Thus, while the Arabs are seen as a part of the anti-imperialistic Third

World, Israel is identified as a unit of the opposition to Third World development.

At the same time there is a growing uninterest in coming to the support of Israel on the part of Western European member states. Reflecting this trend, an analysis of the pattern of voting of the European bloc in 1982 regarding the Middle East indicates that they have been in agreement with the Arab nations 65 per cent of the time, and with Israel 13 per cent of the time.[18]

Israel's Ambassador, Yehuda Z. Blum, in an address to the United Nations on 3 October 1983 noted that the UN had been 'hijacked' by anti-Israeli countries and that instead of promoting peace in the Middle East had become an arena of 'violent rhetoric which has fanned the flames of [the] Arab–Israel conflict'.[19] This seems to summarise the Israeli view of the Organisation in late 1983.

Clearly, Israel regards the UN as an organisation with numerous faults, not the least of which is a substantial and automatic majority anxious to promote anti-Israeli positions. There is, as Israel has characterised it, an 'unrestrained tyranny of an artificial majority' which controls the United Nations through its votes and which can guarantee an automatic majority for any resolution or idea no matter how absurd it may be. Despite this strongly negative perception, Israel remains in the UN and its constituent agencies and bodies. Israel's attitude has been given succinct summary by Abba Eban:

> There is no more disadvantageous arena for Israel than a General Assembly of which twenty member states are Arab, another dozen are Communist and a further twenty are committed by Moslem solidarity to the Arab cause. But I had no reason to renounce whatever opportunity existed for expounding our policies and interests to friendly ears.[20]

Clearly, there is a perception of some value to Israel's continued membership and participation.

The United Nations has served a useful purpose in creating and deploying observer and peace-keeping forces to the region. Units such as UNTSO, UNEF, UNIFIL and UNDOF have served the purpose of separating combatants and of being an observer of developments in the region. For Israel this has been a positive factor, providing support for its position and security without direct involvement of Israeli forces. However, the forces are not fully reliable and Israel sees them as often biased in favour of its opponent. Thus Israel has, at times, insisted on multinational, but not United Nations, peace-keepers and/or observers such as in Sinai after the peace treaty with Egypt and in Lebanon after the PLO evacuation from Beirut in 1982. They are therefore of mixed utility. Other UN bodies associated with various aspects of the Arab–Israel conflict, such as UNRWA, are similarly seen as having mixed value – often removing the onus from Israel for certain actions but also of dubious impartiality and frequently seen as aiding Israel's opponents.

Some Israelis have suggested an alternative to the United Nations as probably of greater value to Israel. Thus, for example, in February 1982, then Foreign Minister Yitzhak Shamir suggested that democratic countries should react to the 'decline' of the UN by forming a 'new organization' designed to protect democracy and freedom throughout the world. He told a press conference that the UN with its automatic majority had become a 'tool in the fight against the democratic world, especially against the state of Israel'. He noted that the truly democratic countries numbered only about 30 out of more than 150 members of the UN and 'therefore we believe the time has come for the democratic countries to organize themselves to protect democracy and liberty throughout the world'.[21] He was to clarify later that Israel had no intention of withdrawing from the UN.

Israel's attitude towards the UN is ambivalent – it questions the utility of the Organisation but shows no inclination to withdraw from it. On the contrary, Israel (and the United States) has gone to significant lengths to prevent its ouster from the UN or any of the constituent organisations of the UN system.

Israel's continued membership in the United Nations seems predicated on the notion that not to belong to an essentially universal organisation would jeopardise Israel's standing in the international system and might lead to questions concerning its legitimacy. There is a psychological dimension in Israel's refusal to allow itself to be 'hounded out' by Arab and Third World efforts. It refuses to allow questions concerning its legitimacy to be given some credence by capitulating to this type of coercion.

Israel's presence in the UN has become a matter of considerable importance in the Israel–United States bilateral relationship. The United States has firmly stated its position that Israel's presence in the United Nations is essential if that organisation is to play a role in the international system. Many of the reasons for the American position comport with Israel's, thus confirming further the continued utility of Israeli participation in the UN system.

On a number of occasions in the past few years the United States has reiterated firmly its position in an effort to affect the outcome of United Nations votes, and has been generally successful. Secretary of State George P. Shultz issued a statement on 16 October 1982:

> The exclusion of Israel from the General Assembly or the International Telecommunication Union in these circumstances would be contrary to the principles of the United Nations. In the case of the General Assembly, it would be a clear-cut violation of the United Nations Charter. Such action defeats the very purpose of the United Nations – to resolve disputes among nations – by creating further conflict and division. It would do grave damage to the entire United Nations system and it would hurt us all.
>
> The exclusion of Israel from United Nations bodies would also be a serious setback for progress toward peace in the Middle East, to which the United States and virtually all members of the United Nations are committed . . .
>
> The United States has always made clear that any attack on Israel's right to participate in any United Nations organization, if successful, would have grave consequences for our own continued participation and support . . .
>
> If Israel were excluded from the General Assembly, the United States would withdraw from participation in the Assembly and would withhold payments to the United Nations, until Israel's right to participate is restored.

The statement of Secretary Shultz, and similar pronouncements by other Reagan administration spokesmen, has been given additional weight by Congress. The Department of State Authorizations Bill for fiscal year 1984, section 115, provides:

> If Israel is illegally expelled, suspended, denied its credentials, or in any other manner denied its right to participate in the General Assembly of the United Nations or any specialized agency of the United Nations, the United States shall suspend its participation in the General Assembly or such specialized agency until the illegal action is reversed. The United States shall withhold payment of its assessed contribution to the United Nations or a specialized agency during any period in which United States participation is suspended pursuant to this section.

The general and somewhat abstract perspective of the value of Israeli participation in the United Nations suggested by Israeli statements is given additional support by specific and concrete advantages of membership.

Israel benefits by its very presence at the heart of the diplomatic world where bargains are struck which may well be to its disadvantage. Israel's participation at the United Nations allows it access to information and permits a more accurate assessment of its international position. Its presence at the UN permits contacts with individuals and nations which might otherwise be impossible due to a lack of diplomatic or political contacts elsewhere. Thus, Israel benefits from access to members of the Arab, Soviet and Muslim worlds which otherwise would be difficult if not impossible to arrange. Israel's Ambassador to the United Nations, Yehuda Z. Blum, has commented: 'This [i.e. the United Nations] is a place where we can meet conveniently. In fact Israel has quite a number of relations here with representatives of countries with which we do not have diplomatic relations.'[22] For example, in 1981 Israeli Foreign Minister Yitzhak Shamir met with Soviet Foreign Minister Andrei A. Gromyko for the first high-level government-to-government contact between the two countries in some five years. Israel's resumption of relations with Zaire and Liberia were initiated through earlier contacts at the United Nations.

Thus, despite the disadvantages and problems associated with United Nations membership, Israel has apparently concluded that non-participation would have greater disabilities and that there are benefits, general and specific, overt and covert, to be derived from involvement in the UN system. Then Foreign Minister Yigal Allon summarised the Israeli perspective in a speech to the Knesset on 23 July 1975 in these terms:

We have experienced a lengthy chain of disappointments from the UN, whether as an instrument for preserving peace in the region, or as the international organization meant to give expression to new criteria of relations marked by peace, respect and mutual cooperation among its members. Nonetheless, we have not despaired of the United Nations, which, as it stands, still constitutes the sole political framework for all the nations of the world. We cooperated . . . in the constructive operations carried out by various bodies in the economic, social and cultural spheres, and the provision of aid to developing countries.

The patterns established thus far seem unlikely to be substantially

altered barring a dramatic change in the nature of the Arab–Israeli
conflict. The relative strengths of Israel and of those opposing it in the
United Nations seem unlikely to undergo significant modification in the
near term. Minor alterations in the positions of some states, and,
therefore, in the positions of the Organisation, might occur.[23] But it is
unlikely that this will represent an overwhelming trend that would
substantially alter the nature of the current relationship between Israel
and the United Nations.

NOTES AND REFERENCES

1. Despite the positive role played by the Organisation in the creation of Israel
   and the importance ascribed by Israel's leaders to United Nations
   membership, there were those in Israel who, from the outset, sounded a note
   of scepticism and caution. Some foresaw disadvantages in having to take a
   public stand on issues which held no immediate concern for Israel, but
   which were contentious between East and West. This was the case during the
   Korean War. Also, there were those who saw in the investigation, to which
   Israel's application for United Nations membership was subjected, indications of a deliberate effort led by the Arab members, and acquiesced in by
   others, to put Israel under a unique form of scrutiny. Thus, a study group set
   up by the Hebrew University of Jerusalem commented, as early as 1954:

   Where the position is unique – is that, in consequence of the avowed
   hostility of the Arab states and their determination to keep Israel isolated
   within and outside the United Nations, the form in which the Palestine
   question has come to be discussed touches directly upon Israel's very right
   to existence . . . This state of affairs, in which Israel has been thrown on the
   defensive, has led to inevitable reaction on the part of Israeli opinion and as
   a cause for dismay and exasperation with the United Nations it must not be
   underestimated.

   Israel and the United Nations, Report of a Study Group set up by the
   Hebrew University of Jerusalem (New York: Manhattan Publishing
   Company, 1956) p. 61.
2. Abba Eban, *My People: The Story of the Jews* (New York: Behrman House,
   Random House, 1968) p. 504.
3. For further details see B. Reich, *Background of the June War* (McLean,
   Virginia: Research Analysis Corporation, May 1968).
4. For further elaboration see B. Reich, *Quest For Peace: United States–Israel
   Relations and the Arab–Israeli Conflict* (New Brunswick, NJ: Transaction
   Books, 1977) especially pp. 83–90.
5. See Bernard Reich, 'The Jarring Mission and the Search for Peace in the
   Middle East,' *Wiener Library Bulletin*, 26 (1972) 13–20.
6. See Bernard Lewis, 'The Anti–Zionist Resolution', *Foreign Affairs*, 55
   (October 1976) 55–64 especially p. 64.

7. Israel dominates the UN agenda and the proliferation of resolutions critical of Israel continues unabated. Of the Security Council's 88 sessions in 1982, 46 were on a topic related to or concerning Israel. In the General Assembly and its seven main committees, debates on the Middle East consumed over one-third of the delegates' time and led to 44 resolutions (compared with more than 80 resolutions between 1973 and 1978 considered by Israel to be 'anti-Israeli').

8. Quoted in *New York Times*, 21 October 1983.

9. *Divrei Haknesset, 1949*, vol. 1, pp. 717–18. Quoted in *Israel and the United Nations*. p. 50.

10. GAOR, 3rd Session, Ad Hoc Political Committee, 5 May 1949, p. 247.

11. Quoted in *Israel and the United Nations*, p. 52.

12. Ibid.

13. Quoted in *Israel and the United Nations*, p. 53.

14. Gertrude Samuels, 'In a Time of Change: A Talk with Israel's New UN Ambassador', *New Leader*, 18 December 1978, p. 9.

15. On this general theme see: Fayez A. Sayegh, *The Record of Israel at the United Nations* (New York: The Arab Information Center, 1957); Sami Hadawi, *Palestine in the United Nations* (New York: The Arab Information Center, 1964); Sami Hadawi, *United Nations Resolution on Palestine 1947–1965* (Beirut: The Institute for Palestine Studies, n.d.) and subsequent editions; and Hazem Zaki Nuseibeh, *Palestine and the United Nations* (New York: Quartet Books, 1981).

16. 'Testimony by Ambassador Jeane J. Kirkpatrick, United States Permanent Representative to the United Nations, Before the Senate Appropriations Committee, Foreign Operations Subcommittee, 7 March 1983' (mimeo) p. 7.

17. Quoted in Juliana Geran Pilon, 'The United Nations' Campaign Against Israel', Washington, D.C., The Heritage Foundation, 16 June 1983 (mimeo) p. 16.

18. Ibid., p. 18.

19. Quoted in *New York Times*, 4 October 1983.

20. Abba Eban, *An Autobiography* (New York: Random House, 1977) p. 496.

21. Quoted in *Jerusalem Post*, international edn, 21–7 February 1982.

22. Quoted in *New York Times*, 16 October 1983.

23. United States Ambassador Jeane Kirkpatrick has noted some optimism about the future in light of the strong approach adopted by the United States delegation under her leadership. The United States has refused to accept routine condemnations of Israel as merely insignificant rhetoric. This has helped to achieve an increasing unwillingness of some Third World states to follow, unquestioningly, the Third World anti-Israel 'line'. Address by Ambassador Kirkpatrick, Washington, D.C., 16 October 1983.

Index